WILD EDIBLE PLANTS

OF NEW ENGLAND

Wild Edible Plants OF NEW ENGLAND

A FIELD GUIDE

Including Poisonous Plants Often Encountered

by Joan Richardson

Full color photographs by Joan and John Richardson
Illustrations by Joan Richardson

Edited by Jane Crosen
with Sue Gawler, *botanical consultant*

DeLorme Publishing Company, Joan and John Richardson, Jane Crosen, and Sue Gawler disclaim any and all liability resulting from the use of, preparation of, ingestion of, or contact with any plant discussed in this book.

ISBN 0-89933-009-6

Plants of the Ocean and Freshwater Marshes

Sea Lettuce

Irish Moss

Dulse

Pickerelweed

Iris (poisonous)

← *Tangle*

Plants of the Ocean and Freshwater Marshes

Fragrant Water Lily

Bullhead Lily

Arrowhead

Long-stemmed Kelp

Marsh Marigold (use caution)

Water Plantain (harmful) ➔

Plants of Marshy Areas

Cattail Stalk

Cattail Flower

Great Bur Reed

Cattail Root (with spring shoots)

Plants of Marshy Areas

Skunk Cabbage (use caution)

Jack-in-the-Pulpit (use caution)

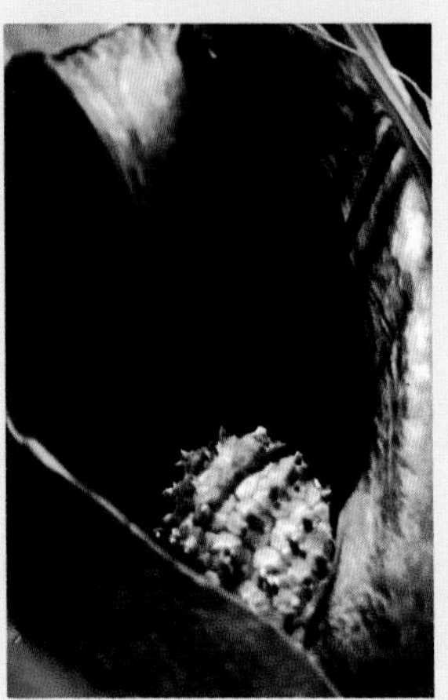

Skunk Cabbage Flower

Large Cranberry

False Hellebore (poisonous)

Plants of the Forest Floor and Shaded Areas

Solomon's Seal (young)

False Solomon's Seal (use caution)

Checkerberry

Wild Ginger

Partridgeberry

Plants of the Forest Floor and Shaded Areas

Indian Cucumber

Spiderwort

Indian Cucumber Root

Bunchberry

Plants of Shaded and Semi-shaded Areas

Blue Lettuce

Wild Lettuce

Jewelweed

Bittersweet Nightshade (poisonous)

Plants of Shaded and Semi-shaded Areas

Wild Sarsaparilla

American Spikenard

Bristly Sarsaparilla Berries (harmful)

Spreading Dogbane (poisonous)

Wild Mint

Plants of Open Areas

Common Milkweed Pods

↑ Purple Milkweed Pods (harmful)

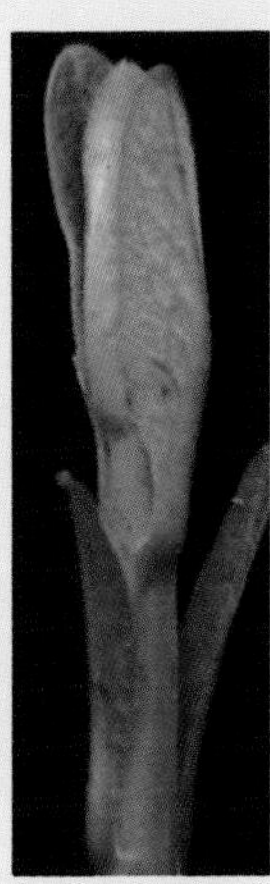

↑ Common Milkweed Shoot

Common Milkweed Blossoms

Purple Milkweed Blossoms (harmful)

← Strawberry Fruits

Strawberry Blossoms

Plants of Open Areas

Chicory

Lady's Thumb (Smartweed)

Yellow Dock Leaves

Pennsylvania Smartweed

← *Chives*

Plants of Open Areas

Sunflower

Lamb's Quarters

Musk Mallow

Strawberry Blite

Black Medik ➡

Plants of Semi-shaded and Open Areas

Bracken Fern Frond (with sori)

Bracken Fern Fiddleheads

Cinnamon Fern Fertile Frond

Asparagus Berries (inedible)

↓ *Bracken Fern (mature)*

Cultivated Lettuce Flower

Plants of Open Areas

Chickweed

Ox-eye Daisy

Bull Thistle

Marsh Thistle (young)

← *Yellow Goatsbeard*

Sea Rocket

Plants of Open Areas

Spiny-leaved Sow Thistle (with seed heads)

Field Sow Thistle

Prickly Lettuce

Dandelion

Ground Ivy

Plants of Semi-shaded and Open Areas

Bladder Campion

Bouncing Bet (harmful)

Pineapple Weed

Night-flowering Catchfly (harmful)

Common Wood Sorrel

Yellow Wood Sorrel

Plants of Semi-shaded and Open Areas

Groundnut

Fireweed

🡅 *Frogs' Bellies*

Sheep Sorrel

Buttercup (poisonous)

Plants of Open Areas

White Clover

White Sweet Clover

Yellow Sweet Clover

Hop Clover

Alsike Clover

Plants of Open Areas

Red Clover

Birdsfoot Trefoil (harmful)

Rabbits Foot Clover (harmful)

Creeping Bellflower

Foxglove (poisonous)

Plants of Open Areas

Field Pennycress

English Plantain

Blackseed Plantain

Poor Man's Pepper

Burdock Flower

← *Galinsoga*

Burdock Root

Plants of Open Areas

Horseradish Flowers

Horseradish Root

Black Mustard

Wild Horseradish

Strawberry Tomato Fruit (Ground Cherries) (Immature)

← *Strawberry Tomato (leaves and flower)*

Trees

Mountain Ash

Scrub Oak

Red Oak

Shagbark Hickory Bark

Black Walnut

Shagbark Hickory

Butternut

Chestnut

Tapping Paper Birch

Black Birch

Yellow Birch

American Hazelnut

Beaked Hazelnut

Shrubs and Shrubby Plants

Shrubby Cinquefoil

Juneberry

Barberry (berries immature)

Common Elderberry

Hobblebush Blossoms

Hobblebush Berries (immature)

Shrubby Plants and Trees

Carrion Flower

Greenbrier

Wild Red Cherry

Staghorn Sumac

Chokecherry

Guelder Rose

Black Raspberry

Wild Raisin

Wild Red Raspberry

Northern Dewberry Blossom

Shrubs and Shrubby Plants

Japanese Knotweed Shoots ➔

Japanese Knotweed Flowers

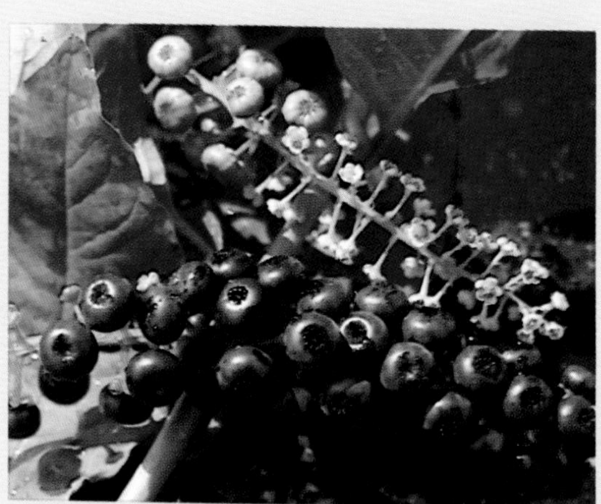

Pokeweed Berries (harmful)

American Yew (poisonous)

Juniper

Shrubs and Shrubby Plants

Wrinkled Rose

Garden Hybrid Rose

Redbud

Dwarf Huckleberry

Highbush Blueberry Blossom

Highbush Blueberry

Shrubs and Shrubby Plants

Purple-flowering Raspberry

Red Elderberry (harmful)

Running Swamp Blackberry

Sweetfern

Mushrooms: The Deadly Amanitas

Panther Amanita (poisonous)

Yellow Amanita (poisonous)

Fly Amanita (poisonous)

The Blusher (use great caution)

Destroying Angel (poisonous)

Mushrooms and Other Fungi

Elm Pleurotus

Common Inky Cap

Sapid Pleurotus

Rusty Bolete (young)

Rusty Bolete (mature)

Mushrooms and Other Fungi

Meadow Mushroom

Skull-shaped Puffball

Cup-shaped Puffball

↑ *Horse Mushroom* ↓

Little Studded Puffball

Mushrooms and Other Fungi

Chicken Mushroom

Scaly-top Polypore

White Lepiota (use caution)

Scaly Lentinus (may be harmful)

←Little Inky Cap

Contents

VIII
Trees, Shrubs and Woody Plants

I

Hunting Wild Plants

Can you imagine a plant which adds the nip of vinegar to a salad, a spinach laced with lemon's zip, or a mushroom flavored like a sizzling, broiled steak? Dream further, and conjure up a free fruit which has a vitamin content an orange might hope to match, a tree fungus which tastes and looks so much like chicken you'd expect it to lay eggs, and an underground cucumber so crisply sweet you'll have difficulty passing woodlands where it might be growing. These are not fairy tales; they're real, and free for the price of your labor alone.

Are They Safe?

Let me first dismiss one idea: You do not need a college education to safely pick of the wild garden around you! Our very early ancestors did quite well without ever seeing a schoolhouse.

This book has been written for a beginner. It contains as few scientific terms as possible. Any plant appearing in this book had to first fulfill certain qualifications: a) it had to have easily identifiable traits, b) it had to have real food value and/or c) it had to be found in great enough numbers to be worth seeking, and d) it had to taste good!

There are many edible wild plants. There are also a certain number definitely known to be poisonous. Between these two extremes there are multitudes of plant species which we really don't know much about, at least concerning their edibility. Be sure you *know* the plant you intend to eat. In our own experiences, we have banished countless specimens, undoubtedly many of them innocent edibles, to the garbage bag or compost pile when we weren't absolutely certain that we had the right ones. It is safer to be cowards.

The plants you eat every day were once wild. It's likely our courageous ancestors employed the trial and error method to find out which ones could safely be eaten. (Perhaps this partly accounts for their limited lifespans.) I'm afraid our family didn't inherit any of their intestinal bravado; the plants contained in this book have been known to be edible for many long years.

Hunting as a Family

We enjoy hunting the wild plants for several reasons. Of course, they provide us with free food. However, I think there are more important reasons involved. Gathering wild food gives us a purpose, an "excuse" to be outdoors as a family. Three out of four in our family hunt deer and other animals, as well; I go along with them and forage for side dishes. If we were ever stranded, it's highly unlikely we'd starve, and I don't mean we'd be able to survive on our stored adipose tissue! Should all the grocery stores and local farms fall to some unnamed plague, or should there ever be a real catastrophe, we would at least be able to eat.

Our children take an active part in hunting foods. Their sharp eyes are a great help, as are their youthful backs. It's amazing how much practical knowledge they have gleaned from our forages, and from having seen their parents (who give the harvest a final going over) carefully inspect, research, and even test various plants. They have observed their parents learning, just as they must do in school, and oftentimes they have been the ones to uncover the important clue which determined whether a particular plant belonged in the pot or the compost pile. It has sharpened their powers of observation and has enhanced their awareness of the living things around them. They are also more knowledgeable of poisonous plants and other hazards.

Nutritional Values

Harvesting the bounty of wild places started us thinking of the vast difference between wild foods and the more sophisticated foodstuffs found at the supermarket.

As our country developed, the people in more densely populated areas found themselves living further and further removed from the food they ate. As the transportation of refrigerated goods over long distances, as well as canning and freezing, became realities, the smaller farms in the less productive areas dwindled and died. Great canneries sprawled where once tomatoes, peaches and peas were harvested for local use. Roads and homes popped up in the fields and woodlands which once supplied us with locally grown, organically raised apples, pigweed, and hazelnuts. Meanwhile, in the broad belts of specialized commercial farmland, the soil was pressured for bigger and better harvests.

It's likely that what we have gained in variety, we have lost in vitamin and mineral content. In order to transport fruits and vegetables to the large freezer plants, canneries, or wholesale markets, it often becomes necessary to pick the harvest before it has reached full ripeness. But we only shortchange ourselves. The immature plant product often has not received its full share of vitamins, minerals, proteins and other nutrients from its parent plant, just as a premature baby is not so richly endowed as one which grows full term. And, with each successive step a fruit or vegetable is removed from nature, its nutritive vitality diminishes. Some nutrients suffer from age, others from exposure to heat and air.

To prevent spoilage, provide "ripe" coloration and flavor, and generally enhance the food product, chemical treatments and processes were developed. Today, because of this, we enjoy summer vegetables in winter, plant products which are not native to New England, and fruits nearly year-round. These *are* benefits. However, while some of the additives are materials actually found in plants, others may be totally strange to all life forms, including us. With the help of technology and chemicals, today's great agricultural areas produce yields unheard of a generation ago. But we pay a price.

Green plants are the backbone of all life. By the process of photosynthesis, green plants, using the energy of light, combine the carbon dioxide given off by animals with water to form simple sugars. "Photo" refers to "light"; "synthesis" means "to make something." Literally, the chlorophyll-bearing green plant makes things from light.

The simple sugars formed through photosynthesis are later combined within the plant's cells to form all the other materials that constitute the living plant. To create fats, oils, pigments, plant hormones, and proteins within its tissues, the plant must draw minerals from the earth. These minerals are vital to plant health. Some, required for special products, are needed only in marginal amounts.

Though we differ in our needs, we too require these basic materials to keep us healthy. We don't have roots, nor are we able to carry on photosynthesis. Ultimately, it is the green plant which must provide these vital materials for us. But, if the soil is leached, year after year, by plants of limited variety and in unnatural numbers, it is bound to become deficient in some of these necessary minerals.

A plant growing in devalued soil may be unhealthy, deprived — and depriving us — of necessary vitamins and food value. And if when the plant dies it does not just stay there and rot, we lose again. There are bacteria and fungi in the soil which very efficiently consume plant and animal remains: this is their nourishment. What remains, a goodly portion, is then returned to the soil in a form usable for other plants growing there. When this does not happen, the ground becomes less and less fertile. Man has developed commercial fertilizers, and no doubt these are good. However, I don't think these commercial fertilizers can ever replace the natural cycle. I don't believe we know enough! Man-made fertilizers contain many minerals, but are we yet certain which of the trace minerals are essential to the plant — and us?

The wild plant may be absolutely loaded with these materials, or barely clinging to life and lacking most of them. However, the wild ones grow in soil occupied by many different kinds of plants. Just as each type of animal seems to have slightly different needs, each of the plant types that you see growing together along a roadside, deep in the woods, or along the quiet edge of a pond needs a unique combination of minerals and has its own talents for absorbing them. Thus, plants that grow wild, diverse neighbors as they are, are unlikely to be competing for the same mineral requirements. And — with few exceptions — when winter or disease reap their dark harvests, the plant remains rot away to further enrich the soil for the next occupants.

Wild Plants and Home Gardens

Many people put in long, back-breaking hours growing their own garden plants, and this is truly worthwhile labor. Some of these people enjoy the work, others feel it is beneficial exercise, and all certainly realize that these foods may be harvested at their prime. The home gardener pretty well knows what has gone into and on these foods. Even if they are home frozen or home canned, they have had to travel less distance than the commercial product, and the result contains only whatever "additives" the family cook decides are needed.

Some people have no land, or lack the time, ambition, or even the health, to do their own farming. Many must supplement what comes from their gardens with produce from the grocery store. Wild edible plants can augment the home gardener, provide for the person unable to plant, or be drawn upon in times of emergency or need, and do it with great flavor while adding real nutrition to the menu.

Many wild plants may be easily transplanted to your garden. In fact, it may be desirable in some cases to raise your own "wild" edibles in your garden patch; some plants that may be confused with harmful species need to be identified when in bloom, yet in many cases they are edible only in their early stages. If you grow these from seed or from root transplants, you'll know for sure what shoots are poking up in your garden!

II

Plant Poisonings

Nature exacts a certain wisdom and discretion from those whom she supports. To reap good meals from the wilds, it is essential to use careful judgment in identifying and preparing the edible plants; for some of the inedible ones (and other parts of some edible ones!) contain substances which can violently affect the human system. People may be poisoned by plants in the following ways:

The plant may actually contain a harmful chemical, and so be inedible to most or all people. Or, the plant may contain materials that could bring about allergic reactions in just a small percentage of people. Doubtless you know someone who cannot tolerate milk, who breaks out when he/she eats strawberries, or who becomes ill from eating shrimp. These individual sensitivities can only be determined by experience. Since we are all different, it is best to eat at first only small amounts of any strange food, wild or not. This is especially important if you have already shown some food allergies.

And then there are perfectly edible plants that "poison" people who are not allergic to them. Such an unfortunate happening is the fault of the collector or the person responsible for keeping the plants fit to eat. (Common garden plants, too, can fall into this category.) If plants (or any perishable food, for that matter) are forced to wait in a hot place, chemical changes may occur and the bacteria of decay may begin to multiply. These changes or the products of bacterial activity may cause problems. This may happen also if the plant is stored in the refrigerator too long, is improperly canned, or is kept in the freezer too long. It's not the plant's fault.

This is not a text on biochemistry! However, it is important to know some facts of life about the poisons contained in the harmful plants if you are to be responsible in preparing wild foods. Should you feel that you might have mistakenly eaten a poisonous plant, call your local hospital or poison control center. ***Keep this emergency number by your telephone.***

Not all poisonous plants are included here. Many plants grown as ornamentals in and around homes, parks and schools are poisonous. An adult, child, or even a pet who has unwisely eaten of a strange garden plant is just as needful of help as is someone who has sampled a mistakenly identified wild "edible." Whether you hunt plants with a camera or for your table, you are wise to know where help may be obtained in a case of plant or other food poisoning.

Poisonous Materials

It is estimated that less than twenty percent of the higher (vascular) plants contain the poisons known as **alkaloids**. Alkaloids most frequently occur in dicotyledons, the seed plants that produce seeds with two food storage chambers. (Split open a bean, and you'll find two parts: This is a dicotyledonous plant.) The alkaloids are most apt to be found in dicotyledons such as the dogbanes, poppies, lupines, delphinium, buttercups, some of the citrus trees, tobacco, deadly nightshade, tomato, thorn apple, poison hemlock, barberry, and even the good old potato, according to chemical analyses. Some mushrooms contain these chemicals, too. This list, by no means complete, should bring some questions to your mind: Some of the plants in this short lineup are regularly found on dinner tables! The point is, sometimes one part of a plant may be eaten, but not the remainder. (Rhubarb is a familiar example. The stems are enjoyed by many, but the leaves and roots are decidedly poisonous.)

Alkaloids have found medicinal uses. Some societies have used their properties in other ways, but, whatever the motive, one is always playing with fire. **Psilocybin** is the alkaloid found in certain mushrooms. It acts as an hallucinogen, but the amount of the alkaloid may vary from mushroom to mushroom, season to season, area to area; hence, use of this alkaloid is an uncalculated risk. Other alkaloids, once used in herbal medicine, have been isolated and duplicated in the laboratory. **Colchicine**, found in meadow saffron, has been employed in the treatment of gout. Others have found no positive uses. **Coniine**, the alkaloid of poison hemlock (not the tree), is believed to be the material that killed Socrates, and (in the past) has been used for dispatching criminals and political prisoners.

How is an alkaloid used within the plant which has produced it? The substance may be a by-product or waste of the plant's life activities, or it may serve a particular function within the plant. While the presence of an alkaloid is sometimes unfortunate for us, it does have a reason for being in the life of the plant.

As for their activity in the human body, whether as medicine or poison, the alkaloids seem to affect mainly the nervous system, although the liver and other organs are known to react. **Purines**, another class of chemical compounds, may be poisonous, but some are strongly stimulating. We use the purine known as caffeine, which we find in coffee, tea, and kola, as well as the theobromine of the cacao plant, as stimulants. It seems little wonder that people who overindulge in these may wind up with problems!

Phenylethylamine, from mistletoe, and **choline** and **muscarine**, from the poisonous amanita mushrooms, are three of the most well known **amines** of the plant world. These powerful substances can be deadly.

More widespread than the alkaloids, but considered to be less important, are the **glycosides**. When stomach acids and enzymes work on these, sugars and carbohydrates are formed. These are harmless. A third product, a glycone, is also produced. It is this material which is believed to be responsible for the problems caused by glycosides. Some glycosides are found in rather common plants.

Some glycosidic plants have a hydrocyanic acid portion. The cyanide-containing materials in almonds, cherry pits and apple seeds are good examples. Tapioca contains this same type of material, but it is leached from the tapioca before you purchase it. Lima beans, which must be thoroughly cooked, are another example. Several grasses that are cultivated as animal foods are reported to contain cyanide-bearing glycosides; these must not, however, be present in large amounts, for certain animals (i.e., cows) are reportedly more apt than others to be bothered. White clover, common vetches, and the pretty hydrangea bush all contain these glycosides.

Some glycosides have a direct action on the thyroid gland, causing it to become overactive (hyperthyroidism); this may even lead to the death of the individual. Such glycosides have been found in soybeans, turnip, kohlrabi, mustard seeds (which also contain mustard oil glycosides), broccoli, cabbage, kale, and other vegetables familiar to most of us. Animals have been killed by overeating of these plants; however, to eliminate them from our diets, at least in reasonable quantities, would leave quite a gap!

The buttercup, which is considered really poisonous, and the marsh marigold, considered a springtime treat, contain similar materials. Some of the uninitiated do-it-yourself plant hunters, as well as children, have come up against the reality of the poisonous nature of the horse chestnut in the past. It, too, contains a glycoside.

It's reported that at least four hundred **heart glycosides** are known, and from their number we can find representatives in our local pharmacies. The wild or garden-grown foxglove, also known as digitalis, is a pretty container for more than ten of these glycosides. Once farmed for herbal practitioners, its use was investigated, and from this study we have the laboratory-produced digitoxin which helps heart patients today. On the other side of the coin, such poisonous heart glycoside-containing flowers as foxglove and lily-of-the-valley are often found in gardens where children play.

There is a group of toxic materials which often will foam, soaplike, in water. They are called **saponines**, and are found in at least four hundred individual kinds of plants; apparently our bodies can tolerate small amounts of some of them. It is believed that in order for them to be truly toxic to us, other materials are required for them to enter our bloodstream. They also seem to vary in their abilities to do harm. Saponines are found in many plants including pokeweed, alfalfa, English ivy, bouncing bet, and beech. Some of the saponines are capable of killing fish, even in small concentrations. Some primitive societies have utilized the toxic properties of saponines in procuring meals for the table.

We need many **minerals** in our diet, some in larger amounts than others. However, plants do not necessarily take in elements in consideration of our needs, and sometimes our individual reactions to plants can be blamed on the soil which supports them. Moreover, plants sometimes selectively concentrate certain minerals, either according to their own needs or the contents of the soil they are growing in. If they are exposed to high levels of nitrates, some plants may store so much of a mineral that they might actually become toxic to many animals. Cases of abortion, faulty thyroid activity, and other problems in animals have been linked to this situation.

Selenium is an odd mineral. Recently there have been reports that it may well be one of the trace materials which we require in very tiny amounts to remain in good health. However, some soils lack this elusive material while others are quite rich in it. Certain plants stock up on selenium if it is available. The "loco weeds" are notorious for this. Little jewelweed, friend to many who suffer from poison ivy, is edible only in its very young stages mainly because of its ability to store selenium, silicon, and other minerals. (It's the old tale of too much of a good thing.)

Oxalic acid and the **oxalates** are found in some plants. Removing them can be a difficult, if not impossible, task. In small quantities, they give the citrus-like tang we enjoy in sorrel and dock plants. If we overindulge in these, or in rhubarb, beets, or purslane plants, we may be looking for trouble. If too much of these materials arrive in our bloodstream, the calcium carried by the blood may form crystals, and these crystals have to be put somewhere. The body's choice of a favorite hiding spot seems to be the little tubes in the kidneys, and the formation of kidney stones is a possible result. (Skunk cabbage and jack-in-the-pulpit contain larger amounts of oxalic acids; this is further discussed in their descriptions.) It seems advisable to include dairy products in a meal featuring any of the plants which are high in oxalic acid. How they knew it, I don't know, but the European cooks have long favored cream sauces or cream soups when making use of many of these plants. Should anyone overindulge without realizing what might occur, the recommended antidote is any material containing calcium, so long as this material is not in itself poisonous. It's doubtful, though, that anyone would eat too much at one sitting. There is apt to be more long-term danger to a person who consistently eats of these plants for many days. While not causing poisoning, large amounts of these plants may reduce the amount of calcium circulating in our bloodstream. Not all our calcium is involved in teeth and bones; several enzyme systems rely on its presence as well.

Most **resins** or resin-like materials are fatally toxic. They do their dirty work inside, affecting the muscles and nerves. Marijuana, water hemlock, mountain laurel and the adult milkweeds contain these, according to reports. Some even irritate externally. Poison ivy owes its reputation to a resinoid, as do the pistachio and cashew nuts. Some resins seem to protect the plant by killing insects. Regardless of their function for the plant, resins usually cause our stomachs to fly into outraged revolt when we partake of them.

Safety in Variety

Fortunately, our bodies seem able to tackle nearly anything as long as it is introduced in moderation and is not definitely a strong poison. I don't mean by this that you should just let nature take its course if a poisoning is suspected; but, given a helping hand, the body seems able to overcome most of our mistakes. There are not too many plant poisonings on record. Yet, every day, we eat potentially harmful foods. In our intake of body-building materials, there is a narrow margin of concentrations which are safe for us. Apparently, the safety-affording fact is that most of us vary our diets from one day to the next.

According to available records, people originally ate a much more varied diet than we do today. As agriculture developed, and certain crops were favored because of their ability to grow in cultivated lands, provide large yields, and because they tasted good, the number of different kinds of plants included in our meals diminished. Later, plant scientists developed hybrid strains which were disease resistant and drought resistant, and which required shorter growing seasons. Many of these "super" plants exist only at our whim. Most were bred with good nutrition in mind, but still the variety grew slimmer.

As you've no doubt noticed in the examples cited of poison-containing plants, many of our crop plants are just as potentially toxic as wild plants. Not enough research has been done on the wild plants, however, to truly come to this conclusion. The majority of wild edibles included in this book are believed to seldom, if ever, cause any problem. They have been used as food for generations (just as have corn, oats and rye, once also wild but now harnessed to the efforts of crop production).

This is the final reason for picking wild plants: to return to a dependence on a greater variety of plants for our health's sake. We can and should do so as intelligent and thoughtful people. In our past, we have thoughtlessly eliminated whole species from our earth. We can thoroughly enjoy and use the bounty of the wild without repeating our mistakes.

Small-flowered Buttercup

Cursed Crowfoot

Wild Indigo

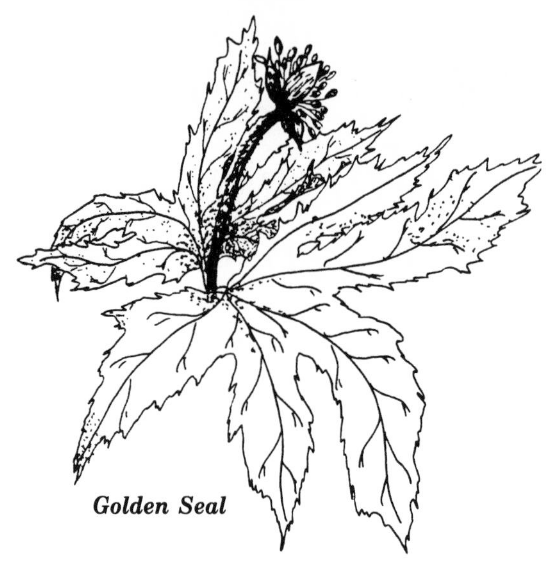

Golden Seal

Cloudberry

Evening Lychnis

III

Identifying and Harvesting the Edible Plants

Plants usually look alike to a beginner, and it takes a while to sort them out. Here is a summary of precautions to take beforehand and while you are collecting your wild edibles, particularly on your first forays:

1) Look through this book and become familiar with its arrangement as well as the plants described in it.

2) Study the photographs and botanical drawings of leaves, roots, flowers, seaweeds and mushrooms to become familiar with plant structure. Most often it is a particular *part* of a plant which is edible.

3) Read about the individual poisonous plants thoroughly, and study the information given on plant poisons and individual reactions.

4) By all means, check a ***number*** of sources if you are in doubt about a plant that almost, but not quite, fits one description. Often a trait that is overlooked by one author will be clearly explained by another.

5) In many cases it may be advisable to cut into or test a plant to be sure of its identity. This is especially important when the plant involved is a mushroom. If, for example, you feel you need a second opinion on the mushroom's identity, a spore print will show the true color of the spores. (A description of making a spore print is given in the introduction to *Mushrooms and Other Fungi.)* Identification procedures for each plant are detailed in the individual descriptions.

6) Discard any plant that does not fit the *whole* description. It is better to waste an edible plant than to poison an entire family with a plant that resembles, but isn't, an edible. In this book we have given space to descriptions and photographs of poisonous species to help in identification and prevent confusion and distress.

7) Carry and store your bounty safely. Particular hints are given in the next pages and throughout the book.

8) Never eat large amounts of any strange food the first time you try it. We all react differently. (See the information on allergies under *Plant Poisionings.)*

If you happen on an unfamiliar term in this book, check both the *Index* and the *Glossary*, for an item is often fully covered in another section.

Hunting and Picking Tips

There are only a few points to remember as you pick from the wild. Of course, first in the list is proper identification. Approach any strange plant with a little fear in your heart—it sharpens your senses of observation! Check off the identification traits to be sure you have covered them all. When you have decided it is an edible plant, be certain the whole plant is edible; otherwise, collect only those portions which you intend to bring to your table. A minimum number of any kind of plant is necessary in any given area in order to continue the species. Be sure you leave enough! A general guideline to heed when collecting the whole of any wild plant is: If there are twelve, you may take up to three; if there are six, you may take one; if there are but three, only observe and enjoy the sight.

Do not collect from areas right next to roadways. These zones are exposed to the exhaust from vehicles as well as materials used on the roadways. We generally try to be at least twenty feet from a small country road, thirty to fifty feet away from a fairly well used road, and over that distance from a highway. We've never encountered any problems as long as we've respected these minimal safety zones. Look for signs of plant damage, either from the traffic, sprays, or industrial wastes. Don't pick near waterways that don't look or smell clean, or which you suspect may be polluted by urban or industrial wastes. Don't pick near any water situated by a dump or in an area heavily used by swimmers or boats. Avoid plants growing right next to hydrants or trees in urban areas, for these are almost certainly puppy stops. Be cautious in picking near anyone's garden, on lawns or in parks until you can determine whether plant sprays have been used in the surrounding area. (These are often carried by the wind into the zones roundabout.) And when you get home, be sure to check each plant again thoroughly for proper identification. Discard any that do not completely tally with the identifiable traits—at least, until you get to know the particular species intimately. Wash your harvest well, but observe any cautions given in the plant entries about soaking.

If you live a distance from your collecting area, or if you must collect on a hot day, remember that heat builds up in a vehicle. Heat increases bacterial activity and quickens the spoilage rate as well as rendering most plants limp and unattractive. An inexpensive cooler and one of those refreezable compartments are good investments.

It is best to keep each kind of plant separated. This is of extreme importance when you are collecting mushrooms, or if you haven't had the opportunity to identify types fully in the field. Plastic bags tend to seal in heat and moisture, and should be avoided. Use the regular paper bags from the grocery store instead. If you're collecting right around your own home, paper bags and a cardboard box are fine. A collecting basket is a romantic reminder of the "good old days," but seems to create a situation where you're likely to mix various types of plants in the one container.

A penknife or a sheathed knife is nearly essential, especially if you expect to hunt unfamiliar plants. (You may need to cross-section them.) A hand lens (magnifying glass) is very helpful for close-up inspection of some plants, especially when you are identifying them for the first time. A trowel may be needed for identification and collection of plants with edible or distinctive roots. Tuck this or a small shovel into your vehicle so you may call upon it when you need it.

Notice where your plant is growing. This book has been arranged as to the typical growing areas of the plants it contains. Check other sections in the book if you do not find your plant classified under the habitat you'd expect.

You'll soon find yourself sprawling on city park greens, ambling along roadsides, and surveying lawns as you drive along. If at all possible, obtain the landowner's permission before trespassing on his property or removing anything. This serves you in two ways: First of all, he too may be a plant hunter and might have been planning on those agaricus buttons for supper or those blueberries for breakfast. You'll be less apt to make enemies. Secondly, many people are curious. They often know the plants on their own land, and will very happily share both plants and information with you in return for your conversation and knowledge. In being neighborly, you'll make lots of new friends and learn many things. Much of the information in this book has been gathered throughout our hunting years in just this way.

Symbols Used in This Book

For quick reference as to whether or not a plant is edible, check the symbol which appears near the heading for each plant (or group of closely related species). Any plant marked with a or / symbol will carry a further explanation or warning, given in bold type under the heading. The warning may state that a plant is poisonous, or may refer to portions of the plant that are harmful, any poisonous plants that could be confused with an edible species, or conditions whereby an otherwise edible plant could be dangerous if eaten.

Generally, these are the meanings of the three symbols used in this book:

—This plant has edible portions which are recommended as food; it may also have other practical uses.

—This plant is poisonous or has poisonous portions, and it is not recommended for use.

/ ***—Some portions of this plant may be edible only under specified conditions or after careful preparation, and other portions may be definitely harmful; this plant may be used, but with caution.***

These basic edible symbols are not meant to be comprehensive, but are provided for initial reference only. The reader is advised to thoroughly read the entire description of a plant before attempting to use any part of it for the table, and to heed any warning given. In many cases, the description will mention another plant or plants that could be mistaken for an edible, and it would be wise to read those descriptions, too. It is also very important to first read the introductory chapters about plant poisons and the recommended procedures for safely identifying, harvesting, and storing wild edible plants.

Mountain Cranberry

Strawberry Blite

Laver

IV

Plants of the Ocean and Seashore

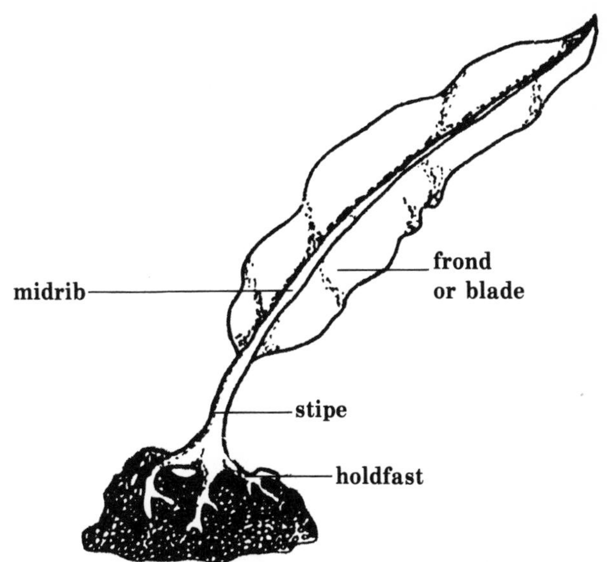

Parts of a Seaweed Plant

SEA LETTUCE 

Ulva lactuca
Photo page #1

Also known as: Lettuce laver, green laver, sea grass
Season: Best in spring; can be harvested throughout year
Habitat: Salt water, ocean front and bays

Sea lettuce! You have seen it churning in the waves after storms, washed up like limp lettuce on the beach, or clinging to rocks, piers, or other solid objects at the shoreline or in bays. It looks good enough to eat, and it is!

The blades of this green alga are a bright, yellowish-green. They are soft in texture, vary in shape, and grow to 8-10 inches in length or more. When the tide is fully out, you'll be able to harvest the fresh plants from exposed rocks or tidal pools or reach down next to pilings to gather them. Their texture is rather like a wet piece of plastic wrap. Grasp them near their base, for they tear easily.

After collecting, if you do not live within a few minutes of the ocean, you must keep the sea lettuce in a cooler. Seal the vegetable in plastic bags with a little water from its surroundings, keep it on ice, and refrigerate it when you get home. It is not advisable to keep fresh sea lettuce for longer than perhaps 24 hours, but it may be dried for storage. (See instructions given for drying dulse.)

When you are ready to use this tasty seaweed, wash the fronds well in fresh water. They may be chopped and added to a salad, soup, or stew. Sea lettuce is nice to serve with seafoods. Small portions which have first been chopped may be added to the pan as you fry meats.

Dried fronds may be chopped and added to stews, soups, macaroni dishes, or cooked with other vegetables. Powdered, dried sea lettuce makes a good salt-substitute seasoning which is nutritious, to boot. You might want to mix in some ground-up peppergrass seeds to create an all-round seasoning mixture.

Though sea lettuce is a bit tough unless finely chopped or well cooked, it is said to be very high in iron, protein, iodine, aluminum, manganese and nickel. Starch, sugar and fat are present, as well as a good supply of vitamins. Reportedly, a higher vitamin content is found in those plants harvested in late spring or early summer, but they are apt to be tougher than those gathered earlier in the season. The best sea lettuce calls for cold feet or boots!

It is fun to try recipes which call for firm land plant leaves, substituting sea lettuce fronds for them. (For example, wrap the fronds around portions of stuffing to make a "stuffed cabbage" with a seaweedy flair.) Just remember to use a recipe that requires fairly long-term cooking.

The seaweeds may well be the food resource of the future. They certainly help both health and pocketbook today!

IRISH MOSS 

Chondrus crispus
Photo page #1

Also known as: Sea moss, pudding seaweed, blancmange, jelly moss, carrageen, salt rock moss, red rockweed

Season: Can be harvested year-round

Habitat: Clinging to rocks in intertidal zone and in area below low tide mark; washed up on beach; ocean and bays

An old acquaintance of people who live near northern ocean waters, this red seaweed looks like a coarse little bush. Fresh, the branches are flexible but firm, though the basal stalk is tougher. When young and vibrant, it varies from the deep red color of cabbage through shades of olive green; as it ages it passes through greens, creams, and then to a nearly white stage. Drying is required to complete this color transition, and it is at this bleached stage that Irish moss is picked to make the delicious and nutritious pudding known as blancmange.

Select anchored plants from clean wave-washed rocks, or those which have just been deposited by an outgoing tide. Seaweeds found in bays are too frequently covered with silt from adjacent land and the rivers that join the bay. These deposits may be contaminated with industrial, farm or domestic wastes. First washed, questionable seaweeds may still be used as compost for your garden.

Picking these plants is a wonderful excuse to go wading! Wait to collect them until just before you go home. They should be bagged in some of their native sea water and kept in an ice-chilled cooler during their trip. Keep fresh water away from them, and, when you get them home, keep them refrigerated. Pick or cut off any little creatures that have hitched a ride. Some organisms live attached to the seaweed; remove these, too. Wash the plants just before use, but don't soak them in fresh water.

If you want to store Irish moss, the plants may be air or oven dried. Use a low temperature and keep the oven door ajar. They will keep well if they are dried to a rock-hard condition, then stored in sealed bottles or kept in the freezer in airtight wrappings.

Irish moss fronds are a bit too chewy raw, although we have slivered the tenderest ends and incorporated them into salad dressings. This seaweed is an excellent addition, finely chopped, to stews, soups, and chowders. As it cooks, the vegetable nearly or fully disappears, but brings flavor, smoothness, and thickness to the dish.

If you intend to prepare blancmange, you'll need the whitest Irish moss you can find. It will be on the beach, and is best found after the very high tides of spring and fall. Pick out any dark pieces, including the pigmented reproductive organs you may find at the branch tips, and rinse the plants quickly. (These deeply colored portions may remain in other dishes, but they would discolor this snowy pudding.) The creaminess of the pudding—and the thickening imparted by Irish moss to other recipes—is due to a gelatinous material which we know as **carrageenan** or **alginate**. You will see these names among the lists of ingredients of many grocery store items. It is the manufacturer's right hand when he needs a material to give a creamy consistency or prevent the formation of ice crystals.

Irish moss is not only flavorful and fun to use, but it's good for you, too. The United States Department of Agriculture (Handbook No. 8) tells us that one pound of this sea vegetable provides a fair amount of protein and a little fat, as well as 4,014 mg calcium, 712 mg phosphorus, 40.4 mg iron, and 12,900 mg potassium. It is nearly as high in sodium as in potassium; though this might at first cause some people to reconsider a love affair with this seaweed, remember that when Irish moss (or any seaweed) is used in a recipe, the amount of salt may be drastically reduced. Also, it is seldom that anyone would eat a whole pound of this vegetable! When you consider that an average can of condensed soup may contain 3,000,000 mg sodium, Irish moss still wears a white hat.

Minerals are delivered to the sea via the leaching action of rainwater, and Irish moss is probably loaded with them. Many of these trace minerals, taken lightly in the past, are coming under renewed consideration as being extremely important in the preservation of our health, especially in times of ecological stress.

Clean Irish moss may be slowly dissolved in simmering water to form a viscous base for a soothing tea that is wonderful for a sore throat; add rose hips, lemon, or honey for flavor. This Irish moss brew is also an effective lotion for chapped hands, and it has been known to ease diarrhea without constipating. Any left over might be used to thicken a gravy or stew.

Irish moss very likely has other uses. And remember, any excess of plants gathered may be used in compost or as fertilizer in your garden—they'll nourish your land plants as happily as they will yourself.

DULSE

Palmaria palmata
Photo page #1

Also known as: Dulce, red kale, Neptune's girdle, dillisk, water leaf, sheep dulse, purple seaweed

Season: Best mid-spring to mid-fall; can be harvested throughout year
Habitat: Anchors to rocks, shells, piers; from midtide to below low tide zone in cool ocean and bay water; may be washed up

One day, while lecturing on the edibility of various seaweeds, I noticed a young man in the class grinning and nodding vigorously. The next day he appeared with a large bag of dried dulse. All my students sampled this Nova Scotian "popcorn substitute," as he called it, and most agreed it was a treat. Dulse is certainly a nutrient-rich substitute for most snacks sold in stores, and you'll even find dulse in some grocery stores. Harvested from spring through fall, it is a free gift from the ocean which need not be purchased. If you get some early in the warm months, it is high in vitamin A. Reaped late in the fall, it is high in vitamin C. Anytime, it's just plain good!

Laver and dulse are very close in appearance, though dulse tends to be more intricately lobed, with tiny branchlets extending from the main plant body. If you confuse these two seaweeds, don't worry, for both are quite edible. Dulse fronds vary in length, depending upon maturity and how rough the ocean has been. Their color ranges from fuchsia red to deep purple-red. You may pluck dulse from the object upon which it is anchored, or select fresh wave-offerings from tidal pools or the surf.

As any seaweed, dulse may spoil rapidly if not kept fresh, moist and cool. Bring an insulated cooler if you must travel a distance after harvesting, and carry the dulse home in cool sea water. (If you use ice in the cooler, keep the dulse with a little of its native water in a plastic bag.)

If you've ever purchased any of the commercially prepared and packaged dried dulse, you'll have noticed that the dulse is unwashed. Dulse may be easily dried, but fresh water before drying will hurt the plant. Dry your dulse between screening in the sunlight, in a propped-open oven set at its lowest temperature, or (briefly) on the top of a wood stove. Don't dry it to absolute crispness. Observe the commercial product: It still has a little ability to flex, but is dry enough to prevent the development of mold. That's what you want. It will take a single layer of dulse about six hours to dry in sunlight.

Dulse has a delicious, nutty-salty flavor and is a very likeable addition in most dishes. Dulse can be baked into bread, fried, soaked or stewed as a condiment, added to soups, included with potatoes, pickled, and even has been used to produce an alcoholic beverage in some parts of the world. And, just on its own, either dry or fresh, dulse is good to eat as a satisfying snack.

Besides being a plant of many uses, it is high in protein, fat, and several vitamins and minerals (such as iodine and phosphorus). It is reportedly quite rich in trace elements, which is understandable when you consider where it grows. Dulse also contains respectable amounts of vitamins B_6 and B_{12}, which may be important in the diets of people suffering from anemia, leukemia, and various cancers.

Like most of the red algae, dulse produces a mucilaginous material and may be added to recipes which require some thickening. The viscous material is called **carrageenan,** and you'll see this name listed as an ingredient in many creamy commercial products.

LAVER

Porphyra species

Also known as: Red seaweed, purple seaweed, purple leaf, red rock tripe
Season: Best mid-spring to mid-fall; can be harvested throughout year
Habitat: Anchored to rocks, shells, piers; usually from mid-tide to below low tide zone in ocean and cool bays; may be washed up

Laver and dulse are often confused. Their color ranges overlap, varying from reddish purples through purples with green or brown tones. Dulse seldom has the characteristic ruffled margin of laver; laver usually does not bear the small branch-like lobes found on dulse. What few distinctions there are between the two plants can be intermingled by wave action. (See the illustration on page 14.)

There is really no problem with identification, for both sea vegetables can be used in the same ways, though laver tends to be a bit tougher than dulse. See Dulse, for all information applies identically to laver. Also, see the picking hints given for Irish moss.

TANGLE

Laminaria digitata
Photo page #1

Also known as: Fingered tangle, kelp, fingered kelp, ocean fingers, sea tangle, horsetail kelp, kombu
Season: Best in spring; can be gathered throughout year
Habitat: Grows attached to rocks or other firm strata in cold ocean water below the intertidal zone

All seaweeds commonly called "kelps" belong to the phylum of plants known as the Brown Algae. They contain brown pigments which tend to mask the green of their food-producing chlorophyll. Tangle is no exception. As shown in the photograph, when first washed up or harvested it is generally a deep umber with olive shadings.

Kelps cling to rocks with tough, root-like holdfasts. Tangle's holdfast may still have a small rock or shells in its grasp when you find the plant. Once you've identified the plant, this holdfast may be removed and left behind. Usually the holdfast is more yellowish in tone than the remainder of the plant. From the holdfast extends a strong stem-like stipe; this is normally flattened where it joins the much-divided blade of the plant. These plants are easily gathered in the spring or fall when we experience the lowest tides. They're best in the spring. (See the other seaweeds for harvesting and carrying hints.)

The fresh blades may be briefly rinsed, inspected for "hitch-hiker" organisms, and then used in a soup or stew. These are pretty tough; sliver them before adding them to the pot. The blades may be cut into convenient lengths and dried in the sun or on the top of a wood stove. They shouldn't become rock hard. Store these pieces in a sealed container in a cool, dry place. When you need to flavor, smooth and thicken a recipe, briefly soak the portions in water, and use as you would fresh kelp.

You'll see this same plant sold in food stores. Sometimes it's called kombu, but it's available free from the clean ocean waters under any name you'd care to call it.

LONG-STEMMED KELP

Laminaria longicruris
Photo page #2

Also known as: Kelp, oarweed, kombu
Season: Can be harvested throughout year
Habitat: Same as tangle

When storms roil the ocean, kelps are often victims of the surging water. In the wake of the storm, go right to the beach to capture an effortless, fresh harvest. Like most kelps, this long-stemmed one grows from the area below the usual low tide mark to well out along the fishing banks.

The blade of this plant begins as a long, flexible frond with ruffled edges. It's thicker up through the center, but has no round midrib at its middle. As the blades mature, they may reach to fifteen or eighteen feet in length. It's seldom you'll see such long ones, though. You'll most often find youngsters, six feet or less in length, that have chosen too insecure a structure as an anchor for their holdfasts. These are tenderer, anyway. Adolescent and mature plants may have blades which broaden into a heart shape at the base, but the other traits will be the same.

The stipe of this seaweed helps to identify it. Solid and round in the area above the holdfast, it is hollow and fatter in the upper areas before its attachment to the blade.

This nutritious plant is used in the same manner as tangle. It's often sold commercially and called by the same name as tangle.

EDIBLE KELP

Alaria esculenta

Also known as: Kelp, winged kelp, honey kelp, sweet kelp, wakame
Season: Can be harvested throughout year
Habitat: Same as tangle

You'd think from this plant's common name that it is the only edible kelp. Not so, but it's one of the nicest and best known.

Unlike tangle and the long-stemmed kelp, this plant's stipe continues through the blade as an evident, strong, central, flattened midrib. The blade is often tattered like a wind-battered flag. Late in the winter and on into the early warm season, secondary reproductive structures, looking like smaller branch blades, develop along the sturdy stipe.

These large plants may be handled in the same way as the other kelps. The blade itself is somewhat pungent, but mellows after drying. The midrib is the star of the show. Sliver it, and add it to a salad, vegetable dish, soup or stew. Its sweetness is what earned this plant the common name of honey kelp. These discs are similar to water chestnuts in their crunchiness. The smaller side blades are tender and nice. These, too, may be used in many dishes, raw or cooked.

Damaged or unwanted portions of any of the kelps may be rinsed free of their salty coating to become a terrific addition to your compost or mulch pile. Reportedly an outstanding source of nutrients for us, these leftovers will nourish land plants with their wealth of sea-derived materials.

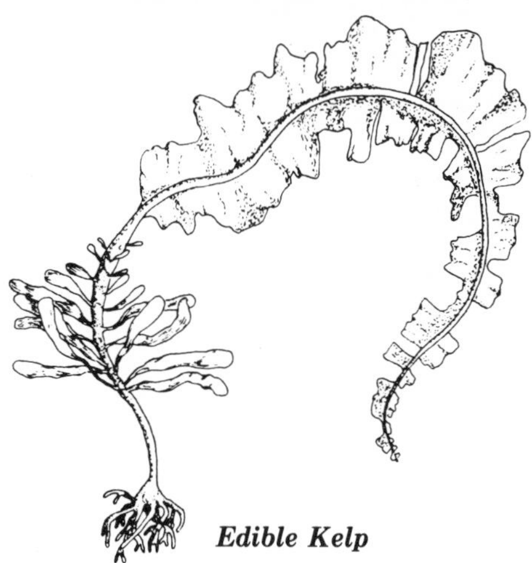

Edible Kelp

SEA ROCKET 

Cakile edentula
Photo page #13

Also known as: Seaside mustard, purple rocket
Season: Summer
Habitat: Sandy edges of ocean and bays, dunes, sandy areas

If ever an excuse was needed to walk the beach or dunes, this is it! Bring some tender sea rocket leaves or pods home with your fishing trophies to make an accompanying salad, or harvest all tender parts to cook as greens. They're good!

When in flower, especially, this is a good beginner's plant and one that even children can easily learn to identify. (Just be sure to check their bounty before casually committing all greens to the pot.)

The sea rocket's stems are thick; the leaves are firm and fleshy, with a peppery taste that tells you it's part of the mustard group. The four-petaled flowers are violet to purple in color. There are few, if any, plants you could confuse this with, but here is one absolutely confirming trait: The unique seedpods, borne on the fat flower stalks that arise from the upper stems of the plant, are plump, round, two-part structures. Each has a point at its outermost end, and bears two seeds. (If you split the pod, you'll find one seed points up, the other down.)

The succulent stems and leaves usually spread out in a recumbent sprawl. The plant is hairless, and the leaves are coarsely, roundly toothed. Once you've become acquainted with it, you'll easily recognize the sea rocket during its growing season.

One of the few plants able to survive the salt and spray conditions of the sand dunes, the sea rocket stores both food and water for other creatures as well as ourselves. Without these and a few other rugged species, the sand dunes would erode. Please don't destroy these plants — they're too valuable to the natural world. Selectively harvest only the portions you will use from a large enough number of the plants so that they will remain established in the area.

Shellbark Hickory *Pignut Hickory*

Common Elderberry

V

Herbaceous Plants of Freshwater Streams, Lakes, and Marshes

PICKERELWEED 

Pontederia cordata
Photo page #1

Also known as: Purple arrowleaf, fishweed

Season: Young leaves in spring; nut-like seeds from late summer into early fall

Habitat: Shallow waters which are quiet or have but little current

In midsummer you've probably seen the stalks of purple pickerelweed flowers decorating the edges of quiet waterways and ponds, tended by seemingly millions of flying insects. Undoubtedly, the shelter afforded by the stems which support the shiny, arrowhead-shaped leaves and flowers (not to mention the dining potential of insects hovering nearby) has caused many fish to linger in the shallow water around pickerelweed. (This is probably what earned this plant the common name by which it is best known!)

At first this plant might seem easily confused with wapatoo (arrowhead), as the overall shape of the leaf is somewhat similar. The veins of this plant's leaf, however, all arise from the junction with the stem and follow the general contour of the leaf. There is no central crosswise "seam" as is found on the arrowhead's leaf. Also, pickerelweed plants have but one leaf, on the flowering stem, whereas arrowhead grows as a rosette, with several leaves coming from one point. Of course, the flowers are easily differentiated. I don't know whether the nut-like seeds produced by the arrowhead's flower are edible by humans, but those manufactured during the warmth of summer by the flowers of the pickerelweed may be eaten directly, used as nuts in any recipe, or ground to form a nutritious flour. They are starchy, and taste rather like potatoes.

These plants generally grow in great patches from the water's edge on out into the shallows. It would be best to first locate a group earlier in the summer when they're in flower and identification is easiest. Get to know the appearance of their four-to seven-inch-long leaves and the slightly fuzzy flowering stalk. If you mark their location and look in your memory, you can capture the early spring leaves, before they've unfurled, and use them as a quickly cooked pot herb. They're reportedly excellent just with a little butter. These young leaves are also good chopped and added to a salad, a possible accompaniment for the cucumber-celery stalks of the young cattail plants which are available at this same time. Add a few sprigs of spring-fresh sorrel leaves and perhaps a few checkerberries the birds missed, and you've a salad fit for your best friends.

IRISES

Iris species
Photo page #1

Also known as: Wild iris, blue flag, specific names for garden species
Season: Blooms in early summer
Habitat: Marshes and wet pastures, gardens

THESE ARE POISONOUS PLANTS

There are many edible roots which wild plant foragers may attempt to gather for table use. ***All iris roots are poisonous,*** and it is important to be able to instantly distinguish them from other roots.

Most people recognize an iris, wild or cultivated, when in bloom. Anyone who has planted them in the garden will know the appearance of the fibrous, dark, underground rootstocks. Since irises grow in the same areas where rushes and cattails are found, it is important to know with full certainty the appearance of the root you are searching for, as well as how the leaves differ from the cattail, arrowhead, or rush leaf.

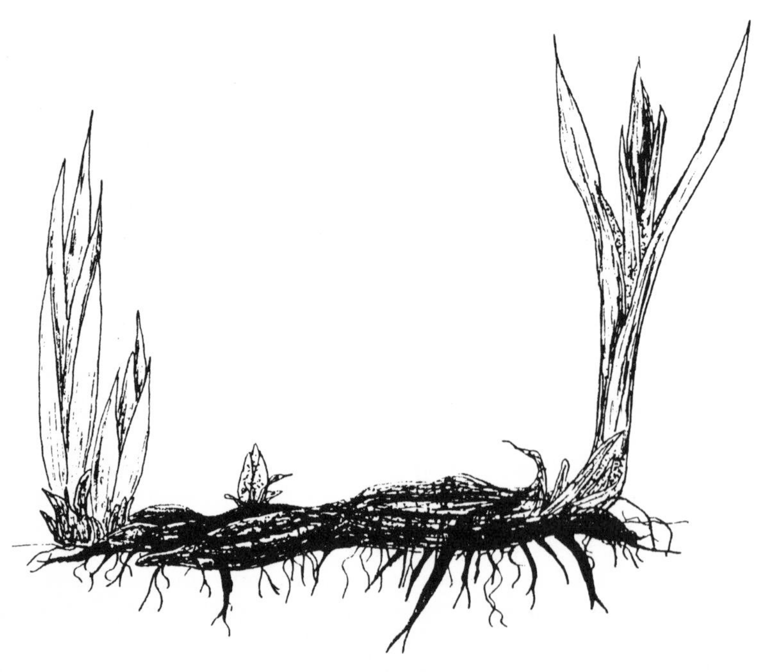

Iris Roots

The gray-green leaves of the iris are sword-shaped, arising from a horizontal, underground tuber or rhizome which generally is found nearly at, or slightly above, the surface of the ground. Normally, it is dark brown and looks hairy. Though the flesh of these rhizomes is usually odorless, the taste is very biting. This should be enough to warn you that you have not found the edible root you seek.

These rhizomes contain a thick sap-like material known as **irisin**. Acting upon the stomach, intestine and associated digestive organs, it may cause severe reactions. Usually the digestive system will react with vomiting and a burning sensation throughout. The skin of some sensitive people is even bothered by irisin. The poison of iris roots is considered potentially fatal, and is certainly best avoided. Irises are lovely plants. But just look — don't bite!

FRAGRANT WATER LILY 

Nymphaea odorata
Photo page #2

Also known as: Sweet white water lily, white water lily, purple-leaved water lily, small white water lily

Season: Young leaves in early spring; blooms in mid-summer; tubers early spring or fall

Habitat: Ponds and lakes, quiet fresh waterways

This water lily blooms after the yellow bullhead lily, generally awaiting the warmth of midsummer to delight our noses and eyes. Its leaves are purplish on their undersurfaces, and usually are in the seven-to ten-inch diameter range, though they may grow larger. The leaves, shaped as circles with a single cleft, generally host small algae and little animals on their undersurfaces.

A breath of sweetness comes from the four-to six-inch flower with pristine white petals and a yellow center. The petals come to definite points, and the flowers float on the surface of the water.

There is another, equally good, white water lily called *Nymphaea tuberosa*, with green-bottomed leaves and more rounded petals. It is usually not so fragrant as its cousin, but is just as edible. This species is, however, not very common as far north as New England, and really should not be picked where it is rare.

You can collect the young leaves, still curled, before they have been made into floating cities by the small living creatures around them. The leaves are usually boiled for about ten minutes and served with a little butter, salt and pepper. They're good mixed with other vegetables or added to a soup or stew.

It seems a shame to prevent their coming to glory, but if you find an area well stocked with these lily plants, do collect some of the unopened flower buds. They may be boiled, like the leaves, and served in the same ways. Better yet, try coating them with flour, dipping them in a little egg which has been diluted slightly with milk, and again in flour. Fry them to golden, delicious morsels and serve as a main vegetable, if you've enough, or as a treat among other fried vegetables.

The seeds can be used like those of the yellow pond lilies (see Bullhead Lily), but the best portion of the fragrant water lily, we think, are the tubers which are produced along the roots underwater. If you don't like the feeling of muddy pond bottom between your toes, a small rake or clam hoe will loosen these tubers. (You cannot just pull them up; all you'll get for your efforts are broken stalks.)

The tubers are the size of what we call "pig potatoes." They will float to the surface as they loosen from the muck. Those that break free of the root system, but not of the mud, probably help to spread the lily family even more than normally. Wash them in the river or pond water, right on the spot, to prevent extra work at home and possibly a clogged drain. They may be used in any of the recipes calling for wild potatoes or tubers. Like most plants, these lilies draw upon their tubers for leaf and flower production during late spring and on into summer, so, once you've located them, harvest these wild potatoes in the early spring or autumn when they're most sweetly stocked with food materials.

BULLHEAD LILY

Nuphar variegatum
Photo page #2

Also known as: Yellow water lily, yellow pond lily, bull lily
Season: Blooms in midsummer; seeds and roots in early fall
Habitat: Ponds, lakes, quiet fresh waterways

As summer begins its climb toward sultry beach days, the yellow water lilies burst into bloom. They never open fully like the fragrant white water lily, but remain in what appears to be a permanent bud stage. If you confuse the bullhead lily with the spatterdock or cow lily, you're none the worse for your confusion; they're very similar, and all three are quite edible.

The bullhead lily has floating, nearly round leaves with a single partition to mark the place where the stem attaches. Their root-like tubers are edible and may be used like those of the fragrant water lily, but you may find the taste quite a bit stronger. This can be tamed by changing the water once or twice. The strong flavor indicates the presence of a material some of the Indian tribes reportedly found useful. (Certain groups dried these roots and used them to treat wounds.)

The root-like tubers may be boiled or roasted, and used like the common potato. The ripe seeds, like those of the fragrant water lily, may be gathered and, when dry, ground into what I'm sure is a very nutritious flour. And, for a delightful popcorn-like snack, try toasting the seeds!

ARROWHEAD

Sagittaria latifolia (Broad-leaved Arrowhead)
Photo page #2

Also known as: Swamp potato, wapatoo, wapato, Dutch potato, duck potato, arrowleaf, Indian potato
Season: Blooms late in summer, tubers best in spring and fall
Habitat: Quiet fresh water

Once identified, this plant is easily recognized. There are several species of *Sagittaria*, but most frequently picked and most easily recognized is the broad-leaved arrowhead.

Long before white settlers came to this country, the Indians harvested wapatoo tubers. These formed a tasty staple in their diet, treated as we do the common potato. The harvesters often did the plants a favor, for as they gathered the tubers some would break loose and further spread these delicious plants. The tubers, ranging in diameter from one inch to the size of a regular potato, are often found several feet away from the parent plant, strung out along the fibrous root system.

The arrowhead-shaped leaves bear distinctive veins. The upper of the three lobes has nearly parallel veins which begin at a point where the stem attaches. At this point of attachment, there's a crosswise "seam." The parallel veins of the two lower lobes arise at this earmark seam. Some leaves will be broad, others narrow, and some may even lack the arrowhead shape. Until you learn the appearance of the tubers you seek, it is best to stalk only those with the typical arrowhead-shaped leaves. The leaves of arrowhead plants grow in a rosette.

Late in the summer you'll find distinctive flowers on a separate stalk. They are white with yellow centers, usually appearing as the pickerelweed is going out of bloom. (Another plant with similar flowers is the water plantain, but these are borne on branched flower stalks.) There are three petals and three sepals on each flower, and many flowers are borne on the stalk. These develop into nutlets, which are eaten by many wild birds, especially ducks and geese. If you have a pond, and wish to attract these wild game birds, by all means consider transplanting some wapatoo into it!

This plant has a bitter, milky juice which is apparent even in the tuber. Heat destroys the objectionable flavor. Wapatoo tubers are best peeled before eating, and most easily peeled after cooking. Clean them well with a little scrub brush before you bake or boil them, cook until fork tender, and you'll have a wild potato which may win you away from the traditional potato!

Of course, this tuber is the plant's food supply. It is packed fullest with flavor and nourishment in the early spring, through the winter, and in the fall. These are the best gathering times, though the water is then certainly chillier than in midsummer. The Indian ladies would root the tubers out with their toes, for they float to the surface when loosened. However, if you don't care for the feeling of lake or stream bottom between your digits, the tubers may be freed of their anchors with a hoe or rake. A little clam rake is a superior tool. Since arrowhead grows anywhere from shoreline to a water depth of five feet, a boat is a good idea. Depending on the water level, the leaves may project from a few inches to a couple of feet out of the water.

If you come across a good harvest of these excellent root products, there are at least two ways to store them. Once excess moisture has been allowed to evaporate, the tubers may be kept in a root cellar. To dry them, string them up in an insect-free, dry place until the moisture has disappeared, and then keep them in mesh bags until needed. The dried potatoes may be boiled, or boiled and then fried, or scalloped. Arrowhead is an excellent plant, along with the cattail, to become friendly with if you are a hiker, skiier, hunter or snowmobile enthusiast. If you are stranded at any time, its roots are a wonderful source of nourishment. Though a little bitter, they may be eaten raw. The brown stalks often remain sticking out of the water throughout the winter, and so, if you are familiar with the appearance of the tuber (and thus unlikely to confuse it with, say, the tuber of the poisonous irises) you can easily utilize this plant (as well as the cattail) in a time of emergency. Just head for the nearest swamp! The trees around a swampy area are generally hemlocks or cedars, offering instant weather protection, as well. You will be sure to find plenty of edible tubers in a swamp. They are exceptional (if you have matches) when baked in the ashes of a wood fire. Even raw, they will at least give you something to live on until help arrives.

WATER PLANTAIN

Alisma species
Photo page #2

Also known as: Marsh plantain
Season: Summer
Habitat: Edges of quiet ponds, ditches, wet and marshy areas

NOT ADVISED — A QUESTIONABLE PLANT

Water plantain is included here mainly because of its superficial resemblance to arrowhead. The flowers are similar, having three petals and yellow centers. They are smaller than those of the arrowhead, and, rather than springing from a single flowering stalk, are borne on branching flower stalks. The leaves, however, lack the distinctive, pointed "arrowhead" shape.

Some authorities state that the roots of this plant are edible after intensive drying and boiling. The remainder of the plant, including the leaves, is not known to be edible, even though the leaf's appearance, and even the plant's name, might lead you to believe it could be used in the same manner as the dry land-dwelling plantains. They are not related at all. I cannot advise using even the root of this plant.

MARSH MARIGOLD

Caltha palustris
Photo page #2

Also known as: Marsh buttercup, American cowslip, king-cup, May-blob, marsh gold, Mary's gold
Season: Early spring to late spring
Habitat: Edges of brooks, ponds, marshy areas and moist woods near water, springs, drainage ditches

THIS PLANT MUST BE EATEN COOKED — IT IS POISONOUS WHEN RAW. DO NOT CONFUSE WITH SWAMP BUTTERCUP OR SMALL-FLOWERED BUTTERCUP!

When you're ready to welcome spring with a feast of wild greens, these plants rival dandelions and sheep sorrel for your attention. They are up early, sometimes before April is fully awake. Look for them first in sheltered wet areas that are open enough to admit sunlight and warmth. The first time you try to hunt these, you may want to wait until their buttercup-like flowers are in bloom so as to easily spot marsh marigold. Make sure the leaves, too, are definitely those of the marsh marigold. There are two harmful yellow-flowered plants, the swamp buttercup and the small-flowered buttercup, that may be found in the same habitat as the marsh marigold. (See the descriptions of the other two plants for clarification.)

The deep yellow flowers are waxy and usually five-petaled, growing in groups at the top of the plant. The lower leaves of the plant have stems, but the upper leaves may be nearly stemless. Before flowering, the plants seldom exceed six to eight inches, but may develop to nearly a foot later in the spring. They'll grow with their feet in the water of melted snow or spring rains, so do wear boots when you gather the early marsh marigold leaves.

You don't want to pull the entire plant from the ground; cut the leaves with scissors or a knife, for the plant does easily slip out of the wet earth. The leaves are usually two to five inches across, heart-shaped to kidney-shaped, and their margins may be wavy or roundly toothed. The leaves, silvery on their undersurfaces, grow in pairs (though the first ones may seem to form a rosette).

Like lima beans, all parts of this plant used as food ***must be cooked***! It contains a glycoside, **helleborin**, which is poisonous. This may be removed by thorough cooking in water. The water from the first boiling of the leaves should be ***completely discarded***. The leaves should be boiled at least a second time, and it is probably a good idea to drain this second water from them completely and even wash them a final time, like spaghetti, in a rinse of hot water. They may be served at this point. They're good with butter, or with a little vinegar. Older leaves may have a bit of a bite to them, and some people like this, but if you prefer them milder, a third boiling will render them less sharp. Adding a cream sauce to them will completely civilize their flavor.

The buds may also be picked and pickled to serve as substitute capers. But, caution must be taken with the pickling juice. It must ***not*** be consumed, for the buds also contain helleborin, and this will have leached into the hot liquid. Drain them, and rinse them lightly before serving.

You may encounter some confusing information if you seek additional data from people or books. In most areas of the northeast, people will understand what plant you're talking about if you use the alternate name of "cowslip." However, even this title can be problematic: In Europe, the plant known as the marsh marigold or cowslip is not the same creature, though called by the same name. The European marsh marigold is found in the open, especially liking sunny hills and alkaline soil. It is a taller plant, with long, pale, oval leaves. The flower color is the same, but the flowers are small, shaped like those of a primrose, and drooping. The European marsh marigold has long been noted there for its medicinal properties, especially as a nerve tonic. The flower heads were used to prepare a tea which was sweetened with honey. This infusion was taken to calm the nerves and treat "fits," and was also recommended for myriad other nerve-related ailments. An alternate method of using this medicinal plant was to eat the flower heads raw. Should people today confuse our marsh marigold with the European plant, a real catastrophe might result! Further research reveals that the European cowslip, in concentrated form, was given as a sleep inducer when pain was present, or as an anesthetic. In concentrated form, our cowslip could produce permanent anesthesia if used raw!

It seems that nothing in this world is perfect, and the same is true of our marsh marigold. It must be cooked—it's not good for a salad. Yet, it is still a worthwhile plant. Reports indicate that it was effective in treating anemia in the past, and so it would seem to be high in iron, and possibly in vitamins too, as is typical of dark-green-leaved plants.

The leaves may be picked until the flowers fade. If you are careful to not strip the plants of their leaves or flowers, more plants will await you each spring. They spread, and, if you can receive the landowner's permission, they will transplant easily to a suitable spot on your own land to produce your very own beautiful marsh marigold garden.

CATTAIL

Typha latifolia (Common Cattail)
Typha angustifolia (Narrow-leaved Cattail)
Photo page #3

Also known as: Cat o'nine tails, Cossack asparagus, swamp asparagus, flags, bulrushes, rushes, swamp bulrush, reed mace

Season: Rootstocks, fall through early spring; stalks, late spring through summer; flowerheads and pollen, midsummer

Habitat: Swamps, marshes, salt marshes, banks of slow-moving waterways, ponds, drainage ditches

Whenever our family passes a cattail-inhabited marshy area, a cry of "There's a grocery store!" is bound to come from one of our children. They love them. So do we. This is perhaps the most versatile, year-round plant of any of the wild ones making their way to our kitchen.

Most people know the cattail, whether it is the broad-leaved variety or the narrow-leaved kind. Both produce a deep brown sausage-shaped spike at the top center of the plant during the summer. Both grow in marshy areas or along the banks of ponds and slow-flowing waters. The broad-leaved cattail is more commonly found in New England.

There are only two real cautions to be observed in picking cattails. First, be certain it is a cattail! The poisonous irises and other narrow-leaved plants grow in the same marshy areas. However, the soft green of the cattail leaves, as well as their arrangement and structure, give them away once you know them, regardless of the season. The evidence of old seed heads adds to the ease of identification. Second, do not pick them from an area too near a heavily used road, or where pollutants are suspected to be in the water. They are probably safe enough at least thirty feet from traffic. Locate a grove growing in a relatively undeveloped or unindustrialized area. Natural materials, such as snails and mud, are harmless and can be washed away. Cattails, you'll find, are seldom infested by insects.

During the winter the rootstocks can be easily recognized. There will be greenish-yellow or yellowish-white shoots already formed and ready to sprout as soon as warmth returns. They may be used in the same manner as the leafstalk, discussed below. Last year's leaves and stalk will help you to locate the root. These are not always easy to dig; downright tenacious, they wrap under and around each other, forming a mat beneath the surface. Gather them from fall through the following spring to provide your family with a palatable potato, or an even better starch.

To serve the rootstocks as a vegetable, wash and roast them as you would potatoes. (Remove any small rootlets first.) They may be peeled and boiled, and even mashed like a spud.

To prepare a nutritious flour, you must peel the rootstocks as soon as you get them home. Slice them into small portions and place them in a large pot or pail of water. Mix and mash them with your hands or a large spoon to release the starch from the fibers. We've found another good tool is a potato masher. The fibers will float heavily in the water, giving it a thickish character. Allow the starch to settle to the bottom as much as possible, and pour off the water containing the fibers. (Watch that you don't clog your sink drain. This water is best poured onto your garden or lawn.) Add fresh water. Allow the fibers and starch to settle once more into their separate strata and again pour off the water. Depending on the size of the batch, you may need to repeat this process once or twice more.

When you feel all the fibers have been separated out, slowly filter the remaining starch mixture through a piece of muslin or flannel. The starch-water will be trapped in the closely woven cloth. For smaller batches, two or three thicknesses of paper toweling in a large funnel may be substituted. As you'll lose some of the starch with either of these methods, you might choose to evaporate the water away by pouring the liquid into a flat pan and exposing it to wind and sunlight or placing it in a slightly warmed oven. Just don't bake it!

If you intend to store the cattail flour for future use, it must be dried thoroughly and stored in a tight container. Slightly damp, it may be used as is in nearly any recipe calling for wheat flour. (You'll want to mix the cattail flour with wheat flour to extend it.)

From late spring throughout the summer, this plant will provide a good source of salad greens, available free before gardens have begun to really green up. Grasp the central leaves and pull steadily. They'll resist, but your efforts will be well rewarded. At the base of the pulled leaves you'll find a solid cylinder, white below blending into the green above. Look closely at the outer tissue of this stalk. It is covered by a mucilage which protects it well. These layers will also show a network of little rectangles. Peel off the outer coverings until these too-tough portions are removed. (Cut them up. These castaways make good garden mulch.) Inside is a tender central area. You'll be able to easily slice six to nine or more inches of this pale lower core. Add these slices to your salad. The flavor of the young cattail stalk is somewhere between that of cucumber and celery.

If your meal calls for a hot vegetable, slice this core crosswise and lengthwise to form carrot-stick-size pieces. Boil until fork-tender and serve with butter, salt and pepper. It tastes like sweet corn!

Later in the summer, try plunking a few slices into the jars when you're making sweet pickles. You can also cook and serve them with a cream or cheese sauce. They can stretch a scanty batch of asparagus when company arrives unexpectedly. They blend delightfully, and cook in the same length of time. Or, for a crunchy surprise, add slices at the last minute when you serve a soup. Pieces of the stalk can also be added as a nourishing vegetable in a stew. The young shoots of the winter roots can be used in all these same ways.

Get to know the locations of several cattail supermarkets. You'll not want to pull the centers of all the plants in any one location. For your own sake, if not for the plants', let a number reach blossoming stage. Feel of the cattail stalks regularly near the upper part of the plant: along about the middle of June you'll find many of them are "pregnant," firm and full-swollen with developing flower heads. (The area marshes will continue to produce flowers through mid-summer.) Carefully peel back the surrounding leaves and you'll find the two parts of the developing cattail flower. The upper part, which will produce the pollen, is a darker green than the lower female portion. Remove the upper male portions of some stalks and scoot them home. Boil them for eight to twelve minutes and serve hot with butter, salt and pepper. They may be eaten like corn on the cob.

Inside, the slim "cob" you'll find will resemble a plastic knitting needle. The outer green edible portions will come away from it easily. Though we haven't tried it, the cobs might make good barbecue skewers.

Our family is a bit lazy, and we prefer to use these cooked flowers in a souffle or other combination dish. They must be separated from the cob first, of course. If enough are available, they are good served with a cheese sauce, or may be mixed with a sauce to top another vegetable.

If some of the flowers sneak into maturity without your notice, be happy. As the upper male portion bulges and turns golden with ripening pollen, stalk the swamp with a paper bag or small plastic bucket in hand. If you use a bucket, cover most of its open mouth with a taped-on lid. Tip the flower tops into your container and strike the stalk several times. The ripe pollen will be deposited for you. Make no mistake, this is a time-consuming job! Children love to help, though, and many hands working will soon produce a sizeable quantity of golden flour. If little fingers have been too forceful, you may find pieces of the plant itself in the amber powder, or other foreign materials that may have accidentally fallen in. A fine mesh will filter these out when you get home.

These are living reproductive cells, packed with the best the plant has to offer. I have no analysis of cattail pollen content, but they are undoubtedly high in protein and many other good things. Pollen has been respected as a health enhancer for ages, and I'm sure cattail pollen is no slouch. Centuries ago, the Olympic athletes, on the advice of their philosophers, used pollen for youthful energy and staying power. Some of our modern Olympic contenders have reported they felt that pollen gave them the little extra edge they wanted. Herbalists and country folk have long touted the benefits of eating pollen-rich untreated honey.

If you can gather enough, this pollen may be used in bread. We enjoy it in pancakes, bread and muffins by mixing it half and half with wheat flour. I think it's good for all of us, and everyone enjoys the golden results. I've even sprinkled a little on salads, added it to hot cereals, let it give salad dressing a golden glow, and used it to thicken and flavor gravy.

It's doubtful you'll be able to harvest all the pollen from the cattails in any one area, and that is just as well. As summer wears thin, the fertilized female portions will develop their fluffy seed heads. Beginning as the familiar brown sausage-like affair, these will ripen into bunches of weathered fluff. The ripe seeds and their fuzzy parachutes will remain on the stalks throughout the winter and be savored by birds of the marshlands. Their pecking releases some of the seeds to further spread these plants.

If it didn't pack down so much, this fluff would make good stuffing for pillows and toys. Indian babies used to nestle in cattail-padded carriers, their bottoms swathed in cattail down diapers. It is a good emergency trick today to pack the fuzz between you and your outer garments if you're away in the woods and in need of extra warmth. It's a good insulator. Or, if your feet are sore from hiking, pack some of this fluff around their abused zones for silky padding.

Char or pluck the fuzz away from the seeds. They are edible, and may be ground to form part of a cereal or a mush. These might be small but helpful additions to the food supply of a lost hunter or skiier.

The leaves of this plant may be woven into baskets or made into decorative items, and so they could also serve to thatch an emergency shelter. Like corn husks, they may be used to make dolls and other toys, or as a fire starter.

If a confused, lost person can find a cattail swamp, it will furnish him with both food and warmth. If he kills an animal and then soaks the seed head in some of the fat, he has a long-burning torch for repelling insects and other wildlife, general lighting, or signaling for help. What more can be asked of a single plant?

GREAT BUR REED

Sparganium eurycarpum
Photo page #3

Also known as: Bur reed, prickly reed
Season: Rootstocks best in spring or early fall
Habitat: Shallow or muddy edges of quiet or slow flowing fresh water

You may find the great bur reed hidden among the larger stalks of cattails, surrounded by water lilies which are nearly grounded. These plants will reach from two to five feet tall, and are most easily recognized when the burs, for which they are named, are in blossom. There are several other common *Sparganium* species, also edible, though smaller.

The flowering stalk is often bent like an accordion, as though a giant frog tried to sit upon it. Roundish flowers are produced at these zig-zag angles. The upper (male) flowers are fuzzy, rather like dandelion heads; below these are the female burs, actually flowers waiting for the pollen of the staminate blooms to be carried by the wind. Nutlets are later produced by the female blossoms, and these are relished by many wild creatures.

Some leaves spring from the base of the plant. These are long, stiff and three-sided, with a keel. Shorter, less rigid, stem leaves alternate along the flowering stalk. Each leaf forms a sheathing at its base.

Under the mud, the rootstocks creep and intertwine, and, in the fall, spare food is stored in tubers. These have reportedly been eaten as potatoes. The intertwining roots make digging difficult, but a muskrat could show you how!

SKUNK CABBAGE

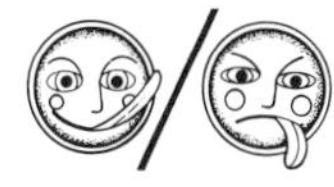

Symplocarpus foetidus
Photo page #4

Also known as: Wild cabbage, marsh cabbage
Season: Young leaves in early spring
Habitat: Marshy areas, bogs

THIS PLANT IS EDIBLE ONLY AFTER CAREFUL PREPARATION. DO NOT CONFUSE WITH FALSE HELLEBORE!

Skunk cabbage is not an easy plant to love. Either the young leaves or roots require repeated boiling or long-term drying before they may be safely eaten. Besides this, the young plant can be confused with the poisonous false hellebore. How anyone found that skunk cabbage is edible I can barely imagine!

I don't think it smells like a skunk. The odor seems more like very strong garlic, to my nose. The plant only really loses this stench upon repeated boilings and changes of water, or on prolonged dehydration. It is reported that some of the Indians found its juice an effective bug repellent, a trick we haven't tried but which I don't doubt!

The leaves look much like elongated cabbage leaves. (Undoubtedly, this is where the plant got its name.) There is never a central stalk as is found on the false hellebore, though the young hellebore plant looks something like the young skunk cabbage. (See the description under False Hellebore.) If you are determined to try skunk cabbage, be sure to familiarize yourself with the appearance of false hellebore.

Oftentimes before the leaves appear the flower of skunk cabbage will have made its appearance. It has no perfume, no flashy colors, nor any other clarion call to attract bees or butterflies. It is its odor which draws insects that would otherwise be found hovering around the dump. You wouldn't even think this was a flower! What appears to be a mottled purplish single-cupped leaf overhangs the spadix, the real flower. This arrangement resembles that of the jack-in-the-pulpit, a close cousin, but in the skunk cabbage this flower group grows close to the ground. Each flower will produce a seed, and these are held within a fleshy fruit as large as an orange. (Apparently, some animals find these fruits tasty.)

Generally appearing after the flower of this plant, the leaves at first form a coiled, cone-shaped structure. Later on they become quite large, reaching up to three feet in length. While this plant does not form heads like the commercial cabbage, it has the netted veination you'd expect to find on a garden cabbage leaf. Later in the summer the leaves seem to disappear in the lush overgrowth of ferns and other marsh-loving neighbors. Look closely, and you'll see that many of these leaves have been eaten, apparently by slugs or insects. The calcium oxalate crystals contained in the tissues of this plant, so terrible to us, must not bother these other life forms.

It is these calcium oxalate crystals which make skunk cabbage so difficult to use. It may take a couple months or more of drying before you can successfully and safely use the leaves or roots of this plant. When we first experimented with skunk cabbage, it was our rationale to follow the advice of those authors who spoke as though they had actually tried the plant, and so we attempted to dry the leaves, though some advised repeated boilings to solve the problem. As usual, faster is not always better. Drying in the oven simply does not do it, at least in our experience! Oxidation over a period of time must have had some effect, for only after a period of over a month and a half, followed by a boiling, did we find the leaves acceptable. Perhaps our tongues are tenderer than most. . . .

The sliced, well dried roots are said to be good. We had an opportunity to try some flour produced from the dried root, and this did give a somewhat cocoa-like flavor to the pancakes made with it.

In the past, extracts from the skunk cabbage have been used in cough preparations and nerve tonics, as well as in preparations to soothe breathing. Herbalists and the American Indians have found many uses for this plant, including treatments for the reproductive system. Perhaps the plant invites further investigation for modern medicinal uses.

JACK-IN-THE-PULPIT

Arisaema triphyllum, Arisaema artrorubena
Photo page #4

Also known as: Indian turnip, wake robin, dragon root, swamp preacher
Season: Blooms in spring; corms best in early spring or fall
Habitat: Damp woods, stream banks, marshy areas

THIS PLANT IS EDIBLE ONLY AFTER CAREFUL PREPARATION

As developers and sprawling new roads have gobbled up "useless" damp areas and woodlands, these plants have become more scarce. Consequently, though it is included in this book as a potential nutritious edible, I recommend that you keep your jack-in-the-pulpit on your "emergency only" list, unless the plants grow in rather large colonies in your area.

Jack-in-the-pulpit seems to be found in two slightly different varieties. In one, the pulpit is green and white striped, while in the other the striping includes purple or maroonish tones. "Jack," who stands in the roofed pulpit, is actually the flower of the plant. A group of brilliant red berries will be produced from this late in the season. You'll find this plant in bloom in the spring, around the time when its cousin, the skunk cabbage, is also producing its flowers.

Standing between one and three feet tall, the plant generally has two leaves; these are most often divided into three lobes, although some may have additional divisions.

At the base of the plant is a swollen structure called a "corm," actually a storage area of the underground portion of the stem. Shaped roughly like a turnip, this gave the plant its alternate name, "Indian turnip."

Unfortunately, like the skunk cabbage, this plant has a rich supply of calcium oxalate. (We've seen slugs contentedly munching away at the leaves. They must have cast iron mouths!) Should someone in your family try to eat any part of this plant raw, or mash the juice onto the skin, they'd be sorry.

We haven't yet found a cache of these plants large enough that we wouldn't feel guilty removing them for experimentation. However, others report that the corms may be sliced thin and then roasted to dryness, whereupon they'll be "corm chips." We know that prolonged drying is necessary to tame skunk cabbage, so I would recommend a long roasting period at a low temperature to give those red-hot oxalate crystals ample time to break down. Regardless of how you choose to roast and dry these roots, if any sharpness remains when you hold a portion in your mouth, it is indication that they have not been treated completely. Large quantities of calcium oxalate can be dangerous as well as a definite irritant.

This is a plant to be handled with caution, but then, so are some of our garden plants. Should food supplies be short, jack-in-the-pulpit is a plant which might help ensure survival. If enough are available, the chips would certainly be a conversation piece, stacked around a tasty chip dip!

FALSE HELLEBORE

Veratrum viride
Photo page #4

Also known as: Indian poke, hellebore, green hellebore, American hellebore

Season: Blooms in late June

Habitat: Same as skunk cabbage — marshes, shady moist areas, stream and river banks, wet pastures

THIS IS A POISONOUS PLANT

Too often, novice foragers in search of the spring leaves of skunk cabbage are not familiar with the appearance of hellebore; if they let hellebore leaves get as far as their table, they could run a definite risk of losing their lives.

The leaves of false hellebore, the "true hellebore" being a European relative, are a lovely bright green in the otherwise drab early spring forest. So are those of the skunk cabbage. The leaves of hellebore first arise from the wet loam, clasped around each other. So do those of skunk cabbage, but there the resemblance ends. The leaves of hellebore are generally odorless. Sometimes skunk cabbage leaves do not give off an odor, especially in their youth or if the weather turns nippy, but more often they bear a rotten onion or garlic-like stench. Look closely at the leaves: the leaf of the hellebore bears nearly parallel veins, and the leaf is folded like an accordion along these veins. The leaf of skunk cabbage has a network of veins, just like the civilized cabbage.

It is in the early stages that these plants can be confused by the inexperienced or unknowledgeable hunter, for later in their growth they are not at all similar. Skunk cabbage is a round, fat plant, its leaves growing from the basal clump and reaching two or three feet in length. The leaves of hellebore may grow to about a foot in length, and, though a brighter green, resemble oversized lily of the valley leaves. However, the upper leaves sprout from a definite central stalk. The entire plant may reach three or more feet in height. The leaves never fully lose their accordion or fan-like pleating, though this is much less pronounced in age. At maturity, the plant looks nothing at all like a skunk cabbage.

In middle or late June the false hellebore may produce a flower spike at the top of the stalk. The flowers, bearing three sepals and three petals, are broken in color only by the six yellow stamens. The pattern of threes tells you this plant is a member of the same tribe as the lilies.

There are many members of the hellebore group. It is reported that the poisonous alkaloids known as **veratridine**, **veratrine**, **cevadine**, **jervine**, and **veratralbine** are present in some of these plants, and suspected to be in false hellebore. These poisons have no detectable flavor, and if they did, it would be outdone by the sharp, biting taste of the calcium oxalate present. This same flavor is to be expected in incompletely dried or incompletely boiled skunk cabbage, and may be less apparent in the young hellebore plant, though we haven't tried it to find out! Also, some of the sharpness of false hellebore might be removed by boiling, or ignored by an overly enthusiastic novice, and enough of the toxic materials eaten to make the person very sick or even cause death.

The symptoms of poisoning include vomiting or gagging, pain in the abdomen, weakness, tremors and spasms of the muscles, lack of coordination, and changes in the pulse. If enough of the toxins have been ingested, more pronounced symptoms result, including lowering of body temperature, loss of consciousness and sight, and shallow respiration. If you suspect someone in your family has mistakenly eaten of these plants, get him/her to a hospital immediately. Do not attempt to treat the victim yourself, since the amounts of toxins present vary as to type of plant and season of the year. If you have any specimens of the plant, or materials which have been regurgitated, bring these along with the patient. If you are a distance from a hospital, immediately call your poison control center for first aid directions.

Cows, horses, and other vegetarian animals will occasionally nibble false hellebore, with disastrous results. This is most apt to happen early in the spring, when the grass is not yet up and around and hellebore is one of the few green things in sight. It is best, therefore, to remove these from any pasture accessible to your animals.

CRANBERRIES 

Vaccinium macrocarpon (Large Cranberry)
Vaccinium oxycoccus (Small Cranberry)
Vaccinium vitis-idaea (see Mountain Cranberry)
Photo page #4

Also known as: Cowberries, marshberries, northern cranberry
Season: Berries ripe from late summer through late fall; last year's berries sometimes available in early spring
Habitat: Cool, moist places and bogs

There are three commonly found wild cranberry varieties, in addition to commercial species which might have escaped into the wild via birds and small animals. All types of cranberries, sharing the same heritage, are similar.

None of the wild cranberries have any hair on their stems. Their leaves — at least most of them — remain on the plant throughout the year. Crush a leaf and sniff: there should be no odor. Most of the cranberries have leaves with smooth edges, and these edges tend to curl toward the undersurface. The entire leaf, ranging in size from one quarter to one half inch long, will be somewhat oval in shape or broadest above the mid-section, and will taper off smoothly and gradually to the short petiole. Turn the leaf over to look for a paler undersurface and a speckling of black dots.

Cranberry plants produce four-petaled white-to-pink blooms in early summer. These flowers will manufacture the deep red, somewhat bitter, acidy fruits which you can harvest and store easily. They make terrific cranberry sauces, though quite a bit of sweetening is required to tame them. The berries may also be frozen for later use. Their collection is a good excuse for late summer and early fall walks.

Look for the large or small plants in marshy areas around sphagnum bogs or ponds that are being overtaken by vegetation. Both species bear fruit from mid-August through late fall, though the large cranberry (*Vaccinium macrocarpon*) is at its peak closer to Thanksgiving while its smaller relative has usually finished bearing ripe fruit during October.

These low plants are creepers. They spread via underground stems, and their mats may cover quite an area. The large cranberry's stems may spread two or three feet from the root system. The large cranberry has evergreen, odorless leaves which are usually paler on their lower surfaces than on their upper; they may even appear whitened beneath. While hunting blueberries, you may notice the flowers.They are beaked in appearance; the four petals recurve, leaving the reproductive parts exposed as the beak. The leaves, having hardly any stalks, are long, flat ovals with rounded or blunt ends and edges that often roll under. Their flowers produce typical red cranberries; use them as you would commercial cranberries. The mountain cranberry, *Vaccinium vitis-idaea*, is similar to the large cranberry, but is found in a different habitat. (See Mountain Cranberry.)

The small cranberry, *Vaccinium oxycoccus*, has very skinny stems, but these may grow to be a foot or more in length. Their leaves have barely any stalk, and tend to be roundly triangular in outline. Like the others, their edges are often rolled under. Unlike the large cranberry, these leaves are often pointed at their tips. They're usually less than a half-inch long, and are alternately spaced along the slender stem. The flowers are shaped like those of the large cranberry, and the leaves are whitened on their undersurfaces. Everything about this plant, except the general leaf shape, would make you think it a small duplicate of the large cranberry. Even its fruits are diminutive, but tasty. You'll just have to work a little harder to gather enough to make the fantastic preserves or drinks they'll provide.

OSTRICH FERN

Pteretis pensylvanica

Also known as: Fiddlehead fern

Season: Early spring

Habitat: Moist areas in relatively wild lands, along shaded freshwater streams

THIS PLANT IS POISONOUS WHEN MATURE

This is one of the most commonly known undomesticated plants, and there is a good chance that it might become overpicked. (With continued utilization of forest lands for housing and recreational development, it is already threatened.) The fiddleheads of this fern are often sold as produce in supermarkets—some people have made a business venture or at least a seasonal sideline of growing, collecting, even canning this largest, most delectable fern fiddlehead. If you, too, gather the fiddleheads of the ostrich fern, please be sure to leave an adequate number to mature into fronds so that the storage organs of the plant may be replenished for the next year's growth.

Look for the ostrich fern along semi-shaded stream banks in undeveloped areas. These plants will not grow along roadsides—they hide from civilization. If you like asparagus-like vegetables and fancy a first wild taste of spring, they are worth seeking. As you hunt them, though, remember to pick only the very young spiral-curled fiddleheads before they unfurl, for, as with any fern, the actual leaves are poisonous.

Ostrich Fern Fiddlehead

This fern's fiddlehead is large, the upper curl often measuring two to three or more inches in diameter. The stalk is firm, and bears an indentation along its inner surface. The whole structure is a deep emerald green. There are no traces of fuzz or hairs. Papery, brown bract-like structures unfurl with the uncoiling stalk.

Early in the spring, before green-up time, look for the withered growth of the previous season. This plant produces two kinds of fronds (leaves). Both varieties of frond resemble a large feather in overall appearance, with the widest part near the upper end. There is one main stem running through the leaf; it is unbranched, in contrast to the frond of the bracken fern. The leaflet-like pinnae go off to both sides from the central stalk.

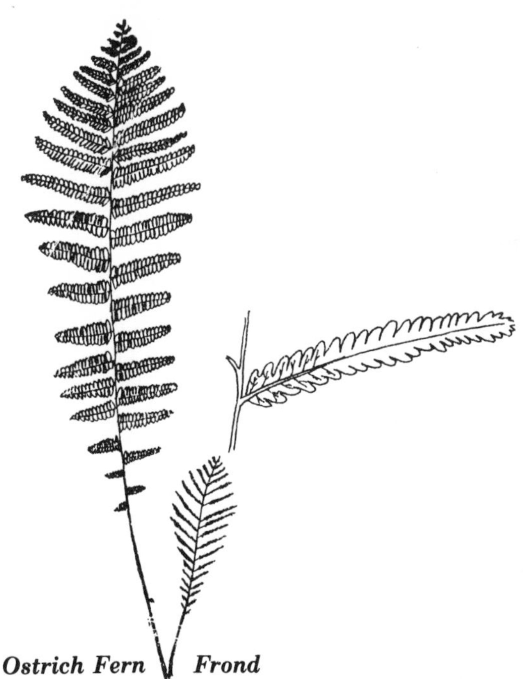

Ostrich Fern Frond

The food-producing, sterile fronds may be anywhere from a couple of feet to a yard tall. Stiff, brown reproductive fronds are also produced. These approximately foot-tall structures may still be erect after bearing the weight of snow, and will beckon to you early in the season. They are minatures, in shape, of the larger fronds. Beneath their feet, the broken sterile fronds will verify the plant's identity.

The two other types of ferns that might be confused at first with the ostrich fern are the cinnamon fern and the interrupted fern. Like the ostrich, the cinnamon fern bears two kinds of fronds, but its fertile frond is rather knobby, and not feather-like at all. Although the effects of winter may tend to darken it, the cinnamon fern's fertile fronds usually retain some of their reddish overtones. The sterile frond of the cinnamon fern is generally widest in outline near its middle; that of the ostrich fern is generally widest near the upper end. The interrupted fern approaches the ostrich fern in overall size. The greatest width of the frond is usually in the middle, but the most outstanding difference is in the location of the spore-producing structures:

there are no separate structures given to spore production. Rather, some of the fronds will develop what looks like a diseased condition, with a few of the pinnae in the middle of the frond becoming knobby and dark. Above and below these spore-producing centers, the pinnae will be normal. Both the cinnamon fern and the interrupted fern have fuzzy fiddleheads; the hairs are light brown to whitish in the interrupted fern, and cinnamon-colored on the fern of that name.

The uncoiled fiddleheads of the ostrich fern may be used raw in salads (see the general warnings given under Bracken Fern), or they may be cooked for about a quarter-hour until tender. They are delicious served in any of the ways you would prepare asparagus. If your harvest is small, use them in soups or stews, spread them among baked mushroom caps, or let them garnish a roast. If you're lucky enough to come across a large batch, they may be canned or frozen — just handle them like asparagus.

VI

Herbaceous Plants of the Forest Floor and Shaded Areas

DWARF GINSENG 

Panax trifolium

Also known as: Little ginseng, ground nut
Season: Blooms in May; ground nuts in early fall
Habitat: Moist areas which receive a good amount of shade; wood edges, thin woods

DO NOT CONFUSE WITH BANEBERRY

This little plant should be picked only when it grows plentifully enough so that its continuation won't be endangered. It is one of the early spring flowers, generally appearing sometime in May. The lacy, round clusters of white blossoms barely reach six inches above the recently thawed ground. Beneath the earth, though, these plants will develop a globular root which can be nibbled raw or cooked.

The true ginseng *(Panax quinquefolius)*, a much larger plant, has been proclaimed as having many curative powers. Its root sometimes takes odd shapes, even

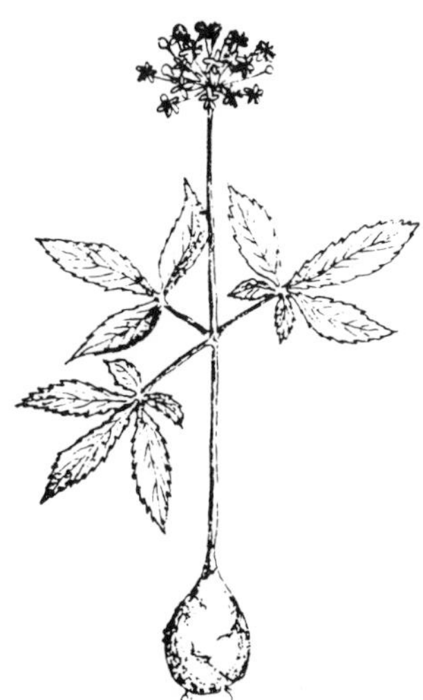

Dwarf Ginseng

to mimicking the human form. The little ginseng has only one shape for its root, but early settlers sometimes utilized it in herbal medicine, too.

Look for three leafstalks which separate from the main flower-bearing stem ***all at the same point***. Each leafstalk will bear three, sometimes five, little toothed leaflets. None of these small leaves will have its own petiole; each is attached directly to the leafstalk. Before you hunt dwarf ginseng, be sure to become familiar with the poisonous baneberry plants. The flowers are very much alike, but the leaves do differ.

Dwarf ginseng is most likely to be confused with baneberry because both plants feature a flower stalk (bearing a cluster of white blossoms) which joins the main stem at its juncture with the three (or five) compound leaves. The ginseng's leaflets, however, are palmately arranged (radiating from a central point), and are more finely toothed than those of the baneberry. The leaflets of the baneberry, on the other hand, are attached directly to the leaf-stalk at intervals (pinnately compound). Once you dig for the root, you will definitely discover the plant's identity: The baneberry's root is long and horizontal, whereas the dwarf ginseng nearly always produces a globular "ground nut."

It will be difficult to collect enough of these little ground nuts to fill a pot. Wash what you have well and add them to quick-cooking wild greens or peas. Once identified for certain, this is a good plant for hikers to know, since the roots are quite good raw.

BANEBERRY

Actaea pachypoda (White Baneberry)
Actaea rubra (Red Baneberry)

Also known as: Cohosh, doll's eyes
Season: Blooms in late spring; berries late summer
Habitat: Moist woods, wooded slopes (areas where dwarf ginseng and wild sarsaparilla grow)

THIS IS A POISONOUS PLANT

The baneberry plants are included here to help prevent confusion for beginning plant hunters who might be stalking sarsaparilla or dwarf ginseng. If an entire family enjoys collecting plants, the children should be shown this one and warned about the pretty doll's eyes berries. Otherwise, a little one might associate these berries with toys instead of the very real danger they present.

The red and white baneberry plants vary only in small details. Both have white flower clusters protruding from the tops of the plants, not unlike the dwarf ginseng. The red baneberry's flower cluster is generally more rounded, while the white baneberry's flower cluster typically takes an oval shape. The flowers have a feathery appearance due to the presence of many stamens in each flower. The plants bloom early in the season, generally in late spring or early summer.

It is the leaves which best distinguish baneberry. The generic name, *Actaea*, comes from a Greek word meaning "elder," and the leaves indeed bear a resemblance to elder leaves. The baneberry plants generally have three leaves. Usually, each leaf is composed of five leaflets. Each leaf has a stalk, but the leaflets are most often stalkless. The arrangement of the leaflets is pinnately compound, and the leaflets themselves are coarsely and doubly toothed. The baneberry flower stem attaches just below the place where the leafstalk leaves the main plant's stem. Neither the white nor the red baneberry is a hairy plant. The entire baneberry plant varies in height from one to two and a half feet, though it may be smaller.

The rhizome is a horizontal, tuberous root. The finer roots that derive from this penetrate downward. Except in odd growing circumstances, this root lacks the bulbous appearance of the dwarf ginseng's root.

Each flower in the cluster produces a berry. The white baneberry typically produces a cluster of white berries, each with a dark purple spot at its end. There is also a variety of white baneberry that bears red berries. The red baneberry generally produces red berries, each with a dark spot at its end, but, complementary to its cousin, there is a variety of red baneberry that bears white berries.

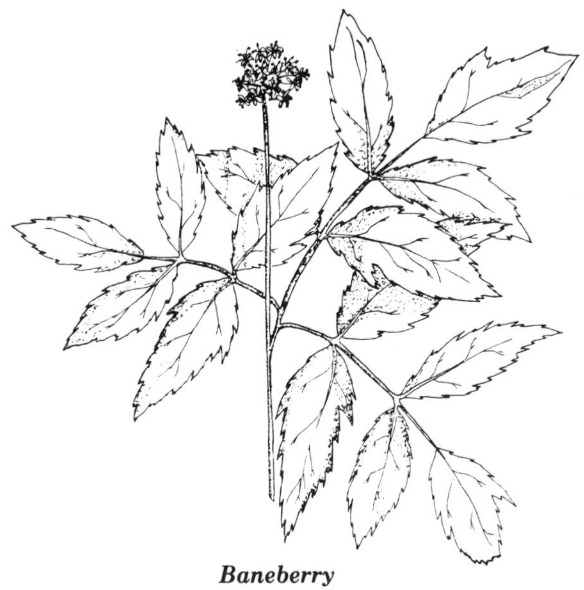

Baneberry

All parts of the baneberry plants, especially the roots and berries, are poisonous. They contain a deadly glycoside. Even six berries is sufficient, reportedly, to cause dizziness, severe cramping and vomiting. A larger number of berries could be fatal. Yet, the berries are attractive; the bright white or red stands out temptingly in the late summer woodland.

One plant that could be confused with baneberry is the wild sarsaparilla. Both plants have somewhat similar leaves, but sarsaparilla has three globular, whitish flower heads which arise from a single, separate stalk. This flower stem springs from the base of the plant, whereas the baneberry flower stem arises from the main plant stem, attaching just below the junction of the leaves.

The plant likeliest to be confused with the baneberry, though, is the dwarf ginseng, whose flower stalk also begins where the three leaves join the main plant stem. The leaves and roots, though, will differentiate the two plants. (See Dwarf Ginseng.)

SOLOMON'S SEAL

Polygonatum biflorum
Polygonatum canaliculatum
Photo page #5

Also known as: Lesser Solomon's seal, great Solomon's seal, sealwort, sealroot

Season: Shoots, very early spring; rootstocks, fall

Habitat: Woodlands, roadsides, gardens, near older homes and homesites

Others may be more showy, but these are perhaps the royalty of the early woodland spring flowers. Arching gracefully above the newly greening forest floor, they soon dangle their creamy bells to summon summer to the woods.

There are few real differences between these two brother plants. The smaller variety, *Polygonatum biflorum,* bears its flowers as twin bells dangling from the arching stalk. These are followed by twin berries which are, unfortunately, ***not edible.*** The larger brother, *Polygonatum canaliculatum*, displays two to ten flowers, but usually four, in each group. This variety is taller and coarser than its dainty relative, growing to between three and four feet tall and overshadowing the little Solomon's seal by a foot or two. Do not eat the berries of this plant, either.

Both plants are found growing in woodlands, old gardens, and near roadsides. Oftentimes Solomon's seal plants, especially the larger ones, are seen among the plants that surround the older homes, having formed graceful clumps around foundations, beneath bushes and trees and along driveways. In looking for Solomon's seal, you may also find some new friends!

The sumac-like leaves spread horizontally from graceful, arching stalks which arise directly from the ground; their entire length is unbranched. The leaves have parallel veins, like those found on grass, iris or lily plants, and alternate along this stem. The flowers, later to be followed by the blue-black berries, dangle from stalks that leave the main stem near the leaf junctions.

The young shoots of these plants are edible, but you must first have located the plant in its maturity to be certain it is Solomon's seal shoots that you are picking. Remove the developing leaves, for these retain a bitter taste. The stems may be cooked for ten to fifteen minutes and served like asparagus. (Don't pick them after the leaves begin to unfurl.)

Since you'll need to find the mature plant for identification, the first plant product you're likely to use will be the underground tuber. These tubers resemble a chain of little fishes, each holding onto the previous one's tail. Every year, a new division of the rootstock is produced, forming nodes; also, each year, the "upstairs" plant stalk leaves a round scar on the rootstock as it finishes its yearly growth. Therefore, you'll find a knobby root, constricted at the end of each year's growth, with the "seals" on its surface from each year's vegetation. If enough plants are available, or if you are in need of food, gather the rootstocks, wash them well, and boil them until fork-tender; they may also be sliced and added to a soup or stew. This is a nutritious food for us, but it does destroy the plant, so gather the tubers only if you can leave a number of healthy plants.

Just be sure to locate and identify the mature plant before picking either the immature shoots or the roots. It would be too easy for an overzealous hunter or a beginner to confuse these rootstocks with those of the iris, mayapple, or another plant.

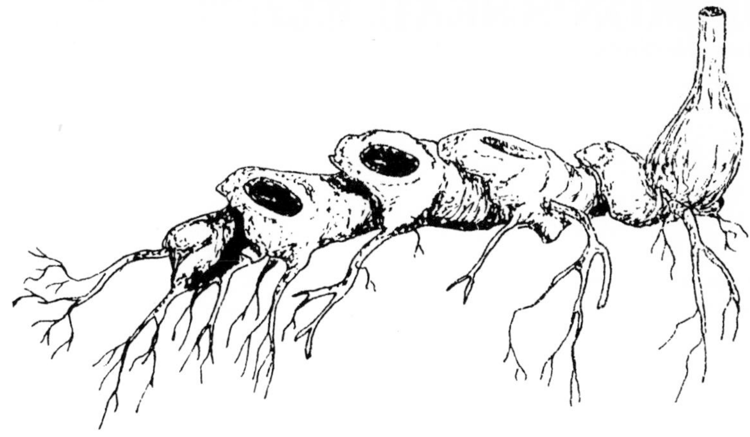

Solomon's Seal Root

Some of these look-alikes may be edible, but others are definitely poisonous. May-apple roots have nodes, but show no "seals" from yearly growth. Occasionally, iris tubers will be marked by constrictions, but no seals, and will have a more fibrous appearance. The plant most likely to be confused with Solomon's seals, however, is the closely related false Solomon's seal, whose roots are edible only after extensive preparation. The root of the false Solomon's seal is more slender and is tinged with yellow, but these distinctions might not be apparent at first. The plants look very much alike when not in flower, but the false Solomon's seal has its flowers in a big cluster at the end of the stem, rather than dangling below the leaves. Be sure to see the description of false Solomon's seal before picking either of these plants.

FALSE SOLOMON'S SEAL

Smilacina racemosa
Photo page #5

Also known as: False spikenard, spikenard, clustered Solomon's seal, scurvy berry
Season: Shoots in early spring, roots in fall; blooms in May
Habitat: Open woods and moist areas in partial shade

ROOT EDIBLE ONLY AFTER COOKING

This graceful plant, often found growing near Solomon's seal, is one of the early spring flowers; it generally begins to bloom sometime in May. The stem is an unbranching arch which often recurves upward at its tip as though displaying, at its apex, the lovely cluster of creamy white flowers. The stalk is finely hairy on its upper surface. Branching directly from the stalk are the alternate leaves, held parallel to the ground surface; they will reach about six inches in length and three in width. They have deeply etched parallel veins, a trait common to members of the Lily family. People seeking the young shoots of this plant must be careful to differentiate between false Solomon's seal and the poisonous hellebores. The hellebore leaves are attached alternately, but circle the stem, whereas these are attached only at the sides of the main plant stalk. The hellebore leaf also has parallel venation, but it is folded like an accordion. The leaves of the false Solomon's seal usually have fine hair on their undersurfaces and either attach directly to the stem or have only a short petiole.

The cone-shaped flower cluster is made up of numerous branches bearing blossoms. The entire flower head may measure from three to six inches in length. Each tiny flower has six petals. The stamens are very prominent, giving the flower a fuzzy or starry look. The blossoms later develop into berries which contain one or two seeds. The berries are at first greenish-yellow in color, then become speckled with red and later turn fully red, often highlighted with purple dots. They remain on the plant until fall.

Underground is a fleshy horizontal root which is reportedly sweetish to the taste. It is rough, and may show scars in the manner of Solomon's seal. If you wish to transplant some of these attractive plants to a compatible spot in your garden, dig the roots late in the fall. This will help you to identify the plant, come spring, in its early growth stages.

Native to North America as well as eastern Asia, this plant is useful as well as lovely. The young shoots, though thin, may be prepared like asparagus, or added to soups or stews. The berries may be eaten raw or cooked, but beware their action on the lower intestine if they are eaten too freely! The berries may be simmered slightly and frozen, or preserved in honey for use as a natural laxative. A few generally do not bother most people, and so they make a good nibble or addition to a conserve, mixed jam or salad. They were known to some of the early settlers as scurvy berries. It seems logical to assume that these berries, like most others, contain high amounts of vitamin C.

The root may be eaten, but ***not*** in its raw state. Since it requires a fair amount of preparation time, most people do not actively gather it today. It would be a source of food in an emergency. It must first be soaked, at least overnight but preferably for about twenty-four hours, in a solution of lye-containing wood ashes and water. The recommended mixture is ½ to ¾ cup of ashes to one gallon of water. After soaking, the root reportedly may be boiled and used as a potato.

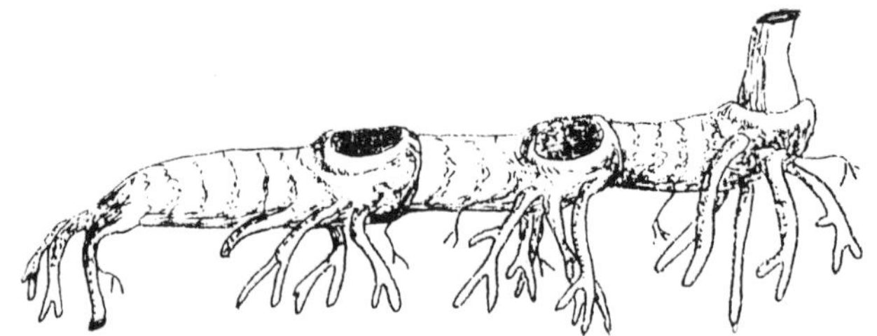

False Solomon's Seal Root

WILD GINGER 

Asarum canadense
Photo page #5

Also known as: Indian ginger, sturgeon potato, hot potato, snakeroot, ginger, Canadian snakeroot, Vermont snakeroot, Asarabacca

Season: Early spring through fall; blooms in May

Habitat: Rich woods, shaded areas; prefers alkaline soils

The two leaves of this plant are its most identifiable feature. They are dark green on their surfaces, lighter beneath, fuzzy and heart-shaped, and will often be seen standing erect like rabbit ears. The leafstalks are hairy; follow them down to a horizontal underground root which is the edible part of the plant. The entire plant usually grows to less than a foot tall, and the leaves will be from four to seven inches broad.

You will seldom spot the flower of the wild ginger plant without really searching for it. A dull purplish brown with red hues, the flower appears in the crotch of the two leafstalks, near the base of the plant, and is often buried by forest litter. If you'd like to see the wild ginger in bloom, look for it during the latter parts of May; this will help to confirm ginger's identity. The flower actually has no petals; the sepals which form the protective coat of the bud become the colored parts of the flower. The three deeply colored sepals unite to form a tube, creamy-colored within, and the seeds are retained here until they ripen.

If you find wild ginger in great enough numbers, you'll be able to dig one or more of the roots. They're easily removed. Their ginger odor will be positive proof that you have found the correct plant, especially when the flowers are no longer present. The roots may be dug throughout the snow-free weather.

These hardy plants spread and may be transplanted to a similar location. Making sure to first obtain the landowner's permission, dig up the plants with some of their native soil. Given a year or two, they'll spread into their new homesite. Though ginger spreads, it is not a common plant; when you find a patch, it will be a large one, but the groups are often quite distant from each other. Remember to take no more than every fifth plant.

Wild ginger is not the same plant as that which is prepared commercially. Its taste is quite similar, though, and the wild root serves as a fine substitute in recipes featuring ginger. Its bite is not as strong as that of the store product, and you'll probably wish to add more than the recipe calls for. The wild roots make excellent ginger candy, and store well candied or dried.

Just as the ginger root of Asia found acceptance not only for its flavor but its medicinal powers as well, so too has the American ginger found similar applications. Early settlers used it as a cough medicine, a relief preparation for stomach distress, and a reducer of fever. Some of the Indian tribes relied on this plant to cure earache.

Wild Ginger Root

GROUNDNUT 

Apios americana
Photo page #16

Also known as: Indian potato, hopniss, wild bean, potato bean
Season: Tubers best in fall; blooms in summer
Habitat: Likes moist, protected areas; grows over other bushes, fences, etc.

This plant, one of the most highly acclaimed wild edibles, was named for its delicious underground tubers. The Indians told the first colonists about these, and early Americans appreciated the groundnut as a staple long before the potato was introduced to this continent. The small, nut-size tubers are best harvested in late summer or fall, when they are at their sweetest. Cooked and served like potatoes, they rival the potato in goodness. Their taste is slightly sweeter than that of the potato; some people consider it turnip-like. Groundnuts may be steamed, boiled, baked, roasted, fried in bacon fat, cooked in chowders, casseroles, or vegetable dishes.

Twining around bushes and over fences and rock walls, this plant bears spikes of flowers; though their brown and pinkish hues are somewhat subdued, the flowers have an attractive appearance and scent. When you break the flower stalk or any of the stems, you'll discover that the plant contains a milky juice. The light green leaves normally have seven leaflets, with six of them paired and the seventh at the tip of the leaf, but these leaflets may vary from three to nine in number. Each has a smooth edge and is not hairy, though the young stems of this plant may be velvety.

The groundnut's seed pods, when ripe, may be boiled and eaten as a vegetable. It's not often you'll find enough to fill your pot, but they will go well with groundnut tubers. They could be included in a mixed vegetable dish or added to a fish or clam chowder.

The roots of this plant are not usually far below the surface of the ground; trace along them to find the tubers. Varying in size, they are often as large as an egg. The groundnut appreciates dampness, and is abundant near the seashore and around inland bodies of water. Point out this plant, and ask your family fisherman to bring home some groundnuts with the day's catch!

INDIAN CUCUMBER 

Medeola virginiana
Photo page #6

Also known as: Indian cucumber root, cucumber lily
Season: Blooms in June; roots best in early spring and late fall
Habitat: Cool, moist woods

This plant is a relative of the trillium, and its parts grow in threes or multiples of three. Normally, the velvety stem, growing one to two feet high, bears a lower whorl of six leaves and an upper whorl of three leaves. The flowers, which appear in June, are not at all showy; you could easily bypass the tiny lily-like blooms that droop, yellowish-green, beneath the uppermost trio of leaves. There are usually six curved-back petals, out of which protrude six stamens and three pistils. Usually there are three flowers, and they each produce a berry-like fruit (inedible) usually containing six seeds.

It is the taproot of this plant which is the edible portion. When you sink your teeth into the sweet crispness of one of these waxy-white roots, you'll wonder why this hasn't been included in your diet before! Generally the taproot is nearly horizontal beneath the ground. It feels like one of the emergency candles bought at the hardware store and is nearly as white, or just a shade creamier, in color. Once washed, it can be sliced into a tossed salad or included in a potato salad; sweetly crunchy, it is a delightful addition to a tuna or egg salad sandwich. Use it as a surprise garnish for any vegetable dish, or serve as a delicious cooked vegetable.

The summer and fall plants are easier to identify than those just sprouting in the spring. Usually, if you find just one, you'll discover a good number of these plants in an area. However, please use common sense, and don't eradicate them all! The roots are sweetest and fattest in early spring and fall, but they're sweet even when the plant is in blossom. Indian cucumber is a terrific plant for hunters and hikers to get to know, for the roots could easily sustain a lost person until help arrived.

These tubers may be frozen or canned; just parboil them a few minutes beforehand. They're a real treat in a stew or soup, whether fresh or from your home stores. Once you've tasted them, you'll never forget them.

SPIDERWORT

Tradescantia virginiana (and others)
Photo page #6

Also known as: Widow's tears, spider plant

Season: Young leaves and stalks, in spring; blooms in early summer

Habitat: Prefers semi-shaded, protected areas—roadsides, gardens (when cultivated), open woods, wood edges, gravelly banks, along railroad tracks

Originally found from Connecticut south and in the Middle West, this plant was cultivated in more northern areas. It proved to be winter hardy, and blithely escaped into the wild. There are several *Tradescantia* species, all edible, with flower colors ranging from purple through blue and pink to white. Their common name is derived from their upper leaves, which spread out from beneath the flower clusters like a spider's legs.

The first spiderwort I saw looked like some sinister alien being glowing in the cool, shaded recesses of a kindly lady's garden. (The original stock of her plants had belonged to her grandmother; the offspring had spread their roots in three states, split and carried away as members of the family moved their households.) Golden "eyes" (stamens) seemed to glare from midnight purple, three-petaled flowers, menacing anyone who might dare to pluck their leaves or tender stems for salad materials or a stew pot.

Whatever the color of the flowers, all spiderworts have these golden stamens. The unopened buds droop, silently awaiting their turn at glory; they begin blooming late in the spring and continue through the summer. The sepals which encase the flower bud are often hairy. The spiderwort's leaves look almost like those of an iris, but do not come from just the base of the plant; rather, they shoot out from the fleshy stems, and there are usually a pair just beneath the flowers. The leaves are indented, nearly folded, over the central vein, and the other veins lie parallel to this like those of grass blades. The leaves may show a little velvet on their upper surfaces.

The flowers may be dipped in egg white and coated with sugar to eat as a fragrant, colorful candy, but the leaves and succulent stalks are the best-known edible portions. Young and tender, they may be added to salads or cooked as a pot herb. Be sure to obtain your neighbor's permission, though, if you spy some in his garden and cannot find wild ones to sample!

CHECKERBERRY

Gaultheria procumbens
Photo page #5

Also known as: Wintergreen
Season: Year-round
Habitat: Woods, clearings, cleared but formerly wooded areas

Most children who have spent any time at all near woodlands know the checkerberry. It's an evergreen plant, a member of the Heath family. The berries are eaten by grouse and partridge, but you'll find them on the plants year-round. The berries from the previous summer are edible the following season. While they are a bit dry, don't hesitate to look for "old stock" — they are still good.

The leaves are aromatic, their bracing wintergreen smell deriving from the **methyl salicylate** oil they contain. (Sniff the commerical rubs for aching muscles, and you'll recognize the odor of methyl salicylate.) The old leaves may be dull and dark green or tinged with red, or even entirely red, but the newer leaves are generally a shiny, lighter green. The leaves have a leathery feel and are toothed with such widely spaced, small teeth that they may at first appear to be not toothed at all. There is a central vein running the length of the leaf. The side veins arising from this midrib curve as they approach the edge of the leaf and rejoin with other side veins.

The flowers are white bells that resemble those of lily of the valley. They dangle beneath the leaves singly, in pairs, or sometimes as a trio. They develop into berries as red as those of holly. If water was plentiful during berry production, the fruits will be large, up to one-half inch across, and the bases will bear a crown of bumps surrounding the little spike that remains from the flower. If the season was drier, the berry will be smaller and may not show the bumps as well, but it, too, will have the basal prong.

The stems of these plants creep along the ground, poking up as what appear to be separate erect plants. Checkerberry plants are never vine-like; there are no tendrils, nor do they climb other plants. Often you'll see only a leaf here and there, peeking out from between the leaves and duff of the forest floor.

The odor of the crushed leaves, crisply minty, is a sure-fire trademark of this plant. Both berries and leaves have the wintergreen flavor. These Christmas-colored berry treats are refreshing hiking nibbles.

Oil of wintergreen, obtained from these leaves by steam distillation, was long used as a rub or poultice against muscle aches, sprains, and joint pain. It was also rubbed onto the chest to alleviate colds. Dried or fresh leaves were used to prepare a tea that was taken both for pleasure and for relief of cold symptoms.

Methyl salicylate (oil of wintergreen) is used as a flavoring in many products, including toothpaste and chewing gum. Checkerberry leaves will only yield so much of this product; most commerical wintergreen oil is made synthetically today from wood alcohol (methanol) and salicylic acid. Naturally produced methyl salicylate is also found in black birch, *Betula lenta.* (See Black Birch.) The birches produced more of this substance than checkerberry, but were exploited to a point where their numbers diminished greatly and profits shrank. Consequently, while natural oil of wintergreen is still obtained from this birch, the chemist today fills most of the spice rack's bottles, provides the wintergreen-warm liniment, and produces the wintergreen-strong muscle rub from his laboratory. (The chemical composition of both natural and synthetic methyl salicylate is identical.)

The plant is called "checkerberry" here to avoid confusion with three plants of the *Pyrola* genus which some European herbalists call "wintergreen." The oval leaves of the *Pyrola* wintergreens originate from the base of the plant, while the checkerberry's grow on the sides and top of the upright stem. These leaves contain a compound similar to methyl salicylate, and were used externally in poultices. A third plant called "wintergreen" in some books is actually pipsissewa (*Chimaphila*). This was used by Indians and early settlers in much the same way as checkerberry: they prepared wet dressings of the entire mashed plant, or drank it as a tea to alleviate joint pains, backache and colds, and to induce sweating.

Since the berries of the checkerberry are somewhat dry, you may enjoy them in combination with other berries in jelly, jam, or a fruit dessert. Sprinkle them over salads for color and flavor, and add some of the tender leaves, too (chopped). Add either slightly mashed berries or chopped leaves to a light-flavored white wine, and allow them to become friends for a day or two. Or, mash the berries a bit to split them, and let them roast for the last few minutes with the meat and gravy when you're roasting pork. It's a pleasant addition.

PARTRIDGEBERRY 

Mitchella repens
Photo page #5

Also known as: Bird berry, little apple berry
Season: Year-round, except when snow-covered
Habitat: Cool, moist woodlands

The partridgeberry plant grows partly hidden beneath pine needles and other duff on the forest floor. Its evergreen leaves are in opposite pairs, dark green and untoothed, and with a distinctive whitish stripe up the middle. In the warmth of summer this plant produces paired flowers shaped like miniature lilies, usually white, but sometimes pink or white tinged with red. Most often there are four curved petals at the tip of the horn, but flowers with five or six petal divisions have been found. Four stamens project upward, while the petals curve outward to reveal the ermine fuzz of four stigmas ready to receive pollen. These paired flowers share fused ovaries, producing edible "Siamese twin" berries. The berry, with its paired flower dimples on the upper surface, is an immediate identification feature.

It is no wonder that birds like these holly-red, shiny berries. Though they are somewhat dry and have several stony seeds, the berries have a pleasant apple-like flavor and are a good woodland snack, available just about year-round. Use the plants for holiday decorations—they may be harvested even in the middle of winter, if you're willing to move the snow and leaf litter. The cheerful partridgeberry plants may be kept in an attractive glass container or woven into your evergreen wreaths.

The berries mix well with other fruits in jellies and jams, and look lovely in fruit cake or muffins. They even serve as a wholesome substitute for the bleached, artificially colored and sweetened cherry in a cocktail! Give them a try, but do leave enough for the little wild food fanciers who rely upon them.

MOUNTAIN CRANBERRY 

Vaccinium vitis-idaea

Also known as: Cranberry

Season: Berries ripe from late summer through late fall; last year's berries sometimes available in early spring

Habitat: Cool, moist woodlands on rocky mountains

While it grows in a very different habitat from its bog-dwelling relatives, the mountain cranberry is otherwise identified and used as a typical cranberry. (For a complete general description of the three *Vaccinium* species found in the wild, see Cranberries.) The mountain cranberry most resembles the large cranberry *(Vaccinium macrocarpon)* in appearance. Its leaves are about the same size as those of the large cranberry, although they may be slightly smaller. Also, the flowers of the mountain cranberry are bell-like, less beaked in shape than those of the other two cranberry species. The berries are smaller and somewhat bitter, but cooking will sweeten them. (NOTE: See the illustration on page 14.)

BUNCHBERRY 

Cornus canadensis

Photo page #6

Also known as: Dwarf cornel, Canadian cornel, low cornel, little dogwood

Season: Berries, late summer and fall, blooms in early summer

Habitat: Completely or partially shaded areas at edges of or within woods

Since it is not all that prolific, this pretty wildflower should not be picked. Removing the berries, though, probably does little harm, except to the birds and small animals who also appreciate them. The plant has a woody, creeping root which runs underground to generate new plants, so the bunchberry does not depend exclusively on its seeds to spread its tribe.

It is related to the much larger dogwoods, and you can see the kinship in both their flowers and leaves. The two- to three-inch leaves are borne on a stalk that seldom exceeds eight inches in height. This stem is woody at its base, but greenly herbaceous above. The leaves of flower-bearing plants generally grow in what appears to be a whorl of six leaves. Of these, two are larger and attached at a slightly lower level than the others. Barren plants usually have only four leaves. These leaves are oval in shape, and pointed at both ends. Usually there are five to seven main veins, and these curve to follow the leaf edge. They're quite prominent. The leaves may be smooth or slightly downy.

During spring and the early summer the plants will bear flowers. The flowers appear to have four white petals, but these are really bracts which surround the multiple true flowers in the center. By July most of these floral structures will have been replaced by holly-berry-red berries.

Bunchberries are bright and beautiful! Each shiny scarlet fruit has within it a central small stone. Our children call them "apple berries," for when you split them the juicy white flesh reminds you of an apple, in miniature. With a little stretch of the imagination, they even taste like a slightly soft apple.

The berries, if not eaten by us or other creatures, remain on the plant well into the fall. This is not a fruit to pick in great quantities for home use. They go well in muffins and pancakes, and may be combined with other fruits and berries. They're a sparkling color contrast when added to salads, too. We haven't tried to freeze them; they never make it that far. Most berries do freeze well, though, and these most likely would. They're probably best preserved in jellies.

These berries are a thirst-quenching trail nibble, even if not heavily flavored, and would be an excellent emergency food for a lost hunter or hiker. And, oddly enough, though these red berries may seem an unlikely temptation for fish, they have reportedly been used as bait for small fishes, which in turn serve as bait for larger ones. How's that, for an edible enjoyed by bird, beast, and fish!

BLUE LETTUCE 

Lactuca floridana
Photo page #7

Also known as: Wild blue lettuce

Season: Young leaves, late spring and early summer; blooms beginning of July

Habitat: Shaded road edges, edges of woodlands and open woods

Originally confined to an area ranging from Boston, Mass., to Minnesota and southward, this lettuce is popping up with greater frequency in the northern states. Constant traffic is a factor in its migration. Once known, this plant can be a boon to campers as well as to everyday households.

It is easiest to identify these yard-high plants when they are in full bloom. The flowers, tiny blue to white starry blooms with light centers, resemble those of chicory, but they're held on branching stalks at the top of the plant. Expect to see them begin to open around Independence Day. The aster-like flowers, as well as the dandelionish leaf form and hollow stems that exude a bitter milk when cut, will reassure you that you've found the right plant.

There are so many plants with leaves that could be described as resembling a dandelion's! In this case, the leaves are deeply cut and grass-green in color, often with reddish tones at their veins. By the time the plant has bloomed, only the very newest upper leaves are fit for picking, and these will still be a bit too tangy for most tastes. At this stage, they're best used as a pot herb; a change of water will tame them.

It is the first tender leaves you're after. Once you know the plant, keep a record of where you've found it. The mature plants shed parachute-borne seeds that travel on the wind. Many of the seeds, though, will take hold near the parent plant—look for the youngsters the following spring. Or, choose a similar location on your own land, transplant blue lettuce or some of the seeds, and you'll have an easily accessible crop of the spring greens.

WILD LETTUCE

Lactuca canadensis
Photo page #7

Also known as: Yellow wild lettuce, tall lettuce, dandelion lettuce, horseweed

Season: Early summer; blooms in midsummer

Habitat: Open woodlands, shaded roadsides and pasture edges, damp areas, along rows of trees and walls

The leaves of this plant are usually like those of a dandelion; they may even be lance-shaped, especially the upper leaves. However, it is the flowers which are a giveaway, if you have ever let cultivated lettuce mature. The yellow blossoms of wild lettuce, like those of dandelion or hawkweed, appear on upper stems in midsummer.

There are several varieties of yellow-blooming wild lettuces. One has leaves with prickly edges, and another shows hairs on the stems and lower leaves. These are also edible.

The spiny variety may be confused with some of the sow thistles, but no problem arises here: the sow thistles are usable in the same ways. They are similar in the overall structure, but have larger flowers. Of course, common cultivated lettuce, *Lactuca sativa*, sometimes seeds from a garden plot and escapes into the wild. Its flower is nearly identical with that of wild lettuce, but the leaves are ovate to lance-shaped and not indented.

The longest leaves of the commonly found wild lettuce may reach ten inches or more in length, while the entire plant may vary from about three feet to well over a man's height. Overall, the plant resembles a dandelion gone out of control, with, instead, small flowers on branched stems. The stems secrete a milky, bitter juice, like the dandelion, and under the plant is a taproot similar to the dandelion's.

The middle-aged leaves benefit from one or more changes of water, though a little honey added to the final water does help. They may also be combined with other greens when served as a pot herb. Very young spring leaves, up to about six inches long, or the blanched leaves of young plants are an excellent salad material, as well as an eminent cooked vegetable that requires minimal time in the pot. Just steam them in their rinse water; the leaves will supply the remaining moisture, and, by not draining, you'll retain all those vitamins and minerals. You may also use these young leaves in any stir-fry dish. If you don't care to boil and reboil the older leaves, simply let them simmer in soup or stew: what would otherwise go down the drain will give itself to the broth.

Horses and cattle often know a good thing when they munch it, and wild lettuce rapidly disappears if it sprouts in their meadow. If you keep rabbits or chickens, watch them gobble up the older leaves—they don't seem to mind the sharpness.

If you allow the milky juice of this plant to stand in the air, it will harden and darken to a brownish tone. At one time, this substance was reportedly sold as an opium substitute! Proven to be a sham, this lettuce extract was discounted as a pain killer; still, some recent authors consider that large quantities of wild or cultivated lettuce may actually soothe the nervous system. Some of the B-complex vitamins, especially, have been shown to benefit the nerves; possibly, lettuce contains enough of these vitamins to have a very direct effect, or perhaps some trace mineral, concentrated, is responsible.

The wild lettuces, blue or yellow, may be canned or blanched and frozen for later use. They are certainly a wild crop worthy of your attention.

JEWELWEEDS

Impatiens capensis (Spotted Jewelweed)
Impatiens pallida (Pale Jewelweed)
Photo page #7

Also known as: Touch-me-not, snapweed
Season: Spring through summer
Habitat: Partly shaded moist areas, rich soil, roadsides

DO NOT CONSUME TOO MUCH OF THIS PLANT AT ANY ONE TIME

There are more similarities than differences between these two jewelweeds. The flowers of both, shaped like miniature cornucopias, are suspended by flower stalks that spring from the leaf axils. Inside the recurved rear spur of each blossom is a drop of nectar to tempt bees. The flowers of the spotted jewelweed, though, are usually a golden tangerine tone, while the pale jewelweed's blossoms are butter yellow. The two species also differ slightly in the shape of the flower and of the spur. The spotted variety generally first blooms late in June or early in July, with its paler relative following a couple of weeks later.

The leaves of both plants, oval with a blunt pointed tip and coarsely toothed edges, resemble those of lambsquarters (see Lambsquarters). The leaves are a dull green, but their petioles and the plant stalks often wear tinges of red, especially at the slightly swollen, often angled, joints.

Once you've seen the plant in blossom, it will be relatively easy to recognize at any time in the growing season. You'll know its ridged stems, translucent as a frosted pale green candle glass. If you wish to transplant jewelweed to your property, it will be happy in a corner which receives some sun during the day. It likes moisture, but not constant wetness. You'll most likely find it growing behind a barn or under a tree's shelter. The plants, a bit weedy-looking, will reach up to five feet tall.

If you locate a patch where you can cut youngsters less than six inches high, these young shoots can be boiled and served like asparagus. If they are very young, one change of water will mellow any bitterness, but if the shoots approach the maximum of six inches, it's advisable to use two waters.

Apparently this plant is a glutton for minerals, and stores high concentrations in its tissues; for this reason, take care not to serve large quantities of jewelweed. The young shoots may be combined with other spring greens or added (in limited quantities) to a soup or stew. For its high mineral content, jewelweed is a good plant to eat, but sparingly — too much could cause an upset. (Cattle poisonings have been reported from herds which consumed large quantities.)

Jewelweed is reported to be an effective treatment for poison ivy reactions, stinging nettle irritation, and allergy-caused rashes. The leaves and stems are ground up (a meat grinder works well), and the green jewelweed juice is applied externally. This extract has been found helpful, used externally, in treating some cases of psoriasis.

The alternate names of snapweed and touch-me-not, as well as the generic name, *Impatiens*, are derived from the plant's impatient jack-in-the-box seed capsule. The ripe, green seed pods will spring open at the slightest touch, flinging the seeds a distance from the parent plant. These seeds are reportedly edible, tasting like butternuts. Let some remain, though, to continue the tribe.

BITTERSWEET NIGHTSHADE

Solanum dulcamara
Photo page #7

Also known as: European bittersweet, woody nightshade, blue nightshade, purple nightshade, red-berried nightshade

Season: Spring through fall

Habitat: Likes to grow on bushes, along shorelines (salt and fresh), and in open woods and clearings, gardens, lots and parks, waste areas

THIS IS A POISONOUS PLANT

This relative of our common potato (*Solanum tuberosum*), black nightshade (*Solanum nigrum*), eggplant (*Solanum esculentum*) and many other edibles and inedibles is a beautiful purple-flowering plant that, late in summer, bears bunches of the nicest-looking red berries ever to tempt a berry lover. Most adults will not pick a berry unfamiliar to them, but many children will; they should be warned about this one.

The vine-like plants trail weakly on the ground or grow up and around bushes, and are woody at their bases. The forest green lower leaves are divided into three pointed lobes, the uppermost lobe much broader and larger than the other two. All in all, the lower leaves resemble rounded arrowheads. The upper leaves may have two lobes or none at all.

The flowers give this plant away. Their form is like that of some of the cranberry plants. Five purple petals curl backwards from the reproductive structures; five fused stamens form a yellow beak protruding from the center of the flower. You can see these flowers from spring through fall, for the plant produces both fruit and flowers throughout the growing season.

All parts of the plant, including the lovely red berries, contain the alkaloid-like material, **solanine**. According to some reports, the fully ripe berries may contain less of this toxin than the remainder of the plant or the unripe berries. However, if enough are eaten, death may result.

I have seen these pretty plants growing in state parks and private hedges. Wild and domestic animals that have eaten of these plants have likely suffered from nightshade poisoning. It would seem a wise precaution to remove the plants, or berries as they form, from areas where pets or children are to be playing.

WILD SARSAPARILLA

Aralia nudicaulis
Photo page #8

Also known as: False sarsaparilla, small spikenard, rabbitroot, shotbush, wild licorice, Virginian sarsaparilla, American sarsaparilla

Season: Spring through summer; roots best in fall

Habitat: Rich, rocky woods, moist but not wet areas, roadsides, fields moist but not wet

DO NOT CONFUSE WITH SHRUB-LIKE *ARALIA SPINOSA* OR BANEBERRY; DO NOT EAT THIS PLANT'S BERRIES

When you find one wild sarsaparilla plant, you'll generally find a whole bunch! Once you've learned to spot them, you'll find them growing nearly anywhere they are sheltered by trees. This is one of the most common plants of the northeastern woods.

The plants vary from about nine to eighteen inches tall. Each features a compound leaf held like an umbrella that protects the three greenish-white flower globes below. Though this plant appears to have three leaves, the compound leaf is actually a single leaf: the leafstalk springs from the base of the plant and then divides into a trio of separate stalks. Each of these three stalks bears three to five leaflets that are usually two to five inches long, oval with toothed edges, and sharply pointed at the ends. The leaves will be fully developed before the flowers appear. (Some plants bear no flowers at all, but most do.)

The flower clusters are arranged like the leaves. A single flower stalk arises from the *basal part* of the plant, then splits near its summit into three separate stalks. On each of these is a round flower cluster; each tiny flower has five petals and five stamens. There are no leaves on the flower stalk.

The plant flowers in late spring or early summer, and the berries ripen by July. Green at first, they will later flush to a purplish-black hue. At the tip of each berry will be the remains of the floral parts, making the berry look like it has a puckered mouth.

All the parts of the plants of the *Aralia* genus are said to have a warm, aromatic taste, but apparently the root of this plant is the only portion commonly used. (The berries are not edible; berries of members of the *Aralia* family contain a poisonous glycoside.) The underground root portion is a large, fleshy, usually horizontal storehouse of flavor. It has been used to impart a flavor to root beers. At one time, sarsaparilla was a favorite drink in America, and you can still find sarsaparilla soda sold today. In the past, sarsaparilla root was used for a health tonic; this may have augmented the sale of sarsaparilla as a beverage, though the flavor is all the sales pitch it needs.

The original sarsaparilla drink was made from the dried roots of several members of the *Smilax* genus. These are tough, climbing or trailing shrubs native to the area between southern Mexico and northern South America, as well as Jamaica and other West Indian islands. The roots of these shrubs were believed to alter body chemistry beneficially. Our sarsaparilla plants were put to the same use, but were found wanting in their effects. Even so, medicinal uses and tonic effects were ascribed to our sarsaparilla plants, and apparently the American Indian tribes, either on their own or through contact with foreign settlers, made use of the wild sarsaparilla, bristly sarsaparilla, and spikenard plants which grow on this continent. In old books, the wild sarsaparilla root is reputed to be equal to the true sarsaparilla root as a tonic.

Regardless of your degree of belief in herbal medicine, the roots of these plants do make a hearty, tasty herb tea. They are best collected late in the season when the plant has had full time to pack them with flavor and goodness. Apparently, some tribes of Indians used them as food when traveling. The roots are strongly flavored, but small amounts, chopped, could be added to a salad, casserole or vegetable dish for a real change of pace.

To use wild or bristly sarsaparilla or spikenard (see the next two entries) to make your own cough medicine, make an extract of the root and sweeten with honey. The sliced, bruised pieces of any of these roots may be used to brew a hearty, stimulating tea with good flavor. As you would before picking any plant root, be certain to make positive identification. Many plants have similar root structures, and you may be wise to tag actual specimens for reference.

BRISTLY SARSAPARILLA

Aralia hispida
Photo page #8

Also known as: Wild elder
Season: Same as wild sarsaparilla
Habitat: Dry roadsides, woods, lawn edges and ditches, waste places

DO NOT CONFUSE WITH SHRUB-LIKE *ARALIA SPINOSA* OR BANEBERRY; DO NO EAT BERRIES

The bristly sarsaparilla looks like the wild sarsaparilla's big brother. This plant, though, is much branched and, while the leaves and flowers closely resemble those of wild sarsaparilla, the flower stalks arise from the same stalk as the leaves. There are generally *three* globular flowers on each flower stalk, and the flowers are positioned higher than the leaves.

The leaves are compound, normally with three to five leaflets shaped like those of wild sarsaparilla. Some of these leaflets will have thumb-like divisions, and a pair of leaflets is usually found where the leafstalk divides to form the three leaflet stalks. The overall impression of the leaves is their similarity to the elder leaves. ***Do not confuse these with those of the baneberry plants.***

The plant reaches from one to three or more feet tall. Probably its most telling characteristic is the presence of bristles, especially on the lower, somewhat woody and often reddish-hued stem. Though they are not as menacing as those of the rose or brier, it is advisable to wear gloves when handling this plant.

Bristly sarsaparilla spreads via its fleshy underground root; a whole group, if located in loose, sandy soil, may be pulled up at one go with their interconnected rhizomes intact. Of course, thin but do not strip an area of these plants.

The roots of this plant are used in the same manner as the wild sarsaparilla's. (See Wild Sarsaparilla.) The berries, nearly identical to those of the wild sarsaparilla, are inedible.

AMERICAN SPIKENARD

Aralia racemosa
Photo page #8

Also known as: Spice bush, spignet, Indian root, life-of-man, old man's root, old maid's root
Season: Blooms in mid-summer; roots best in fall
Habitat: Rich, rocky woods and wood edges

DO NOT CONFUSE WITH SHRUB-LIKE *ARALIA SPINOSA*; DO NOT EAT BERRIES

This is a relative of wild sarsaparilla; you can see the family resemblance in their leaves. However, while small specimens are found at two feet tall, the spikenard ranges to hale and hardy plants six feet or taller!

Like the wild sarsaparilla, spikenard's leaves are usually separated into three parts, each part with five or more leaflets. Each leaflet is heart-shaped, doubly toothed, and finished with a finely pointed end. The leafstalks attach to the dark green or reddish main stem. The entire leaf may reach a length of three feet.

Branching from the axils of some of the leaves and the end of the stem are the flower stalks, but these flower clusters are not globular as in the smaller sarsaparilla plants. At first glance they look a little like the flower stalks of meadow rue. Roughly conical or cylindrical, the clusters of fuzzy greenish-white flowers are borne on a central stalk, and will later produce reddish-purple inedible berries. The flowers of this gracious Aralian giant are generally seen later than those of the smaller sarsaparillas; they grow in the depths of the woods in mid-summer.

The main stem of this plant lacks any bristles, but is larger and thicker than those of the other relatives. The root is proportionate to the size of the plant: spicy, aromatic, and big! If the plant you have found grows in a very rocky area, you may not get the entire root intact. One root, though, is sure to go a long way in making teas and beers, or whatever you have in mind. As with the other members of this group, the roots are best gathered in the fall. They may be dried, but the larger ones should be split to facilitate drying without decomposition. Seal them well in a tight jar to retain their spiciness.

There is a long record of medicinal use behind this plant. Even in the late 1800's, spikenard roots were still employed to alleviate chest congestion, asthma, rheumatism and even skin problems. (Collection of these plants for pharmaceutical uses provided some people with extra income, but must have thinned the spikenard population considerably.) Spikenard roots were found to contain a saponin, which was named **aralin**. Many saponins have the ability to break down the membranes of platelets, hastening the formation of a clot. Though spikenard berries are considered inedible, some Indians reportedly used a salve prepared from this part of the plant for treating wounds.

For many years, spikenard found its way into spring tonics. The mashed roots of this plant joined those of burdock, dandelion, and others, each adding their flavors and benefits to the brew. For a down-to-earth pick-me-up, why not try one of our ancestors' favorite elixirs of vitality?

CINNAMON FERN

Osmunda cinnamomea
Photo page #12

Also known as: Osmunda fern, rusty osmunda, cinnamon osmunda
Season: Spring through early summer
Habitat: Roadsides, open woodlands, along shady edges of streams and ponds

THIS PLANT IS POISONOUS WHEN MATURE

The cinnamon fern looks like its name. Its fertile frond (or fronds) looks like a cinnamon-colored firebrand sticking upward from the rosette of grass-green sterile fronds. The bottoms of its stalks, too, seem to be dusted with cinnamon: the rusty-colored fuzz they bear is what remains of the silvery-rusty velvet that encased them as fiddleheads.

The fiddleheads (tightly curled-up developing leaves) are quite edible if you're willing to remove the hair and cook them in at least two changes of water. Most of the fuzz on the stalks can be rolled off between your dry hands, but we find it easier to not bother with the immature leaf's curled knob at the top — the hairs are very bitter, and persist in clinging to the fiddlehead itself.

Several other ferns have fuzzy fiddleheads. The surest way to gather cinnamon fern is to locate the plants at maturity and hunt the fiddleheads in exactly the same spot early the next season. This species is one of the first ferns up in the spring.

This fern requires considerable time in cooking, so you might do well to first parboil the fiddlehead stalks separately for about ten minutes, then cook them to tenderness in a soup or stew. Remember, though: ***Never eat any fern after the fiddlehead has begun to open up, for the mature foliage is considered poisonous.***

COMMON WOOD SORREL

Oxalis acetocella (Oxalis montana)
Photo page #15

Also known as: Sour grass, pink wood sorrel
Season: Summer
Habitat: Prefers semi-shaded areas; woodland clearings, roadsides

Though not as common as the yellow wood sorrel, this variety may be used similarly—in salads, cooked with other vegetables, or served as a lemony iced tea.

The flowers are borne on individual leafless stalks, and their color best distinguishes the common from the yellow wood sorrel: The five petals are basically white, but darker veins or stripes give the flower a violet to pink tone. Each petal has yellow shading at its base, near the flower's reproductive structures.

The clover-like leaves are very similar to those of the yellow wood sorrel. Each leaf has three broad, heart-shaped leaflets. A tiny nibble, after the other traits check out, will confirm that you've found common wood sorrel, for the leaves have the same agreeable taste, lemon-tart, as those of yellow wood sorrel and dock. The flavor is due to the presence of oxalic acid. (See Sheep Sorrel and Yellow Wood Sorrel.)

VII

Herbaceous Plants of Fields, Roadsides and Open Places

STRAWBERRY 

Fragaria virginiana
Fargaria vasca
Photo page #9

Also known as: Wild strawberry, running strawberry, wood strawberry, little wild strawberry

Season: Late spring to mid-summer

Habitat: Pastures, fields, wood edges and open areas in woodlands, lawns, waste areas

The lovely, tasty little wild strawberry that will survive nearly anywhere is a cousin to the rose. While the rose has more leaflets on its leaf, and showier flowers, the fruits of both plants are exceptionally high in vitamins, and you can see the family relationship when you look closely at the leaves.

When the fruit is on the plant, you can't miss identifying it. Just like the commercially grown or garden berry, but smaller, these wild fruits may reach three quarters of an inch in length; most will grow to about a half inch. It takes a lot more picking to fill your pot with these, but they are sweeter and more fully flavored than most garden strawberries.

A few struggling strawberry plants growing on a steep, impossible-to-mow bank on our front lawn gave us an idea: Looking around our property, we gathered a large number of strawberry plants that were in effect weeds among the grass, and transplanted them. Our improvised strawberry bank now provides many loads of fresh-picked berries for breakfasts and desserts! They bear over a period of weeks, given enough moisture, and mellow to deep red-toned ground cover as fall approaches.

Reportedly, the stalks are edible (if you can bear to sacrifice the berries the plants would otherwise yield). And nearly anytime during their growing season the fresh leaves may be brewed for an excellent, vitamin-C-rich tea. To get the fullest quantity of this vitamin, though, it is best to let the strawberry leaves steep for a day in unheated water, then drink this as an iced tea. A little honey, and lemon if you like, is all that is needed to round out the flavor. The leaves may be dried for future use.

The fruit, too, may be dried, stored, and enjoyed as a candy leather: Mash the fruit, line a cookie sheet with aluminum foil, and spread a layer of strawberry mash (no thicker than half an inch) into this. Covered with netting or cheesecloth, the mixture may be dried in the sun or in a low-temperature oven to a leather-like consistency. (You may wish to add another fruit — banana is a compatible one — to stretch the berries and improve the texture.) To prevent the cut-up fruit leather strips from sticking together, wrap them in waxed paper or coat them with sugar. They are wonderful as a snack, or may be soaked or stewed just enough to top a cheesecake, stir into desserts, or drizzle over pancakes, ice cream, yogurt.

Of course, the fresh fruit may be canned or frozen. You could make a batch of strawberry ice cream, without the artificial colorings and flavorings, with some of your crop. If you have had a real harvest, make strawberry jam or jelly to give someone else the bounty of summer during winter's doldrums. Complement it with a holiday-colored package of dried strawberry leaf tea, and watch eyes light up!

To prevent vitamin loss, avoid soaking the little berries or simmering them any longer than is necessary. A little sprinkle of sugar and a short stay in the refrigerator will bring out their juice and sweetness. Don't hull them until just before you plan to use them if you want to prevent juice loss. If any of your berries go a bit mushy or your last pickings of the season seem somewhat overripe, blend them with milk and a little plain yogurt or ice cream to make a terrific milkshake.

Just how good are these little sweeties from nature's garden? Wild strawberries are especially rich in vitamins A and C, potassium, calcium, and contain some B vitamins. As the vitamins are incapacitated by heat, fresh or frozen berries will give you the greatest nutrient boost.

SPREADING DOGBANE

Apocynum androsaemifolium
Photo page #8

Also known as: Wandering milkweed, milk ipecac
Season: Spring through late summer
Habitat: Woodland edges, roadsides, pastures

THIS IS A POISONOUS PLANT

Don't be fooled by this lovely, common plant! It and its cousins — Indian hemp, intermediate dogbane, and the shrub known as oleander — are all very poisonous. Every plant hunter is well advised to know the dogbanes — and keep a safe distance from them. Spreading dogbane is included here as an example of this family mainly because in its youngest stages it might be confused with milkweed or some of the other edible plants found along the edges of fields and roads.

Dogbane prefers shade during part of the day, but will grow in pastures where it receives shelter from other plants or bunches of its own kind. The flowers are beautiful pink and white candy-striped bells. The smooth-edged, dark grayish-green leaves grow in pairs on stems that usually have a reddish hue. Fortunately, soon after the plant erupts from the ground, it distinguishes itself by branching, its leaves sprouting from short stalks. While the plant lacks hair, a careless milkweed hunter may be tricked by its milky juice; the early shoots, however, are much slenderer than those of the chunky common milkweed or knotweed.

Intermediate dogbane is believed to be a hybrid between spreading dogbane and Indian hemp. The flowers are lighter, often white, but the leaves look much like those of spreading dogbane. Indian hemp, also with milky juice, may bear a little fuzz, but is more typically hairless. It has greenish-white flowers and leaves much like those of spreading dogbane. The stems are erect and covered with a fibrous bark. Overall, Indian hemp is larger than the dogbanes.

All of these plants bear a milkweed-like seed pod which releases fuzzy, parachute-transported seeds.

Several toxic substances reside in the dogbanes. Symptoms of poisoning by dogbane or Indian hemp may include fever, increased pulse, coldness of hands and feet, dilation of the iris, a change in color of the membranes of the mouth and nose, and excessive perspiration. Depending on the amount eaten, death may follow. ***If poisoning is suspected, contact a hospital!***

MILKWEED

Asclepias syriaca
Photo page #9

Also known as: Silkweed, butterfly weed, monarch flower, rosy milkweed, pink milkweed, common milkweed

Season: Spring through late summer

Habitat: Waste places, fields, roadsides; tolerant of poor soils

DO NOT CONFUSE WITH OTHER MILKWEEDS OR DOGBANE; MATURE PLANT NOT EDIBLE

The word "weed" should be deleted from its name! Milkweed is a plant to treasure for its versatility, strength and beauty. The next time you are in a patch of blooming milkweed, close your eyes and savor its fragrance carried on the warm July breeze, the very essence of locust-strumming summertime.

Don't look for milkweed in damp meadows, though; this is the habitat of the purple milkweed, unknown as to edibility. (See the following entry.) There are several varieties of milkweed; it is the common dusty-rose flowering milkweed we've come to love. Look for this in areas which are relatively open and dry, where you have seen the pinkish blossoms in previous seasons.

The young stalks, up to six or eight inches, are an outstanding vegetable. Though it is difficult to recognize many plants in their young stages, especially the first time you try, milkweed is easier than most: With young leaves held close against the sturdy green stems, the shoots look much like asparagus stalks with leaves. The young leaves have a broad paddle shape, a promise of their mature form, and will already be thick for their size. A most important identification feature is the dense white nap on the lower surfaces of the leaves, even when young. The poisonous dogbanes have somewhat similar stalks with paddle-shaped leaves; dogbane, however, is not at all fuzzy, and quickly branches, which milkweed never does.

Removing a leaf or cutting the stem of milkweed results in the flow of a sticky white latex. This thick sap neither tastes good nor is it at all good for you, and the shoots are usually boiled at least once before being served as a vegetable. Some people do eat the shoots raw without ill consequences; we don't, having heard of cattle that have been poisoned by eating freely of the mature plants.

The shoots up to four inches tall do not contain too much of the latex and, boiled for twenty to thirty minutes, they're delectable with butter, salt and pepper, or peeking out from under any creamy sauce.

The slightly larger, four to eight inch stalks contain more latex. To get rid of it, place your "wild asparagus" in a ceramic, stainless steel or lined pot, cover with boiling water, and allow the water to return to a boil. Keep this simmering while you boil a second change of water; then pour off the milkweed broth and add the fresh batch of hot water. If the stems still show a large amount of latex, repeat this process a third time. After this, only a few minutes' more cooking is required, and they'll be as good as the baby sprouts.

Though these young stalks first shoot up in spring, you'll be able to harvest them until midsummer. The plants you've cut early in the season will send up new shoots, for their roots are large and well supplied. If you overpick an area, though, the roots will be sapped of food and will die. You don't want to pick all the shoots, anyway! The harvest is not over when you have had your fill of the little stalks; why, it has only just begun!

Watch your milkweed patch for the appearance of the flower buds during July. When the buds are full with the developing flowers, but have not yet begun to show color, snip them from the plants and rush them to your kitchen. Make a fritter batter and coat them with the batter. (A little nutmeg added to the batter is good; finely chopped onions will give zip, and chives add their own interest.) Deep fry these to a golden brown, and you have summer flavor in a nutshell. They're great! These heads are also excellent when cooked like broccoli, just steamed. Snip a few of the flower heads apart to release the individual buds and add them to a chowder or stew for interest and nutritive value.

To be sure plenty of milkweed will be available for next summer's enjoyment, let a decent number retain their blossoms. Besides, you have a third harvest waiting. These lovely deep rose blossoms will fade to a pale tan or cream color and then droop; in a week or so, after the flowers have left their stalks, a pod will begin to grow where each flower had been. Keep an eye on them. When they become about an inch and a half long, and are still firm, snip them from the plant. The pods may be sauteed with meat, onions, or whatever, batter-dipped and deep fried, or stir-fried with Oriental-style vegetables. They may be cooked whole or sliced. Pods that feel spongy to the touch have already begun to form the beautiful silk that will transport the developing seeds on the wind; these have sneaked beyond a usable stage. Be happy, though; they will become next year's supply of vegetables.

The shoots may be canned, the shoots and pods may be blanched and frozen, and the pods may be dehydrated for storage.

Milkweed has had other uses in the past, and is presently under further investigation. Evidently, the roots of some varieties were used to achieve temporary sterility by Indian women who did not wish to conceive too soon after childbirth. The latex of one variety of milkweed has been used to fight skin infections. It would seem these plants and their relatives had greater use in earlier herbal medicine, for the genus is named in honor of the Greek god of medicine, Asclepius.

During World War II, the fluff which accompanies the seeds was collected and used to fill life preservers. This would be an inexpensive filling today for additional floating boat pillows. (They would need to be watertight to keep the fluff from matting down.) The seeds should be removed from the fluff, for they might decompose if not completely moisture-free.

Many trials were proposed and conducted to try to make a rubber from this plant's latex, and recently it was announced that this plant is being investigated as a possible source of oil from which home heating oil and gasoline could be made. The seeds contain approximately 20% oil. If this is accomplished, we'll see vast fields of milkweed and the monarch butterfly will be in heaven! (This is the plant that the beautiful insect feeds upon.)

Like most wild edibles, milkweed is good for us. It is a fine source of vitamin C (though it won't put orange trees out of business). Versatile in the kitchen, it makes the sticky fingers you'll get while gathering it well worthwhile. Milkweed's many uses will keep you busy for at least half a year!

PURPLE MILKWEED

Asclepias purpurascens
Photo page #9

Also known as: Red milkweed, marsh milkweed, woods milkweed
Season: Spring through late summer
Habitat: Wet or damp meadows, woods

EDIBILITY UNKNOWN — NOT RECOMMENDED

Pick your common edible milkweed from dry meadows, and you'll avoid risk of getting the purple milkweed. This variety, bearing reddish-purple flowers at maturity, is unvouched-for as to edibility; it may be as safe as our common dull rose flowering milkweed, but it is not mentioned by other authors, and we have never tried it.

This variety looks very much like *A. syriaca.* Its leaves, though, are slightly narrower, and the pods lack the warts found on those of the edible milkweed. The underneath of the leaves, and the pods, are downy, and the plant produces the same milky latex as seen in the edible milkweed; it would be difficult to separate the young shoots.

Habitat is the most direct key to identification. We've found the purple milkweed close to streams or marshes or in very damp meadows. It is also known to grow in woodlands; you'd seldom find common milkweed there — it prefers sunny meadows.

CHICORY

Cichorium intybus
Photo page #10

Also known as: Ragged sailors, coffee plant, blue corn plant, blue sailors, succory, wild bachelor's buttons, blue dandelion, blue daisy, Barbe de Capuchin
Season: Early leaves in spring; roots best in late summer and fall; blooms in summer.
Habitat: Fields, roadsides, waste places; alongside gardens and railroad tracks

The sight of this plant's cheerful flowers, borne on tall terminal stalks, still brings a salty breeze to mind: as a child, I knew chicory by another of its names, "ragged sailor."

The illustration shown is not true to form; the flowers have been severed and placed across the leaves to give a close-up of both leaf and flower. The leaves near the base of the plant resemble those of the dandelion, though they are not as a rule so deeply lobed. The upper leaves are lance-shaped, and the flower stalks stick up like knobby sticks from the center of the plant.

The flowers are usually found at the top. The plant blooms over an extended period, producing only one or a few full-blown flowers each day. Most of the time these blooms are light blue, but sometimes they are pinkish or even white. The petals have squared, toothed tips.

Chicory has so many similarities to the dandelion! The sap, like that of the dandelion, is milky; beneath this plant, too, is a firm, tough taproot that, slow roasted to a deep brown and then ground, is an outstanding coffee. Blend it with regular coffee for a mellower, less expensive brew, but be cautious — chicory is a lot stronger than the coffee bean!

The young leaves may be gathered and boiled for six to ten minutes as a vegetable. They're quite good served with butter and salt and pepper or a little vinegar. The underground whitened portions of the leaves are excellent in salad; they have a bitterness which offsets the flavors of cucumbers and salad dressings.

This is a direct relative of endive, its name coming from the Egyptian name, *chikouryeh*. Chicory is believed to have migrated to this continent from Europe. It has certainly found our soil to its taste! It can easily be moved into your own yard, via either seed or transplantation, and makes an attractive background planting. Pick the leaves in the early spring, allow the flowers to ripen seed for the next year, and then salvage the late summer and fall roots for coffee. You can enjoy this happy cycle year after year.

WILD MINT

Mentha arvensis
Photo page #8

Also known as: American mint, water mint, corn mint, field mint
Season: Spring through summer
Habitat: Low, damp areas, shores of woodland streams, and run-off areas

The mints are easy to know and love. They all have square stems, paired leaves, a minty aromatic odor when stems or leaves are broken or crushed, and small flowers in shades of pale violet. There are many other plants in the Mint family with some of these characteristics, but the familiar, strong mint fragrance is the key criterion that tells you you've found a mint.

There are many other varieties, too, of edible mint, including bergamot and the mountain mints (*Pycnanthemum* species). The flowers of the mountain mint tend to grow in more widely spread, flat-topped clusters at the top of the plant; flowers of the *Mentha* species will grow more compactly in spikes or against the stalk.

Common mint is easily found: look along stream banks or other damp areas. The stems do not branch, but are hairy-fuzzy. The paired, pointed-oval leaves are like those of most other mints, all of which have toothed edges. The flowers of the wild mint are found in tight clusters at the leaf axils. The plants usually grow about a foot tall, though they may double this height in some locations.

The fresh or dried leaves of any variety of mint make a delightfully refreshing tea. Serve after a meal, for mint is a well-known friend to digestion. Add the freshness of chopped mint leaves to a salad or to boiled and buttered new potatoes, along with fresh chives or parsley. Delicious! Mint leaves in a sauce are a famous accompaniment to roast lamb. Store their flavor in a jelly to brighten winter, or make a cooling mint-ade drink for summer use.

Another closely related Mentha is peppermint (*Mentha piperita*), which looks a lot like wild mint; the plant, though, usually shows some branching and the leaves taste hot when chewed. The flowers are located at the uppermost parts of the plants. Peppermint, too, likes wet soils.

Spearmint (*Mentha spicata*) is branched like peppermint, and its flowers arise from the axils of the paired upper leaves. The spearmint's leaves are almost directly attached to the plant stalk; the wild mint's leaves have petioles, whereas spearmint's leaves appear to just about lack them.

Any of the mints may be used in the same way as common mint. Mints root easily in water, and you may easily start a mint patch of your own.

LADY'S THUMB (SMARTWEED)

Polygonum persicaria
Photo page #10

Also known as: Redleg, spotted knot grass
Season: Early through late summer
Habitat: Waste places, pastures, road edges, gardens

The smartweeds, related to other members of the buckwheat family, are mostly herbs. They bear alternate, lance-shaped leaves. All possess swollen joints along their stems, just above which will be found a thin sheath surrounding the stem. The size and edge of the sheath helps in distinguishing one smartweed from another.

Many of the smartweeds are very sharp or peppery in flavor, and their juices may make the mucous membranes of the mouth, eyes and nose smart — hence their name. None of the smartweeds are known to be poisonous.

All the smartweeds produce similar, sometimes erect and sometimes drooping, long flowerheads. Colored in shades of green to white to rosy pink, the blossoms are found at the ends of the plant stalks or sometimes in the axils of the leaves. They usually have five petal-like sepals.

Lady's thumb stands out from the other smartweeds in easily distinguishable ways. Its leaves bear brownish or dark reddish splotches about midway up the blades; like inkblots, these vary in shape from circles to arrowheads. The sheaths above each joint have fringed edges, and the stems may show red tones. The flowers, blooming anytime through the summer and on into Indian summer, are usually a delicate pink.

We have found young lady's thumb leaves a delightful addition to soups, stews and other cooked vegetable dishes. I've added them chopped in little bits to whipped potatoes in place of parsley, and their flavor has been good; the heat from the potatoes probably tames their juices, which are otherwise rather acrid when raw.

The smartweeds grow nearly everywhere, and probably deserve more experimentation than we have given them thus far. Even herbal medicine has seemingly ignored the smartweeds in this country, though a relative known as bistort was used in Europe as a gargle, mouthwash, and as a curative against dysentery.

If you would still rather weed lady's thumb from your lawn than cook up its nutritious leaves, at least transfer the plants to your compost heap: smartweeds are reported to be excellent soil builders.

YELLOW DOCK

Rumex crispus
Photo page #10

Also known as: Curled dock, wild rhubarb, narrow-leaf dock, wild spinach, wild pie plant.

Season: Spring through fall

Habitat: Fields, lawns, gardens, roadsides

Equal to lamb's quarters in both familiarity and availability, the wild docks have been used for centuries. At least a dozen members of this group made their way to our shores with early settlers from Europe and Asia. Dock plants are now found throughout North America, even in Alaska. Prized in the gardens of Europe and cherished here in the Great Depression, dock largely fell out of use in American kitchens as commercially available vegetables became abundant. Yet these wild greens are all around us, just waiting to be recognized and used. Yellow dock is the most easily recognized member of this group of useful plants. (Many of the broadleaf docks are more bitter in flavor.)

The docks belong to the same genus as sheep sorrel; they too contain oxalic acid, and their leaves have the same lemony tang — cooked, dock leaves taste like spinach to which a few drops of lemon juice have been added. The large leaves quickly fill a pot, for they range from a few inches to a foot or more long, and up to a couple of inches wide.

Although they would take no prize at a flower show, the yellow dock's blossoms are an aid in identification. Spikes of them form at the tops of the plants, held from knee-high to a yard above the ground. These greenish spires turn reddish-brown as the seeds mature. Each of the many flowers produces a tiny, roundly triangular, winged seed; the shape and structure of the individual seed helps to differentiate between the varieties of dock. Look for the stiff, umber brown seed stalks of the previous season when you are stalking the spring greens.

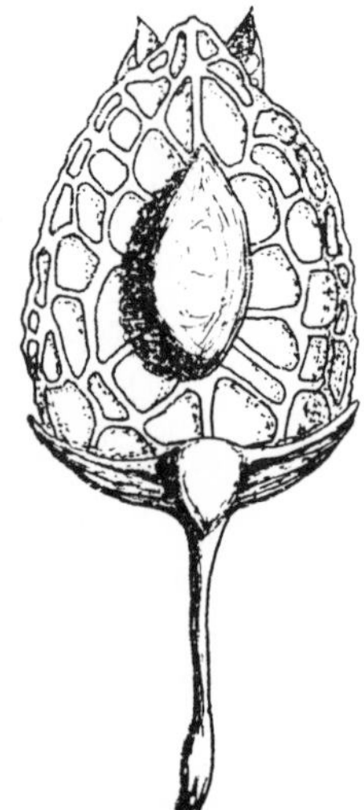

Yellow Dock Seed

Two other traits help to identify these early spring greens. The leaves have a characteristic vein arrangement: A central, main vein runs strongly along the central axis of the leaf, and branch veins shoot off toward the leaf edge, recurve, and rejoin with other branch veins, forming a scalloped pattern near the leaf edge. This leaf edge is somewhat wavy in yellow dock. Look also at the base of the leaf where it joins the main plant stalk: each leaf's petiole will enlarge to form a translucent sheath that surrounds the plant stalk.

There is a final trait, also shared with sorrel, that helps in identifying the flowerless, seedless young plant: if a leaf is injured by insects, dryness or other forces, it often develops a red pigmentation.

The young spring leaves are the best. Later in the season other hunters will have attacked the older leaves, for they seem to be appreciated by the insect world also, and the tiny upper leaves may be all that are left for you to forage. That's just as well, for the older leaves tend to become quite strongly flavored and require a change or two of water to tame. As the plant matures, the stems, which were quite good in the spring, become tough. At this time they are best used as a sham rhubarb; they make a nice pie!

The abundance of spring and summer may easily be stored. Dock will freeze or can well; handle it as you would spinach. Its likeness to that garden vegetable is remarkable, the only difference in taste being the lemon tang. A comparison of their nutritive values when raw (from U.S.D.A. Handbook No. 8) is interesting — little wonder, that an alternate name for yellow dock is "wild spinach"!

100 g. portion:	*Dock (Yellow)*	*Garden spinach*
Calories	28	26
Protein	2 g	3.2 g
Calcium	66 mg	93 mg
Iron	1.6 mg	3.1 mg
Phosphorus	41 mg	51 mg
Sodium	5 mg	71 mg
Potassium	338 mg	470 mg
Vitamin A	12,900 I. U.	8,100 I. U.
Vitamin C	119 mg	51 mg
Thiamine	0.09 mg	0.10 mg
Riboflavin	0.22 mg	0.20 mg
Niacin	0.5 mg	0.6 mg

Besides being good-tasting food, the docks were reputed to have other virtues. The roots were gathered for pharmaceutical purposes, and some of the Indians of this continent prepared a flour from the seeds. These plants are related to buckwheat, and so it is not surprising that their ground seeds make a valuable flour. Though other uses for dock may have been lost through the centuries, its food value and flavor can certainly be appreciated by today's cooks — for free.

CHIVE

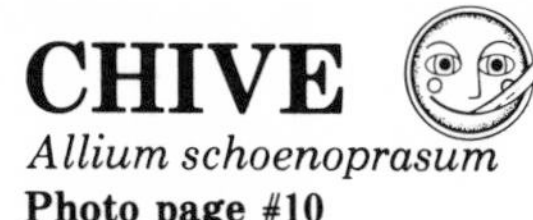

Allium schoenoprasum
Photo page #10

Also known as: Garlic chive
Season: Spring through fall, year-round in greenhouse or flowerpot
Habitat: Lawns, fields, waste areas

You'll know you have wild chives in your backyard if you smell onions as you mow the lawn. Look for the tubular, dark green leaves imitating grass in your lawn. They may be garden chives that have escaped the orderly rows of civilization, or wild ones spread by seed from someone's field. The domestic variety grows larger, as shown in the photo, whereas wild chives seldom exceed seven inches in height. Let them grow to maturity, and sometime in May you'll see the pretty globe of violet flowers announcing that they intend to spread farther yet.

Note that the leaves are hollow and stand erect. Each tiny flower that contributes to the attractive lavender ball is a bell with six petals; you'll notice a purple line running the length of each petal. The surest identification is the onion-like odor of the cut plant. The kinship of chives and onions is shown even in the two brownish flaps of tissue that once covered the bud and now hang beneath the flower: they look like the outer skin of an onion.

The Latin name means, "an onion with leaves like a rush." Chives are purported to have the antihistamine properties of onions, and in past years they were used as a tonic and to improve the appetite. This they surely do! Chopped chives will enhance the flavor of many foods, and can add dash and character to even a sandwich.

If you would like to let your chives "do their thing," but don't want tufts of tall wilderness interrupting the clipped smoothness of your lawn, transplant them. They seem to do especially well in rich soil that receives sun only about half the day.

While not generally used as a pot herb, chives can be added to other greens. Snip them into a cheese or white sauce that is destined to cover another vegetable — they'll add interest and aroma. You can keep on clipping all year if you bring a few indoors in a flowerpot. This green flavor king may be dried and stored, too, and added to soups, stews, spaghetti sauce, casseroles, and souffles, all winter long.

Not everybody loves chives. Dairy farmers are more than happy if you offer to remove them from their pastures: When the cows indulge themselves, the flavor shows up as a stale onion-y flavor in their milk. The cows may be happy to nibble this tasty herb, but the consumer doesn't appreciate the aftereffects! Chives go best of all with dairy products, though; they add a savory snap to cottage cheese, herbed soft cheese spreads, creamy dips.

Chives add not only flavor but vitamins and minerals to your menu. They are especially high in vitamin C, vitamin A, and potassium, and also contain calcium, phosphorus, iron, and several of the B vitamins (thiamine, riboflavin, and niacin).

SUNFLOWER

Helianthus annuus
Photo page #11

Also known as: Common sunflower, wild sunflower

Season: Blooms in summer; seeds ripen in fall

Habitat: Open areas, waste places, dumps, near bird feeders, pastures, fields

Centuries ago, this native South American plant became important in the lives of North American Indians. Never entirely out of the picture, the sunflower is today becoming significant in the diets of nearly everyone in this hemisphere. As the call for more natural, basic nutrition has been heard throughout our land, diligent research has found not only just why sunflower seeds are so nutritious, but how to use this plant in new ways.

Science and nature have collaborated to breed many varieties of sunflowers. Hardy giants may reach ten or twelve feet toward the sky, and competitions are even held to see who can raise the largest sunflower. Some varieties, or those grown in poorer conditions, may reach to only a foot or more; their flowers are proportionately smaller.

Search for runaway giants, or grow them yourself. Their plump, power-packed seeds are well worth the effort. You will know the plant without question when you see the flower. The central disc, flat or rounded, is brownish and will be filled with the nubbins of seeds as it hangs its head at maturity. Except for those pecked by birds, or snatched by humans, the mature seeds would eventually fall to the ground where they are quickly gathered by mice and other small animals.

To glorify your own pantry, cut the heads free when they are hanging and pregnant with seeds, but before the seeds have fully loosened. The heavy flowers may be kept in mesh bags or laid out on a dry surface in a temperate area until the kernels are fully ripe. At this point, the seeds may be separated out and the remainder consigned to your compost pile. Any missed seeds left among this fertile material will likely sprout at the first opportunity.

The outer hulls aren't eaten — even the bluejays discard them. Shelling is the hardest part of the preparation. You can do it by hand or by cracking them with your teeth; hulling devices are sold by several firms. Find the method that suits you best.

Those tasty inner seeds are well worth the effort! According to the U.S. Department of Agriculture (Handbook No. 8), a pound of these hulled nuggets will yield 2,540 calories of food energy. These are not empty calories! You'll receive about 108.9 g protein, 214.6 g fat (much of which is in the form of polyunsaturated oils), 90.3 g carbohydrate (including some excellent fiber), 544 mg calcium, 3,797 mg phosphorus, 32.2 mg iron, 136 mg sodium, 4,173 mg riboflavin, 24.7 mg niacin, and a small but measurable amount of vitamin C. Interestingly, while the dormant seed contains little of this vitamin that human beings and only a few other animals cannot manufacture for themselves, the sprouted seed soars in vitamin C content. This is one very tasty way of using sunflower seeds.

Whole or shelled raw sunflower seeds may be sprouted. (See Alfalfa for sprouting hints.) These seeds will need rinsing on an average of twice a day. They're usually ready in one or two full days, or when the new sprout is about the same length as the original seed. Use them in salads, nearly any cooked dish, as a garnish for soups, or to add a sweetly crunchy texture to a sandwich. You may find them disappearing before you have a chance to use them, for children find them as irresistible as cookies once they have tasted them, especially if they are unaware that the sprouted seeds are good for them!

Polyunsaturated oils are recommended to help prevent many complications, including circulatory troubles. These same oils carry the oil-soluble vitamins, A, D, E, and K, which reportedly are found in good supply in the sunflower seeds.

Fatty acids are one group of the building blocks that make up fats and oils. It has been recognized that the body can manufacture some of the fatty acids it needs from other kinds. Those it cannot manufacture are called "essential" fatty acids. Linoleic acid is one of these, and, according to the U.S.D.A., it's found in sunflower seeds at the rate of 135 g per pound of the hulled product. This is right near the top of the list for grains and seeds, insofar as this fatty acid is concerned.

Why are these fatty acids so important? Not very long ago, scientists discovered that they were not only needed to keep cell membranes strong but also were used in the making of materials called **prostaglandins**. These prostaglandins apparently are manufactured throughout the body by all cells, according to their needs. They act like hormones or chemical messengers to regulate bodily activities. Some of these materials are involved in the regulation of blood pressure, the secretion of stomach acids and enzymes, and control of the timing of digestive processes, among other things. The proper use of cholesterol and other fats seems to be dependent upon one or more prostaglandins. These also seem to be directly involved in fertility, and linoleic acid appears to have a large role, according to recent reports, in the body's manufacture of prostaglandins.

When foods are cooked, the quality of vitamins and minerals diminishes. The beauty of sunflower seeds is that they are excellent raw, as well as roasted or included in cooked dishes. When fully dry, the raw seeds may be stored in closed containers. They will keep quite a long time, especially if cool; their vitamin E content helps to keep the fats and oils from becoming rancid.

A tasty nut butter can be made from the seeds, roasted or raw, and this has a good shelf life. It's a tasty alternative to peanut butter, and makes a tempting sun-butter-and-jelly sandwich; try it layered with toasted cheese. Sunflower seeds may also be dry roasted on a cookie sheet to a light, golden brown (use a moderate oven). When you have just taken them from the oven, drizzle the hot seeds with tamari (soy sauce) or Worcestershire sauce; this will sizzle and quickly dry. These savory nuggets are almost too good!

JERUSALEM ARTICHOKE

Helianthus tuberosus

Also known as: Tuberous sunflower, wild sunflower, Canada potato, sunflower artichoke

Season: Blooms in summer; roots best in late fall and early spring

Habitat: Likes dampness but not excessive wetness; found at roadsides, waste places, near streams and ponds, along fences

This sunflower hoards hidden treasure! Its tubers were discovered by native citizens of this country long before settlers arrived. The Indians cultivated these plants for their delicious tubers, but, like many other garden plants, they escaped to grow where they liked. The colonists quickly adopted them and exported them to Europe, where they were a hit. ("Jerusalem" is possibly a corruption of the Italian name given them.)

The Indians ate the flower heads, too, boiled and served with marrow. The Jerusalem artichoke's flower heads are smaller than those of the common sunflower; they average about two inches across and may sometimes reach three or more inches in diameter. Many flowers may be borne on the upper branched stalks of a single plant, and the flowers have yellowish centers. The leaves are narrower than those of the common sunflowers. Otherwise, this plant closely resembles the other sunflowers. If the yellow-centered wild sunflowers are also present, it will be the tubers that confirm the artichoke's identity.

Jerusalem Artichoke

Do not dig the tubers while the plant is in blossom; the growth of the plant will have drained their sweet goodness. Locate and identify the plants as they bloom, then lurk in the sidelines until late fall, when the roots have been repacked with nutrients for the next season's growth. If you're certain of their location, the tubers may be left in the ground until next spring and harvested for an early-season treat. A better idea, perhaps, is to move a few of the plants into your own garden, if you've room, and grow your crop where you can be a lazy forager; then you're certain to know for sure that you are picking the right tuber. One caution: Do not plant them near irises or other garden plants having poisonous tubers or bulbs, for, when the greenery has left for the winter, it is difficult to tell them apart. Read about wild irises, too, before you collect any Jerusalem artichokes!

The tubers are quite wrinkled in appearance, with a thin brown skin. Dispel any doubts about their identity at the supermarket, where Jerusalem artichokes are sold seasonally. They are best scrubbed and then cooked right in their skins, and rival the potato as a root vegetable; the flavor is sweeter, the texture wetter, than a potato. They're delightful as a scalloped potato or in a potato salad, baked or pickled. And do try them raw — they are crisp, sweet, crunchy and delicate. Cooked or raw, Jerusalem artichokes will hold their own against any garden vegetable for flavor and adaptability.

The stored food consists primarily of a carbohydrate called **inulin**. Apparently, inulin is not so rapidly broken down into sugars by the body, and it has long been a recommended carbohydrate for diabetics and dieters. Jerusalem artichokes not only yield fewer calories than a potato, weight for weight, but are a good source of B vitamins, potassium, phosphorus, trace minerals, and vitamin A.

A few people have begun to seriously grow Jerusalem artichokes, for they are reported to produce adequate tons of marketable tubers per acre. Perhaps this native crop of North America may once again become an important crop here.

LAMB'S QUARTERS

Chenopodium album
Photo page #11

Also known as: Pigweed, goosefoot, wild spinach, white goosefoot, smooth pigweed, white spinach

Season: Late spring through summer; seeds, late summer

Habitat: Gardens, waste places, dry woods, roadside; mainly where soils have been disturbed

A friend of ours reminisced how, as a girl, she was given two baskets when her mother sent her to weed the garden. One basket was for the "good weeds," and the other for the "weeds." Into the first she would place such edibles as purslane, dandelion and pigweed; the others weren't salvageable for human fare.

Pigweed, or lamb's quarters, is found nearly everywhere. The shape of its leaves and, especially, the talcum-powdered appearance of the young growing leaves gives it away. This mealy powder, most noticeable on the undersides of the leaves as the plant gets older, repels water, but disappears upon cooking. The leaves themselves are bluish-green, delicate to the touch. The stem is fleshy, tender in youth, and often ridged or grooved.

Later in the year, usually at the beginning of August, the plant will produce a very unspectacular flower head, rather like that of dock or ragweed. Green at first, it will later turn to brown or reddish tones. The flower stalks often remain on the plant throughout the rest of the year, their black seeds giving sustenance to many birds. A healthy, mature plant may produce as many as 50,000 to 75,000 seeds, and lamb's quarters spread rapidly and thoroughly throughout the North American continent when it was accidentally introduced from Europe and Asia by the first settlers. Anyone who has planted a garden knows all about this prolific plant!

The leaves of the upright, well-branched plant are alternately placed. While the upper leaves may lack teeth, the lower ones are roughly triangular in shape and coarsely, roundly toothed. The plant may stretch to three or more feet in height.

They're easily identified—you'll have seen them everywhere. Lamb's quarters is probably second only to the dandelion as a commonly eaten weed, and many people don't even think of it as a wild plant—rather, as a friendly stray. There is one caution to be observed when you first go after this plant: If, when you have crushed and sniffed a leaf, ***it smells like turpentine, you've not found lamb's quarters,*** but an inedible relative. Leave it alone.

When picking any wild plant, you should know something about the area and its soil. Plants of the Chenopodium group growing in high nitrate (very heavily fertilized) areas may be ***potentially poisonous due to high nitrite concentrations*** that may be present in their tissues, especially if they have been sprayed with non-toxic herbicide 2-4D. The plant stores the excess nitrates in a converted nitrite form, and there have been cases of poisoning in animals. Be sure to pick lamb's quarters from ordinary untreated soils or from areas whose history is known to you.

If you are already familiar with these plants, then you know how nice the young leaves can be in a salad. These plants contain none of the bitterness found in some wild foods. The tender stems and leaves of plants under nine or ten inches tall can be briefly boiled and served as spinach, the plant it most closely resembles in flavor.

Lamb's quarters will continue to provide delicious greens throughout the summer. Clipping (or picking from) the plants forces them to continue production of young leaves. The uppermost leaves on larger plants are also usable as cooked greens, but the stems gradually become tougher and less palatable. The older plants' leaves, especially, are best boiled with a strip of bacon or a small bit of salt pork. Add a little squirt of vinegar at the table for a change of pace. With a sprinkle of lemon juice, the greens will remind you of dock. In fact, lamb's quarters go well with dock, if one or the other is found in small numbers in your picking area. Sheep sorrel or wood sorrel greens may also be added to the batch, as may the leaves of galinsoga or jewelweed.

This green is not only a versatile, flavorful vegetable, but even outclasses spinach as a storehouse of protein, calcium, phosphorus, iron, vitamin C, and great amounts of vitamin A, not to mention all the minerals pulled out of the earth by its strong taproot. The nutrient counts for lamb's quarters are comparable to those of dock. (See Yellow Dock.)

The seeds, while very small, are produced in such numbers that they may be fairly easily gathered. (As with any other plant, leave some seed-bearing adults to continue the tribe.) The seeds may be ground and mixed with wheat flour to make pancakes, muffins and breads. They lend a buckwheat-like flavor and an interesting darkness and richness, and probably fortify the flour immensely.

MUSK MALLOW

Malva moschata
Photo page #11

Also known as: Cheese plant, field mallow, mallow
Season: Summer
Habitat: Fields, gardens, roadsides

DO NOT CONFUSE WITH WILD GERANIUM OR CRANESBILL WHEN NOT IN BLOOM

You are most apt to see this showy plant in a field, and think it an escapee from somebody's garden. The plant is often close to two feet tall, and the pink flowers range up to two inches in diameter. Not often does such a gorgeous plant offer such good eating!

The flowers and, especially, the leaves of this branching plant might at first remind you of those of the wild geraniums. Other wild mallows may have leaves full enough to look a little like window-box geraniums, but those of the musk mallow are much more delicate. The palmately cut, feathery leaves may range from two to four or more inches in width.

The petals of the pinkish to white flowers are nicely scented, and are haloed beneath by short triangular green sepals. The pistils and stamens are grouped into a central projection that is elevated above the five petals. If you are familiar with the hibiscus of warmer climates, you'll see a resemblance.

The seed pods are flat discs that resemble a Gouda or Edam cheese in shape, and are even segmented just as these cheeses are usually sliced. The plants of this group are often called "cheese" because of this. Raw, the fruits may be nibbled or put into salads. They may also be added to soups and stews or to a cooked vegetable melange.

The young leaves make a fine pot herb by themselves, or may become part of a mixed pot, stew or soup.

STRAWBERRY BLITE

Chenopodium capitatum
Photo page #11

Also known as: Blite, strawberry spinach, goosefoot, strawberry goosefoot, Indian strawberry

Season: Late spring through summer

Habitat: Waste areas, roadsides, cleared or burned areas, woodland clearings

This is a close relative of lamb's quarters, and a perfect substitute for it. The upper leaves of strawberry blite often look powdered, as do those of lamb's quarters, and this is the first identification trait to look for. The leaves are similar in appearance to lamb's quarters', but tend to be more triangular—they may even be arrowhead-shaped. One warning: If, when you have crushed and sniffed a leaf, ***it smells like turpentine, leave the plant you've found alone***.

Certain identification, at least the first time, is easiest when the plant blossoms in early to mid-summer. The round clusters of blooms sprout from the leaf axils and upper stalk and soon develop into a fruit that looks very much like a berry. These berries are the source of some of its common names: they're a bright red, showy against the soft green of the leaves. Strawberry blite will grow from one to two feet tall. (See the illustration on page 14 as well as the photo.)

In the unproductive stage shown in the photograph, this plant might be confused with another similar plant, orache (*Atriplex patula*). Like strawberry blite, orache's leaves are excellent served as a cooked spinach. If you're uncertain whether you've gathered strawberry blite or orache, it is best to cook the leaves. With either plant, pick the young, tender parts. Strawberry blite's youngest leaves are tasty in salads.

These plants might make an attractive addition to your kitchen garden. The berrylike fruits, too, can be added to your menu. They add sparkling color to a salad, though they have little flavor; you might mix them with fruits whose flavors will carry them along.

BRACKEN FERN

Pteris aquilina
Photo page #12

Also known as: Pasture brake, brake, hog brake, bright greens, Wa-ra-be (Japanese), eagle fern
Season: Spring through summer
Habitat: Open woods, fields, roadsides; very common

THIS PLANT IS POISONOUS WHEN MATURE; FIDDLEHEADS EDIBLE AFTER COOKING

This common fern has been eaten in many countries through countless centuries. The hunters of some Indian tribes ate it exclusively when hunting deer in the spring so that the deer, which foraged on bracken fern, would find it difficult to scent them as they approached. Bracken fiddleheads are eaten on a wide scale in New Zealand. And in Japan and Korea these ferns are used in great quantities and are often eaten raw; marinated, they are relished as a condiment. There are plenty of wild plant connoisseurs here in New England who enjoy them year after year. Some find the fiddleheads nearly tasteless, while others liken the flavor to that of delicate young asparagus. Try some, and see what *you* think.

Fern fiddleheads are so called because, as the young ferns first come up, their fronds are curled like the design at the top of a fiddle. Besides bracken, there are several other ferns which are edible at this stage, though some are not so good. It would be wise to get to know what you are looking for.

Important: ***Do not pick these baby ferns after the upper parts begin to unfurl!*** Not only will the flavor be bad, but the results may be worse; the fern leaves are poisonous to cattle, horses, and people. The fiddleheads, however, are harmless and delicious.

The bracken fern fiddleheads roughly resemble a "chicken fist" (see photo). There are three curled-up knobs that would later form the three portions of the frond, or leaf structure, of the plant. There seem to be two slightly different varieties of bracken fern in the northeast; both are good. The fronds look identical, but the fiddleheads are subtly different, just different enough to give an amateur hunter second thoughts. One variety of fiddleheads will bear a velvety white bloom. Overall, this fiddlehead is grayish-green, with a slightly darker shade on the stem when the short hairs are removed. At the base of each of the developing parts of the three-sectional frond you'll see a black spot. The second variety has the same coloring except for these spots (nectaries), which will be brown rather than black and will look more elongated. The velvet fuzz that covers the entire fiddlehead will have some cinnamon coloring in this second variety, especially near the top of the fiddlehead.

Many of the other ferns' fiddleheads will have appeared before you see those of the bracken fern. This gives you fair warning of when to begin looking! Cropping up one at a time from the roots, these will continue on into the summer, giving you plenty of picking time.

The first time you hunt bracken fern, you might want to wait until late May. At this time some of the fronds will have matured, while fiddleheads will be found nearby. The fronds range from one to four feet tall and are a light grass green. The stems will be darker or even brownish in tone. The frond is divided into three equal or nearly equal leaves, each of which is roughly triangular in shape. These leaves are further divided into little leaflets. The lobes of these leaflets are so cut that the indentation does not reach the stem or midrib. The three-part fronds arise individually from underground rhizomes, not as a cluster.

The reproductive structures (sori) are found on the reverse side of these leaflets. The edges of the leaflets curl under to form an edging channel that holds the sori. In newly-grown fronds these may be difficult to see; they begin as silvery structures and turn dark brown as the season progresses.

The most distinguishing characteristics of the bracken fern are the color of the fiddlehead, its lack of scaly covering or long hair, and the fact that the stalk of the fully grown plant, partially grooved in the front, is usually just about equal to the length of the frond itself. Also, the stalk of this fern separates into ***three*** portions (1½-2 feet high). A final reassurance will be the presence of black or brown spots at the bases of the leaves. We have often noticed a variety of red ants busily sipping of the sugary material produced by these nectaries. We've seen no other roadside fern so visited. These must be the "pop shop" of the fern world! (Though the sight of munching ants may deter you from picking some specimens, it will at least give you a visual memory for identifying the plant.)

Many people remove the curled-up leaves-to-be, cooking only the tender stalks picked while they still snap easily away from the lower structures. They are best at this six-to-nine-inch stage, and the upper uncurled frond is fine to eat, too. Once the leaves have begun to uncurl they become bitter, a reminder that they are actually poisonous.

Some people cook the fiddleheads for only a few minutes, but we have found them better with longer cooking — sometimes thirty minutes or more. Though they are quite edible raw, it is advisable to cook them. The raw fern contains the enzyme thiaminase which, if eaten in large quantities, could destroy the vitamin thiamine (B_1) in your body. This enzyme is deactivated by heat. Recent studies suggest that the consumption of quantities of raw fern in such countries as Japan is linked with the high incidence of stomach cancer in these countries.

If you find that you are really taken by the flavor of raw bracken fern and worry about the thiaminase, you might help offset its presence by conscientiously eating thiamine-rich foods. Some of these are oatmeal, whole-grain rice and wheat, organ meats, pork, potatotes, beans, peas and asparagus. Brewer's yeast, very high in thiamine, might not be appreciated in the family's salad, but wheat germ might be "sneaked in." Don't worry too much — thiaminase is believed to be of concern only if eaten regularly or in large quantities.

One last embarrassment exists for these plants. Most ferns contain tannic acid, and it is probably this which oftens gives their cooking water a brownish hue. Tannic acid tends to constipate if strong amounts occur in the diet; cooking your fiddleheads in a second change of water will quiet any effect and let you thoroughly enjoy this delicious and abundant wild vegetable.

ASPARAGUS 

Asparagus officinalis
Photo page #12

Also known as: Wild asparagus
Season: Spring through early summer
Habitat: Sandy, well drained soils, especially alkaline or neutral soil; old gardens and farms (escapee from cultivation)

Nearly everyone knows asparagus. If you are unfamiliar with its appearance, check the illustration on a package of frozen asparagus or a can of this delightful vegetable.

This member of the lily family originated in Europe, Asia and Africa. Brought by pioneers to the North American continent, asparagus was soon adopted by native Americans. In the Middle East, asparagus is gathered in vast quantities after the first rains. Lucky plant hunters here, too, can share in asparagus's bounty.

Like most other plants, these hardy perennials develop from seeds spread by wind, birds, water, and people. A plant hunter who has missed the delectable wild asparagus in its prime may choose to harvest the seeds and plant them around the homesite to promote an easily reached stand of asparagus. (Gardeners purchase first year "crowns," which are planted and yield a good crop after two years' growth.) We have found that asparagus grows best where neither weeds nor grass are removed; just be careful when mowing near the half-hidden stalks, or the entire crop could be chopped away by one false move of the mower.

To allow the plants to replenish their roots' supply of stored food, let your asparagus go to seed after about the first of July. Some of the seeds may be spread to neighboring fields, where they might grow as well as they would coddled in the garden.

Wild asparagus belongs to a genus of plants that includes both woody shrubs and herbaceous perennials, as well as some vines. Most of these are not hardy to frost, but they share a common characteristic in that they lack true leaves. In place of leaves, which are reduced in this case to scale-like structures, the stems and branches take on the responsibility of photosynthesis, producing food for the plant. Most of these types of plants also require a dormant period, brought on by either drought or cold, in order to continue life.

There are several varieties of cultivated asparagus plants. Most have been specially bred to resist their natural enemies, and they do not differ much in appearance. Asparagus-gone-wild closely resembles the civilized version, and you'll find it poking up early in the season. The best way to find the tender stalks is to keep track of where you may have spotted last summer's mature shoots (too woody to harvest) with their feathery, fern-like tops. When the first green appears in the grass, start stalking these patches! The shoots, under moist growing conditions, will be tender up to eight or ten inches tall. The long winter's wait will have been well worth it — nothing can outclass the flavor of fresh-picked asparagus spears rushed home and served hot with butter or hollandaise or sliced raw into a salad. If you continue to harvest from the same rootstocks, they will continue to produce new shoots. If you've located more than one picking site, you'll be assured of many good potfuls and a freezer banked against the rest of the year. Just observe the early July cutoff to ensure an equally splendid crop next season.

You'll know picking season is over when stem-like structures spring from the axils of the scale-like "leaves" and begin to branch into the delicate ferny tops that resemble the common house plant known as asparagus fern. Asparagus plants are male or female, each sex producing bell-shaped yellowish-green flowers. The female plants will later produce (inedible) berries, which start as green pea-like fruits and later turn red. Each berry usually contains three seeds. (These seeds have reportedly been roasted and ground to form a coffee substitute; some authors, however, warn that they may be poisonous raw, so the product is probably not worth the effort or risk.)

If you want your own asparagus patch, collect these berries and sow them in well-drained soil. You haven't much choice about the sex of the plants thus produced, or even those from purchased crowns, but it is interesting to note that male plants produce more shoots while the females deal in quality — they produce larger shoots.

In the past, asparagus was known as a diuretic and was often prescribed to ease kidney maladies and body puffing. Most effective raw, it was considered helpful even when cooked. The fern-like tops, too, were also used to prepare a tea that served these same functions. One of the amino acids that the body takes in or manufactures from various sources is **asparagine**, first isolated from asparagus. Asparagine is found in the juices of most plants and is in highest concentration in germinating seeds and other areas of intensive growth; the fast-growing asparagus shoots are certainly high in this amino acid. Who knows, this vegetable may someday serve in other ways than as the feature of a gourmet dish.

Asparagus is certainly worthwhile from a nutritional standpoint. The U.S.D.A. Handbook No. 8 tells us that a 100-gram portion of raw asparagus, though 91.7% water, contains 26 calories, 2.5 g protein, .2 g fat, 5.0 g carbohydrate (including .7 g fiber), 22 mg calcium, 62 mg phosphorus, 1.0 mg iron, 2 mg sodium, 278 mg potassium, 900 I.U. vitamin A, 0.1 mg thiamine, 0.2 mg riboflavin, 1.5 mg niacin and a good 33 mg vitamin C. That's not bad for the leafless stems we snatch from their cradles!

CHICKWEEDS

Stellaria media (Common Chickweed)
Cerastium vulgatum (Mouse-eared Chickweed)
Photo page #13

Also known as: Chickweed
Season: Early summer through fall
Habitat: Lawns, gardens, waste places, roadsides

The chickweeds are adaptable, invading harsh areas and lush gardens with seemingly equal ease. In a dry, inhospitable zone such as a gravel parking lot or driveway, they'll sprawl crab-like, reaching out a foot or more. In a lawn or garden, where the living is easier, they'll reach upwards in competition for sunlight.

When weeding, oldtimers would remove them from their gardens, as a harvest rather than a throw-away plant. The young, tender leaves of the common chickweed are a delightful addition to an early season salad, and the older leaves are fine as a cooked vegetable. The fuzzy leaves of the mouse-eared chickweed are eaten cooked only.

The leaves of these plants are found in pairs on the lengthy stems. The common chickweed's leaves usually have petioles, though the youngest ones or those near the flowers may appear to lack them. Their petioles may bear some fuzz or hair; both the leaf and petiole of the mouse-eared chickweed are fuzzy. The long oval leaves of the mouse-eared chickweed lack petioles.

The fuzziness of the mouse-eared variety is certainly a quick identification guide, and the flowers of these two chickweeds are also distinguishable. In both chickweeds, the green sepals are visible directly behind the white petals (viewed head-on). The sepals of the common chickweed are slightly longer than the petals, while the sepals of the mouse-eared chickweed are equal in length to the petals. The flower of either variety has five petals, split so that there appear at first glance to be ten. The common chickweed's petals, narrower than those of the mouse-eared chickweed, are split nearly to the base; the petals of the mouse-eared chickweed are broader and are split only midway.

The common chickweed, especially early in the season, is a nice salad herb, with a taste as delicate as the dainty leaves look. (The earliest chickweed is usually tender enough that the leaves may be left on the stalks.) The leaves, particularly when raw, are rich in phosphorus and iron; these may also be used as a garnish or as an ingredient in a healthful drink of herbs and greens blended with water.

OX-EYE DAISY

Chyrsanthemum leucanthemum
Photo page #13

Also known as: Common daisy, field daisy, bruisewort
Season: Summer
Habitat: Fields, roadsides, gardens, pastures

DO NOT MISTAKE THE LEAVES OF THIS PLANT FOR THOSE OF WATER HEMLOCK OR OTHER CUT-LEAF PLANTS

Yes, you can eat the daisies — a part of them, anyway; the tender light green leaves of the good old daisy may be nibbled raw in salads or combined with other greens in a cooked mixed vegetable dish. There are, however, many daisy-like flowers, so be certain that you have this familiar friend of our roadsides and fields.

First blooming in early summer, the flower is easily recognized for its cheerful yellow central disc surrounded by twenty-five (more or less — count 'em!) white petal-like rays, the flower head measuring one and a half to two inches across. The leaves are irregularly lobed, sometimes toothed, and deeply indented, particularly the lower leaves. A biennial, the daisy normally flowers in its second year.

Aphids, too, find the tender leaves delicious, but the older leaves and the remainder of the plant contain a bitter sap. At one time this acrid material was prescribed for gout. Poultices made of the crushed leaves were applied to bruises, sprains, and skin eruptions, and a tea made from the leaves was used on wounds. A salve made from the pulp of the leaves was important in European herbal medicine. The leaves were also used somehow in cleansing the nasal passages.

Dairy farmers don't welcome this harbinger of summer. Though the cows will usually avoid its bitter mature foliage, any leaves sampled will impart a bad flavor to their milk.

Do go after the light green youngest leaves of the daisy, the sunny flower that brightens highway enbankments as well as it does your backyard. Just be sure to pick out of reach of sprays or exhaust fumes.

THISTLES

Cirsium vulgare (Bull Thistle)
Photo page #13
Also known as: Common thistle, large thistle

Cirsium pumilum (Pasture Thistle)
Also known as: Hairy stemmed thistle, field thistle, great thistle

Cirsium muticum (Marsh Thistle)
Also known as: Barren thistle, swamp thistle
Season: Summer
Habitat: Fields and pastures, open woodlands; the marsh thistle prefers damp areas

Thistles are considered a plant pest by gardeners, farmers, ranchers, hikers, and homeowners alike. But there *is* something you can do about the thistles that infiltrate your yard: Eat them! All varieties are reportedly edible, once you get around the spines. (Also see Sow Thistles.)

While the young leaves may be used in salads or as a cooked vegetable, the bother of removing the spines puts most people off. The young stems, however, are very good either raw or cooked. Peel them and slice them into crunchy little rounds to throw into a salad, coat with batter and deep-fry, or slip into a mixed vegetable dish, soup, or stew. You won't be disappointed!

The thistle is a biennial plant. During its first year, it will produce merely a prickly rosette of low leaves. (Only in the second year does the flower stalk sprout up with the familiar flower.) The roots of the first-year plants may be collected in late summer or fall, washed well and peeled, then boiled in a couple of changes of water. Some people enjoy the roots as a carrot-like vegetable.

The thistle head, in nearly all species the characteristic purple or purple-red flower, later produces dandelion-like seed puffs that are carried on the wind to further spread the tribe. And this hardy plant does spread! If you would rather not have it around, the persistent removal of stems and leaves may prevent the flowering (and spreading) of the plant; if this is unsuccessful, you can at least take advantage of the thistle's usefulness.

Whether it is despised or utilized, the lowly thistle has a special skill: The flower head contains a material that can curdle milk and aid in the cheese-making process. Quantities of mature flowers are thoroughly mashed and pounded to release the rennin-like material they possess. This chestnut-colored liquid is very strong — only a small amount is needed to curdle large quantities of milk, even though the substance is already diluted by the water added to release it as the flower is mashed.

You may find, after all, you can do more with thistles than admire their handsome flowers and curse their prickly leaves.

YELLOW GOATSBEARD

Tragopogon pratensis
Photo page #13

Also known as: Vegetable oyster, yellow oyster plant, goatsbeard

(See the following description)

SALSIFY

Tragopogon porrifolius

Also known as: Oyster plant, purple oyster plant, purple goatsbeard
Season: Early through late summer
Habitat: Gardens, pastures, roadsides, fields, waste places

These two garden escapees are nearly identical except for their color, and may be used interchangeably. Yellow goatsbeard is, of course, yellow, while salsify is a pretty violet or purple tone. The alternate names for both plants were no doubt inspired by the mild, sweet oyster-like flavor of their cooked roots.

You may have admired these plants many times without being aware of their usefulness. You may have seen some growing in your own neighborhood, right under your nose! They were cultivated years ago, and still are in some areas, for their delightful flavor; some gardeners grow these biennials only for their attractive appearance. You may find them in fields, pastures, and along the roadside, blooming without the support of a proper garden.

Both plants are easy to spot when in blossom or in seed. Their blooms, usually held one and a half to two and a half feet above the ground, look almost like those of a giant hawkweed or dandelion, except for the green spikes that form a crown beneath and around the petals.

The leaves, which alternate up the flower stalk, are thick and grasslike, coming to a sharp — often curled — point. The flower buds are goblet shaped, becoming tipped with yellow or purple along the rim as the flower prepares to open. Normally there is but one flower on each flower stalk. The overall appearance would almost lead you to think these plants were related to the carnation, but they are actually in the Composite family.

After the flower is fertilized, the bracts that formed the spiky green crown turn backwards and droop, and the seeds slowly mature. Each seed is carried by a fuzzy parachute, and the entire seed head most closely resembles that of the dandelion.

If you obtain some seeds and intend to grow this tasty vegetable at home, do not expect flowers until the second year. These plants will flower during late June or July and produce their puffy seedheads from late July through August or into September.

It is the first year's plants, though not so colorful as the second year's, that seem to produce the best "oyster" roots; in the second year, the root is apt to be far more fibrous. The root is the edible portion by which the plant is best known, but the tender young leaves and bases of the stems, as well as the top of the root, are very edible. The salsify you might find in your neighborhood market is the same plant as that you'd find growing wild, though the cultivated grocery store item will usually have larger tap roots.

To serve an excellent wild vegetable, prepare the uppermost section of the root and the bottom few inches of the rosette of leaves. The roots require a good amount of cooking, and if they are gathered late in the summer it is wise to change the water once. (As the plant matures, the taste becomes somewhat bitter.) Boil until fork tender, and serve with butter and spices. The oyster roots and leaves could be used in a casserole; they are sumptuous with a little bacon fat added to the cooking water and crispy bits of bacon garnishing the top of the dish.

This plant contains a milky juice that, when evaporated, forms a gummy material. Some of the early users of the plant found this a good chewing gum to alleviate indigestion.

These plants (as well as the mustards) are often bothered by a type of fungus known as a rust, which produces white blister-like patches on the leaves. While this rust would probably not be harmful, it certainly indicates that the leaves are not in any condition to supply you with all the nutrients they'd have if uninfected. Leave such specimens alone.

When you first search for these plants, you'll need the blossoms to assist you in identification. By the time the plant blossoms it is too late to use the roots, which are excellent in spring. But you have not necessarily lost out. Mark their location and wait until after the early frosts. Collect some roots then, and enjoy!

SOW THISTLES

Sonchus asper (Spiny-leaved Sow Thistle)
Sonchus arvensis (Field Sow Thistle)
Photo page #14

Also known as: Spiny dandelions, yellow thistles
Season: Summer
Habitat: Waste places, roadsides, dry areas and along bays

These have the bristly appearance of the common purple thistles insofar as their leaves are concerned, but they lack spines on their stems. Otherwise, the spiny-leaved sow thistle means business! You will have to clip the spines from the leaves before you can use them; you needn't bother to remove the field sow thistle's weaker spines.

Like the dandelion, these plants have yellow flowers that yield silky seed puffs. The flower stalks of the sow thistle, however, will often branch to produce more than one flower. The plant has a bitter, milky juice, and the older leaves will require several changes of water. The young leaves are much better; still, in preparing them as a cooked green, you may want to change the water once. If you have located a patch of these plants the previous season and can get the tenderest new leaves as they emerge, these may even be eaten raw. Be certain of identification, though.

If you're looking for a vegetable to extend others in your pot, these are a good addition. They are also excellent in a soup or stew. We've seldom found enough at one gathering to serve as a potful by themselves, but you may be luckier.

PRICKLY LETTUCE

Lactuca scariola
Photo page #14

Also known as: Beach lettuce, thorny lettuce, thistle lettuce
Season: Early spring to mid-summer
Habitat: Dry places, along ocean zones and bays, roadsides, fields

At first you might think you've spied regular wild lettuce, for this plant has the same tiny, dandelion-like yellow flowers. The spiny leaves and stems, however, will tell you it's a different plant altogether. The leaves usually do not have any indentations, but they do have the same milky, bitter sap characteristic of the yellow-flowered lettuces. This tang is apparent even in the young leaves, and a change of water is required to make them palatable to many people.

The leaves are good extenders for salads or mixed vegetable dishes, and are usable in soups or stews. Choose only the youngest leaves, and trim off the stiff spines.

We've most often found them in areas close to the ocean, where the ground tends to be somewhat dry and inhospitable for most plants. Chopped, these leaves are good in fish or clam chowders; bring some home with your spring catch.

DANDELION 

Taraxacum officinale
Photo page #14

Also known as: Red-seeded dandelion, lion's tooth, common dandelion, blow tops, blow balls
Season: Early spring through late fall
Habitat: Fields, pastures, lawns, gardens, roadsides

There are surely not too many people who don't know the common dandelion, or who haven't heard that the young spring leaves of this plant are both an excellent pot herb and a good salad material. The dandelion has been lauded for its high vitamin content in many magazine articles, and none of it is fiction. There are several varieties, their differences probably unnoticed by the finicky gardener who tries to wrest their sturdy taproots from the ground.

"Pieces of eight" is what my mother used to call them. We seldom picked them out of our lawn, and their brassy yellow flowers brightened the grass from early spring through their last valiant reproductive efforts in the fall. The broken leaves and flower stems exude a bitter milky juice, one identifying feature of this plant with the lion's-toothed leaves. Once the flowers are open, everybody recognizes this plant, but it's then too late to pick the greens unless you resort to this little trick: Try blanching the greens. Grasp all the leaves and place them under an upside-down pail or other container. The root, still in the soil, will continue to supply the plant with water and minerals, but, out of the sun, the chlorophyll will disappear; so will most of the bitterness of the mature leaf. This bleached vegetable is probably not so high in vitamin content as the early spring green leaves, but it is good in salads or incorporated in a cooked dish.

The fully-opened blossoms may also be harvested. (This will please tidy-lawn neighbors.) Probably their most famous use is for dandelion wine. The flower buds may be boiled for a few minutes, alone (if you have enough) or with other vegetables, and served with butter, salt and pepper. The sunny bud adds interest and flavor to a stew or soup, too.

If you would rather remove the dandelions from your lawn, don't throw the roots away — they make a good coffee substitute. Bake them until they're brown and dry all the way through, using a slow oven, then grind and prepare them like coffee. Since the root stores the food for the plant over the winter, coffee made from the mature roots would presumably be very high in vitamins and minerals. These same roots, though they are bitter and call for more than one change of cooking water, may be sliced after washing and peeling, boiled until tender, and served like carrots. The young spring roots, having survived winter's frosts, may be washed, peeled, and sliced, and eaten raw as a munch or in a salad. These may also be stir-fried, or pan-fried with potatoes.

At nearly any time in the summer you can root up the pale lower portions of the leaves to stretch a vegetable dish or stew. These and the flower buds may be combined in fritters, or dipped in a batter and fried.

When October and November draw their icy curtain on the growing season, it's time to begin picking dandelion greens again! Once the leaves have been exposed to a frost they lose most or all of their bitter flavor. Often, after the first frosts have relaxed their hold in the glow of Indian summer, the dandelions will make a last effort to sprout new leaves. Don't pass these up, for they're just as tasty as the spring youngsters. If, by any chance, in spring or fall you've picked leaves which are a bit too tangy for your taste, a change of cooking water will render them palatable. Cooking a little bacon or salt pork with the stronger-flavored leaves seems to work wonders, too.

Are dandelions worthwhile nutritionally? The raw greens, low in calories, contain good amounts of protein, calcium, phosphorus, iron, sodium, and some B vitamins, are high in potassium and vitamin C, and are just bursting with vitamin A. Cooking diminishes their vitality somewhat.

If you eat of the dandelion frequently or in great quantities, you may notice one of its medicinal virtues: The root of this European import, especially, is a rather strong diuretic; presumably it is this quality that earned it its English nickname, "piss-in-bed." In the old world, the root was collected for medicinal purposes as well as for a coffee substitute even into the early twentieth century. The fall root, with the milky juice at its bitterest, was considered the best. An infusion of the leaves was taken to relieve a variety of internal disorders.

Delight of the wild food fancier and bane of the sod farmer, the dandelion promises more uses than most of us care to take advantage of. Become a dandelion lover, and you'll go a long way toward stretching your food budget and adding a boost to your diet.

GROUND IVY

Glechoma hederacea
Photo page #14

Also known as: Gill-over-the-ground, lawn ivy
Season: Spring through fall
Habitat: Fields, lawns, roadsides

The cooked leaves of this little plant are a fine accompaniment to a wild meal of more substantial edibles. The leaves, too, may be dried for use as tea. Ground ivy is very common, and you can easily stockpile enough dried leaves for winter teas and gifts for friends, as well. In a tea, it blends well with other wild herbs, or may stand alone with a bit of honey or sugar, and perhaps a touch of lemon, orange, or even vanilla. It's a nice partner for rose hips.

This pretty plant is part of the Mint family. You can smell its perfume, perhaps, when you cut your lawn. The paired leaves are opposite on the stem. In the axils of the leaves will be one or more tubular violet to purple flowers. The lower three lobes spread and are dotted with darker purple. They may bloom from spring through frost, depending on water supply and the richness of the soil. The base of the flower and the leaf surface may be somewhat fuzzy, and the leaves themselves may show some of the purple toning of the flower.

Four Similar Summer Plants

As summer unfurls its golden days, the following four plants decorate the roadsides with masses of white blossoms. Where states and cities trim these hardy weeds back with mowing machines, they'll quickly regrow once the worker's back is turned. If necessary, they'll persevere until August to bring their seeds into the world, but most bloom abundantly during June and July.

This is at first a confusing group for the beginner. These plants, all from the Pink family, are strikingly similar; they all have opposite leaves, and flowers that project from cylindrical bases. You must get nose-to-nose with them to clearly distinguish the edible bladder campion from the remainder of the group. Once you have learned to identify it, though, you'll wonder why you had any trouble.

BLADDER CAMPION

Silene cucubalus
Photo page #15

Also known as: Inflated campion, edible campion
Season: Summer
Habitat: Roadsides, along railroad tracks, gardens, waste places, fields

DO NOT CONFUSE THIS WITH THE FOLLOWING THREE NON-EDIBLE OR HARMFUL PLANTS

Bladder campion has leaves up to three inches long, borne in pairs on stalks that range from one to two feet tall. The entire plant is smooth, hairless, and often covered with a bloom or powdery coating. The important keyword to remember for identifying bladder campion is ***hairless*** — it is its hairlessness that most certainly differentiates it from evening lychnis and the night-flowering catchfly.

The leaves are long and oval, with a rather pointed tip. The stems are branched, and each apex generally bears many flowers. The slender stalks at the top of the plant bear a pair of bracts, or leaf-like structures, below the flower petioles. The green portion of the flower, or calyx, which covers and hides the ovary, resembles a little balloon or melon. At first pale green in hue, this rotund structure later fades to a nearly translucent tan or grayish-tan; it is patterned with a network of croshatched veins. Projecting from the crown-like tip of the calyx are five petals. Since these are divided into two lobes, the incision reaching at least halfway down the petal, there may at first appear to be ten petals. Three long styles and stamens protrude from the white halo of petals.

Though not much of this plant can be used, it is found in such abundance in some areas that it can provide an early season vegetable. The young shoots and leaves, when the plant is still quite short, may be gathered and cooked as asparagus. They may have a slightly bitter, but not objectionable, taste; this is due to the presence of a small amount of **saponin** in the plant. If the leaves are picked too late, when fairly large, the bitterness will be unpleasant. This is a warning that the levels of saponin have built up in the plant, and you are about to give your digestive system a difficult time.

Since in the early stages the bladder campion may be difficult to distinguish from the inedible soapworts (such as bouncing bet), this is a plant to transfer to your own garden weed patch if you intend to try the young shoots. Gather the seeds late in the summer, and put them to bed in an area of your property that approximates the conditions in which the parent plant was found. Though there is still a chance you might confuse the bladder campion with its look-alikes, starting your own patch certainly diminishes the odds. As the plants sprout the following spring, you'll become acquainted with their appearance as youngsters; even though a bird may have dropped a foreign seed into your patch, you'll know the bladder campion by the numbers of nearly identical babies that will have sprouted. If you're still hesitant about using the nourishing greens, you'll be able to watch the plant's entire growth cycle and confidently recognize them the next year.

EVENING LYCHNIS

Lychnis alba

Also known as: White campion, evening campion
Season: Summer
Habitat: Roadsides, along railroad tracks, gardens, waste places, fields

NO PORTION OF THIS PLANT IS EDIBLE

Like the bladder campion, evening lychnis has five notched petals on its flowers. You will instantly be able to tell this plant apart from the bladder campion by noting the presence of sticky hairs on its stem. The plant grows to the same measurements as the bladder campion, and its leaves, too, grow in pairs. They are narrow and oval, with pointed tips. The plant flowers at night or on cloudy days; the blooms may still be open if you spot this plant early in the day. The flowers are either male or female. The stamens of the male flower curve back onto the petals like little horns. The calyx of the female flower is fuzzy, swollen, and light green, with darker green veins; it lacks any network of veins, translucent appearance, or true melon shape that characterize the bladder campion. (See the introductory paragraph preceding this group of look-alikes, and study the illustration on page 10.)

NIGHT-FLOWERING CATCHFLY

Silene noctiflora
Photo page #15

Also known as: Sticky cockle, clammy cockle
Season: Summer
Habitat: Roadsides, along railroad tracks, gardens, waste places, fields

NO PORTION OF THIS PLANT IS EDIBLE

Named after Silenus, a Greek god who was often pictured as a slavering drunkard, night-flowering catchfly is known for the wet, sticky secretions it exudes to trap insects. The clammy, hairy surface of this plant will immediately inform you that you have not found bladder campion. (See the introductory paragraph preceding this group of look-alikes.)

The catchfly is much like the bladder campion in overall appearance, but the flower has several variations. The calyx of this white, five-petaled flower is more cylindrical in shape. Green with darker veins, this calyx has branching veins and other veins that cross between them, but these do not form a fine network as on the bladder campion. (The veins are coarser, the crossing veins fewer.) The calyx also has five large teeth that taper to fine, long points. The petals are deeply notched; the flower has the same arrangement of stamens and styles on the pistil as bladder campion. The bloom is large and handsome, usually white (though it may be pinkish) and up to an inch in diameter. It opens only at night or on cloudy days.

BOUNCING BET

Saponaria officinalis
Photo page #15

Also known as: Hedgeweed, fuller's herb, wild sweet William, lady of the night, lady of the gate, woods phlox, sheepweed, soapwort, soap plant, Boston weed, scour weed, sweet Betty

Season: Summer

Habitat: Roadsides, along railroad tracks, gardens, waste places, fields.

THIS PLANT IS NOT EDIBLE, MAY BE POISONOUS

Like so many of the plants commonly found in grassy meadows, bouncing bet, too, is an immigrant. It arrived from Europe with the early settlers, and, according to reports, the Indians quickly discovered the plant's special skill and used it as a cleanser. You see, bouncing bet is high in the glycoside known as **saponin**. The saponin produces a lather in water, and is an effective soaping agent if you're away from home and need to clean yourself or your dishes. Just be sure to rinse well; any soap-like product, from good old grandma's lye soap through modern detergents and back to bouncing bet, can be a severe irritant to the digestive system. The saponin may affect the fatty contents of the cell membranes, and could actually be destructive or poisonous.

The flowers of bouncing bet may be white or pink. Though the petals are notched, they are not so deeply cleft as those of the bladder campion. They also fold back, or reflex, toward the calyx. Looking closely, you may see a horn-like projection of the petal where it narrows to enter the inner parts of the flower. The flowers have a spicy odor, and you'll see some that seem to have been so excited about attracting insects, they have actually produced double petals. The calyx is not swollen like the three previous plants mentioned, and while the pistil has ten stamens, it only has two styles.

Otherwise, bouncing bet is of about the same size and construction as bladder campion; the leaves are in pairs. This plant, too, is ***free of hair***. Bouncing bet is most easily distinguished from bladder campion when the plants are in blossom. (See the introductory paragraph preceding this group of look-alikes.)

In the past, some herbalists have used extracts of bouncing bet to treat liver problems, digestive disturbances, and asthma. Considering the effects that the saponin may have when taken internally, this seems a risky choice. Apparently, though, bouncing bet is safe to utilize as an external cleanser.

PINEAPPLE WEED 

Matricaria matricarioides
Photo page #15

Also known as: Pineapple plant, mother's nut
Season: Early through late summer
Habitat: Unpaved driveways, roadsides, barren and waste places

This rugged individual seems able to survive in the most unlikely places. We've seen it sprouting from cracks in sidewalks, along curbings, and from fissures between rocks. It prefers a good amount of sunlight, but seemingly cannot compete where good growing conditions allow numerous other plants. Often the plant is small, and since there is no showy flower, it goes unnoticed. Should the pineapple weed find a happy situation, it will grow to about a foot and a half tall, but most often lingers around the six inch mark.

The pineapple weed is a close relative of tansy, yarrow, ox-eye daisy and chamomile—it's part of the Chrysanthemum tribe. A newcomer to the adventure of hunting wild plants will be instantly reassured by the scent of this one. Squeeze or crush the leaves or flowers: There will be an immediate, unmistakable, crisp and familiar fragrance of pineapple!

The leaves are deep grassy green to yellowish-green, depending upon growth conditions; cut and doubly cut, they have a feathery appearance. As for the flowers, they don't look like flowers at all! The yellowish cone-shaped structures utterly lack petals or rays. When the flower has passed, an unhandsome gray or tan cup-shaped receptacle remains to mark where the little "pineapple" had been.

The plants bloom throughout most of the warm season, then quietly fade from insignificance to oblivion with the first cold snaps.

You probably won't have to go far to find your first pineapple weed. Check along your driveway or around ball fields, playgrounds, or parking lots. Wherever it would seem a plant would find difficult growing conditions, even among the rocks at the seashore, you may well find pineapple weed. Of course, don't pick these plants where they have been exposed to pollutants from automobiles or industry.

Leave some of the flowers to form seed, but don't hesitate to pick more than you'll need for your day's use—they may be dried and stored for later enjoyment. It doesn't take many of the stalks, flower and all, to make a wonderful hot or cold tea that tastes and smells like pineapple. Simply pour boiling water over the weed and allow the stalks to steep for a few minutes. Your nose will know when the tea is ready! Strain out the plant materials and serve this delicious brew hot with a little honey, or chill and serve as a refreshing iced tea. Combine pineapple weed with rose hips or another tea herb for a terrific, flavorful tea.

A close relative, German chamomile (*Matricaria chamomilla*), which yields an oil known as **matricaria** or **anthemic acid**, was used as an herbal remedy for uncomfortable bloating and gas. It was also known to relieve teething pains and earaches in children. I suspect that pineapple weed might contain the same substance, for we have found it an excellent brew to top off an over-abundant meal or to soothe an unsettled stomach. Regardless of these fancied or actual values, pineapple weed tea gives a happy, flavorful surprise to your tastebuds.

YELLOW WOOD SORREL

Oxalis stricta (and relatives)
Photo page #15

Also known as: Sourgrass, sour clover, trefoil, yellow shamrock, sour trefoil, scurvy grass, sleeping clover, sour shamrock

Season: Spring through late summer or early fall

Habitat: Likes partly shaded areas: wood edges, fields, waste areas, lawn edges

This pretty little plant is native to both North America and Europe. Pink, white, and violet edible varieties are also found; in New England, yellow wood sorrel is most common and most easily found by the beginning plant hunter.

These plants will fold their shamrock-like leaves to protect them from the glare of full sunlight. Once the coolness of shade revives them, they regain their elfin delicacy. Each leaf usually bears three heart-shaped, light grass-green leaflets, and the five-petaled flowers, each about a half inch across, are buttercup yellow. The whole plant seldom exceeds eight inches in height. A taste confirms that you've found wood sorrel—it has the same lemony flavor as sheep sorrel.

This tart flavor, so delicious in salads and cream soups, is due to the oxalic acid content common to all sorrels. (See Sheep Sorrel; oxalic acid is generally described under *Poisonous Materials.*) The sorrels are tangy additions to many dishes, but consideration must be given to the possible effects of too great an intake of their oxalic acid. To be on the safe side, include dairy products with a meal featuring any variety of sorrel—food rich in calcium will offset the tendency of quantities of oxalic acid to form crystals in the body.

Yellow wood sorrel's nutritional goodness includes vitamin C, phosphorus, and potassium.

The leaves of this plant can make a luscious green bed for a cottage cheese salad, and are a fine addition to tossed salads, soups or stews. Nibble on yellow wood sorrel if you're out hiking, biking, or jogging—the tartness will quench your thirst. Indeed, a tea steeped from these leaves is very refreshing, iced, on hot summer days.

Throughout Europe and this continent, wood sorrel has been used in sauerkraut, mock rhubarb pie and even wine. Easily identified, the wood sorrels are also more resistant to bugs and drought than the other types, and thus are available throughout a longer season. Just be moderate with your portions, or else your stomach may scold you!

SHEEP SORREL

Rumex acetosella
Photo page #16

Also known as: Common sorrel, sour grass, lemon leaf, field sorrel

Season: Spring through fall

Habitat: Clearings, meadows, lawns, roadsides

Several plants bear the name "sorrel." Most are related, belonging to the genus *Rumex*. The clover-like wood sorrels, however, though they taste like sheep sorrel and its relatives, do not belong to this genus. (See Yellow Wood Sorrel and Common Wood Sorrel.)

The arrowhead or lance-shaped leaves will help you to identify wild sheep sorrel. Though some leaves may lack the definitive points of a sharp arrowhead, they will at least have the rough shape of a worn arrowhead. The lush new growth will be celery-leaf green, but older leaves damaged by frost, drought, or insects may show brilliant scarlet tones.

The poisonous bittersweet nightshade has leaves that might be described as arrowhead-shaped. However, nightshade is a vine-like plant, whereas sheep sorrel produces a rosette of leaves and no wandering vine-like parts whatsoever. Though sheep sorrel's taste is an identifying trait, it is better to rely on appearances. ***Do not attempt to taste nightshade!***

The flowers of sheep sorrel are a further aid in identification. The tiny individual flowers are rather like those of some of the grasses, and they are found in great numbers on upright spikes; a flower spike will arise, aften branching into two or more flower heads, from the rosette of leaves at the base of each plant. Cream and reddish-green in color, the flowers are attached closely against the spike. Now that you know what to look for, you may notice masses of sheep sorrel in fields and lawns from May on. The flower spikes show as rusty-red patches amid the green of the grasses. Once you have identified the plant in all certainty, you may nip off the flower spikes to extend the picking season for the leaves. A cautious nibble of the leaf will confirm that you've found sheep's sorrel: it will have a tart, lemon-like flavor. If this flavor is not present, ***do not eat the plant***.

Sheep sorrel was once thought to be an indicator of acid soil, and indeed it does prefer more acid soils. However, it will grow as well in neutral or even alkaline soils. The plants certainly like to grow beneath evergreen bushes! If the flower stalks are kept nipped back, this sorrel will provide an attractive, edible ground cover in these areas.

In Europe, sheep sorrel was known as *oseille*, and you'll still find recipes calling for this in European cookbooks. In this country, too, sheep sorrel is used in salads, stews, soups, and as a pot herb—the leaves require only a few minutes' cooking before they may be dished up as a delicious vegetable, served simply with butter, salt and pepper. (You could also let sorrel serve as a lively companion to blander vegetables.) Sorrel leaves may be steeped in hot water, and the tea sweetened with honey and chilled. This "lemonade" is a delightful, vitamin-rich summertime drink. For future use, dry (or blanch and freeze) the leaves and add them to winter stews and soups.

Sorrel extract has been used like rennet in the past to coagulate milk for puddings or junkets. It was even used medicinally in days of yore—to treat inflammation of the kidneys, intestinal ulcers, liver complaints, and boils.

French sorrel (*Rumex acetosa*), cultivated in Europe, may also be found here growing as a runaway in the same conditions you'll find sheep sorrel. This variety closely resembles sheep sorrel, except for its larger flowers and upper leaves; the "ears" of the leaves are broader, point more directly downward, and embrace the stalk. Their flavor is the same. The domesticated species does not spread by runners, as do the wild varieties, and while the sheep sorrel's leaves are generally from one to three inches in length, the garden variety produces leaves up to a foot long.

One word of caution must be mentioned concerning any of the sorrels, dock, and even spinach: All of these contain some amount of oxalic acid, the substance responsible for the lemony tang we appreciate in these plants. ***Excessive consumption of oxalic plants over an extended period of time may interfere with the body's abil-***

ity to absorb calcium. (Oxalic acid binds with calcium.) It might be wise to consider adding dairy products to meals containing any of these plants, for the accompanying calcium presumably might cancel the effects of the oxalic acid. Interesting, that the old French recipes using sorrel were cream soups and sauces! Other plants that contain oxalic acid are purslane, rhubarb, and beets.

Sheep sorrel offers great quantities of nutrients to us if we partake in moderation and with due awareness of oxalic acid's long-term effects.

FROGS' BELLIES

Sedum telephium (purpureum)
Photo page #16

Also known as: Common sedum, live-forever, frog plant, evergreen orpine, orpine, rosy orpine
Season: Leaves, late spring through early summer; tubers, fall or spring. Blooms in late summer.
Habitat: Fields, pastures, sunny road edges, waste places; likes moisture but not excessive wetness

"Frogs' bellies," you may wonder, "what a weird name!" Once you see children playing an old game with the leaves, though, you'll always remember this plant and its common name: If you find and identify frogs' bellies, pluck a leaf, rub it between your thumb and forefinger until it is translucent but not mangled, and the layers of the leaf will separate. Blow on the open end, and you'll inflate the leaf like a little green pillow, or frog's belly!

This plant's coarsely toothed leaves are distinctively thick and fleshy. The only look-alikes are the little plants known as hens-and-chicks (not edible) and a close relative called roseroot (*Sedum rosea*). Frogs' bellies is a far taller plant, reaching a foot or more in height, than hens-and-chicks, which spread outward on the ground in a tight greyish-green "bouquet" of little one-to two-inch rosettes. The roseroot's leaves look like those of frogs' bellies, except they do not have teeth. A row of leaves

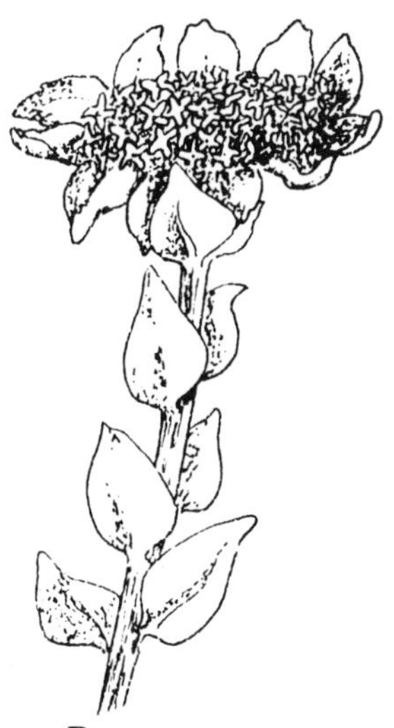

Roseroot

surrounds the flower head of roseroot like a saucer beneath a cup. Roseroot's flowers are either purple or yellow, and the petals are usually in groups of four. Roseroot, however, will not be found in the same habitat as frogs' bellies. It dwells on rocky cliffs, especially along the coast and in the mountains. Although it may be locally abundant and is sometimes grown in gardens, roseroot may be sparse in some areas. Use common sense if you find this plant; leave some to spread in the area. Its leaves may be eaten in the same manner as those of frogs' bellies, raw in salads or as a pot herb.

The juicy leaves of frogs' bellies alternate up the fleshy stem or grow in groups of three; the stem may be whitish or purplish in hue. These plants grow nearly anywhere, forming neat bushy clumps that look as though someone had purposely planted and regularly tended them. In fact, they originated as garden border plants, and are terrific as such; if you fancy the leaves and transplant some frogs' bellies, you'll have picking grounds within a few steps of your door. (Just be sure to dig up the entire bunch of storage tubers for your transplants; these comprise the basic root system of this plant.)

Once you've identified the plant, you'll not forget its appearance. From mid-to late summer you can expect to find this plant producing pink or pinkish-purple, five-petaled flowers in groups at the top of the plant stalk. At this stage, however, the leaves will be too chewy to bother with. Earlier in the season you can pluck the tender, juicy upper leaves and add them, sliced, to salads. (They are also delicious if marinated for a day or two.) They may be served with other cooked vegetables or by themselves, if you've enough plants to pick from. (Harvesting helps to retard the toughening of the leaves.)

The tubers of this plant are also edible—harvest them in late fall or early spring. Those growing in sandy, loose soil are most easily handled. Separate, wash and clean them. They may be boiled like a potato and served with butter or sour cream, or even pickled.

Though frogs' bellies are garden escapees, they are so commonly found today that you'll often find them listed with well-known wild flowers. The plant spreads quickly and easily, and is difficult to eradicate from an area. Stems of these hardy plants have been known to revive and grow after surviving very discouraging conditions. No wonder the species has earned the name of "live-forever"!

Buttercups

All members of this group of wildflowers (*Ranunculus*) contain a biting, easily evaporated material called **anemenol**. In great enough concentrations, this material may blister the skin badly; lesser exposures will result, depending on individual sensitivities and the variety of buttercup, in rashes of varying degrees of intensity. Consumed internally, it may cause severe inflammation of the digestive system. Apparently, anemenol is absorbed into the bloodstream of some mammals, for when cows partake of buttercups, they may produce bad-tasting, off-colored milk, and their milk production may lessen, according to reports. This chemical must be quite volatile, for burning or crushing the green plant will release it into the air.

The buttercups have been included in this book because a beginning plant hunter might possibly confuse their yellow blooms with those of the shrubby cinquefoil or the marsh marigold. For safe and certain identification, the most common species are outlined below.

The members of this group of plants typically have about five sepals, three to eight petals, and many stamens on each yellow flower. Most often the plant has a rosette of leaves near its base, with other leaves, different in shape from the basal leaves, alternating up the stem. The upper leaves are usually attached directly to the stem.

COMMON BUTTERCUP

Ranunculus acris
Photo page #16

Also known as: Tall field buttercup, bitter buttercup
Season: Spring through fall
Habitat: Pastures, meadows, edges of woods, roadsides

THIS IS A POISONOUS PLANT

This is the very buttercup many a youngster will hold under another's chin to see if he likes butter. It is poisonous, like the others in this group, if eaten. Consequently, families with small, exploring children might be well advised to remove any buttercups from their yards, regardless of how attractive the cheerful, yellow, shining flowers may look.

These plants usually grow close to three feet tall, with long, bare branches that bear individual bright yellow flowers. The leaves are cut into divisions like fingers, each roundly toothed or lobed, with three to seven "fingers" per leaf. The stems are hairy, and if you cut through them you'll find they are hollow. The plant's juice is very bitter, so most people won't persevere in sampling the leaves.

The shining five-petaled flowers first make their appearance in late spring or early summer, and may last until the first frosts. Their seeds are spread by small birds and little animals like mice and chipmunks, who eat and carry them from one place to another.

CURSED CROWFOOT

Ranunculus sceleratus

Also known as: Marsh buttercup
Season: Summer
Habitat: Marshes, wet meadows, swamps, damp ditches, river banks

THIS IS A POISONOUS PLANT

This plant grows about half as tall as the common buttercup and has smooth stems. The lower leaves may be either entire or divided into three lobes that are less deeply cut than those of the common buttercup. The stem, sturdy and hollow, branches freely. The flowers are small and yellow, with both the sepals and the small petals bent backwards (reflexed). This variety contains large amounts of anemenol, and is capable of blistering the skin—don't get too close. (See the preceding introduction to this group, and study the illustration on page 9.)

SWAMP BUTTERCUP

Ranunculus septentrionalis

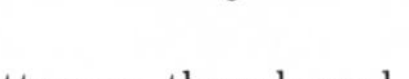

Also known as: Marsh buttercup, three-leaved buttercup, three-leaved crowfoot
Season: Spring through early summer
Habitat: Swamps, wet areas; prefers shade

THIS IS A HARMFUL PLANT

This buttercup grows to about a yard in height, and has a coating of velvet on its stems. Its lower leaves often are divided into three separately stalked leaflets, each of which is coarsely and roundly lobed and toothed. These lower leaves are known to send down roots where they touch the ground. The upper leaves are usually stalkless and arranged in whorls of three around the stem; those just below the flowers are usually lance-shaped, and may be entirely unlobed or untoothed.

Swamp Buttercup

This buttercup has the typical yellow, five-petaled flower. The petals are broadest at their outermost ends. This plant flowers during the same season as the marsh marigold and is likely to be found in the same areas. While moose reportedly find it flavorful, the swamp buttercup is not a food for humans, for it contains the same material as the other members of the buttercup group. (See the preceding introduction to this group of related plants.)

SMALL-FLOWERED BUTTERCUP

Ranunculus abortivus

Also known as: Woods buttercup, small buttercup
Season: Early through late summer
Habitat: Woodlands, shaded areas

THIS PLANT IS POISONOUS

Since this plant begins blooming when the marsh marigold is at its peak and may be found in similar situations, it is wise to be somewhat familiar with this plant. These buttercups are rather low-growing individuals, seldom exceeding one and a half feet in height.

The stems are nearly hairless. The basal leaves may be up to one and a half inches across, with fairly short leaf stems. The leaf margins have rounded teeth, and an inexperienced plant hunter could take them for leaves of the marsh marigold. Later, the plant will unfurl upper leaves shaped like a crow's foot, usually with five divisions, and the marigold hunter will no longer find it confusing to tell the two plants apart. The very topmost leaves are usually divided into three lance-shaped segments and attached right to the stalk. Once these upper leaves and the small yellow flowers appear, it will be clear that this plant is a variety of buttercup. (See the introduction that precedes this group of related plants, and study the illustration on page 9.)

The Clovers

Trifolium, the Latin name of this genus, means three leaves, and when we trace our language back to this same root we find presumably, the reason why the English common name for those plants is clover: Hercules carried a three-knobbed club, and *clava* was the Latin name for such a weapon. It is believed that the name for the three-leaved clover derived from this. (So, apparently, did the symbol for the suit of playing cards we call "clubs"!)

There are many varieties of clover as well as some three-leaved plants that we call clover, though these are not related to the true clovers. Almost all are edible, though some are tastier than others; some have certain characteristics and thus special uses in our diets and households. The true clovers (*Trifolium* species) belong to the legume family. Some of them may be native to America, but the sweet clovers (*Meliotus*) and others grown for agricultural purposes have origins in Europe and Asia.

Clover is a valuable addition to lawns. Besides weathering drought and coolness well, it helps to replenish the nitrogen that other plants remove from the soil. Clover will even withstand the salt-infused sand that passes for soil at roadsides, and highway departments depend upon clover to cover bare slopes without demanding frequent mowing. Clover will transform barren wastelands so that they are tenable by grasses and shrubs, yet it prefers cool, moist climates. Where there are lush growths of clover, you may assume that the soil has good amounts of potassium, phosphorus and calcium, for clover requires these minerals.

Be cautious, however, about picking roadside clover: While it will have all the nutritive value of the plants growing in a farmer's field or your own back yard, it may have an additional mineral supplied by automobile exhausts—lead. You don't need that one! Some towns use herbicides to clear roadside weeds, and the wind can carry this from nearby sprayings. Avoid picking clover or other wild plants from industrial sites; generally, any plant coated with dust or other materials is best left alone.

The early leaves of most clovers (before the plant has flowered are nice raw in salads or cooked as a pot herb. The plants blossom early in the season, but you can still find young, just-opened leaves throughout the summer. They will not be as good as the first spring crop, but they are tasty. However, as spring passes into summer and the leaves gear up for the food production necessary for forming seeds, they become tougher. These older leaves are fine as a cooked vegetable, though a bit chewy. They are best cooked with other vegetables or added to a long-simmering stew or soup. Cooked, chopped clover leaves are excellent, too, in a cheese sauce. The Indians, who valued clover for its many uses, passed on these tricks to us: They sometimes cooked the leaves in layers, moist after a washing, between hot stones. They also soaked the leaves in salt water for a few hours before cooking to render them less chewy. (Prolonged cooking in salted water helps, too, but lessens the nutritional value.)

The flowers have been used to flavor cheese (Gruyere, for example) while it is being made; those who make their own cheese at home might like to experiment with this. The flowers have also been used to add a delightful aroma to pipe tobacco, and some Indian tribes went so far as to dry the leaves and use them as smoking material. In Ireland and Scotland, as well as other European countries, the dried flowers and seeds were ground into a nutritious flour which was used in breads. Some people even use the seeds to grow refreshing (and healthful) salad sprouts! (Be certain that any seeds you sprout have not been treated with chemicals beforehand.)

Carefully dried flower heads, picked before the florets are fully opened, make a wonderful sachet; a gift of these will bring summer to someone you care about, year-round. Blossoms picked at the height of their glory on a dry day may be dried, then crushed into small pieces. (To retain their freshness, store the blossoms in clean, dry jars.) A teaspoonful of the dried blossoms steeped in boiling water and sweetened with honey makes a refreshing tea. Add a little mint or another herb for a variation of this soothing, flavorful tea.

A plant puts its best efforts into its flowers and seeds, for these ensure the next generation. The pollen contains many essential nutrients and vitamins, especially vitamin A. Pollen has an ancient reputation as an enhancer of health. Today we know that the body requires an adequate reserve of vitamins and minerals in order to successfully fight viruses and bacteria, and it makes sense that clover blossoms have been used in cough syrups and spring tonics, too, for the flower contains the pollen of the plant.

For many years the clovers, red clover especially, have been extolled as having beneficial effects for cancer victims. (This is described more fully in books devoted to herbal healing.) Clover blossoms have been used to soothe nerves, promote restful sleep, and balance bodily functions. The plant was also supposed to restore fertility and cleanse the blood; this last surmise was not far off the track, for we now obtain from sweet clover a powerful drug, dicumarol, that has proven effective in treatment of thrombosis. (See White Sweet Clover and Yellow Sweet Clover.)

The clovers, first the true clovers and then the sweet varieties, are described individually in the following pages. Only specific identification traits and uses are mentioned for each member of this useful group of plants.

ALSIKE CLOVER 

Trifolium hybridum
Photo page #17

Also known as: Swedish clover

(See the following description.)

WHITE CLOVER

Trifolium repens
Photo page #17

Also known as: Dutch clover
Season: Spring through fall
Habitat: Lawns, roadsides, waste places, any open area

One might at first take the alsike clover for a variant of the typical lawn-planted white clover. Both range from pink to white in flower color. There are only three apparent differences between this and white clover: The leaves of alsike clover do not have chevron marks, and the flower-bearing stems branch from the leaf stems. The seeds are a shade of olive green.

The leaves of the white clover show chevron marks, and the flowers are most often white, though they may be tinged with pink. The blooms are borne on separate stems, rather than branching from the leaf-supporting stems, and the seeds are generally a shade of golden tan.

Both of these fragrant clovers were imported from foreign shores. Both tend to be low-growing plants, and are excellent not only for the table but for lawns. Bees that visit them produce one of the best honeys. Both alsike and white clover begin blooming in May, and will persevere until the approach of winter. When you collect the blooms, be sure to let some of the late ones mature to continue the tribe. (Be sure to see the introduction to the clovers for general information and suggestions for use.)

RED CLOVER

Trifolium pratense
Photo page #18

Also known as: Tall clover, purple clover
Season: Spring through early fall
Habitat: Pastures, fields, roadsides, any open area

This is the large, rangy, purple-red flowering clover often planted as a soil retainer by highway departments. Farmers, too, know it as a top-notch pasture plant for their animals.

The plants first bloom in May, and their large, fragrant flowers call all the bees for miles around. The leaves are usually marked with chevron stripes. Given good growing conditions, a single red clover will form a small bush, so these hardy plants are better off thriving in meadows than in well-trimmed lawns.

An import to North America, red clover is now found nearly everywhere, and was even adopted by Vermont as its state flower. The red clover, like the others, relies upon bees to continue. When the plants were introduced in Australia, they failed to flourish until bumblebees were also provided! Here's a happy triangle of mutual benefit—we, too, enjoy the excellent honey the bees produce from red clover.

Often, red clover will scorch in mid-summer, only to revive for a second flush of tender growth as Labor Day approaches. This doubles the picking season if you want to gather young leaves for salads or vegetable dishes. (See the general introduction to the clovers for tips on preparation and use.)

RABBIT FOOT CLOVER

Trifolium arvense
Photo page #18

Also known as: Rabbit ear clover, fuzzy pink clover
Season: Summer
Habitat: Waste places, pastures and fields, roadsides, open areas

NOT EDIBLE

Though it is a pretty little plant, this is one clover not recommended for human consumption. It is included here to make sure no one confuses it with late white or alsike clover.

The leaflets of rabbit foot clover are softly silky and noticeably smaller and narrower than those of the other clovers. There are no chevron marks on the leaves, so you'll know it is not white clover; the flowers are lengthier, fuzzier, and more deeply colored pink than those of the alsike clover. These flowers have been known to trouble cattle who eat to many of them: the soft blossoms can contribute to the formation of hair balls in the animals' stomachs. That should be enough to keep you away from them!

HOP CLOVER

Trifolium agrarium
Photo page #17

Also known as: Yellow clover
Season: Early summer
Habitat: Open places, roadsides, pastures, fields, lawns

There are actually three kinds of edible yellow-flowered clover, two of which look very much alike. The true hop clover (*Trifolium agrarium*) is an erect plant that blooms in May, at about the same time as do the red, white, and alsike clovers. The flowers fade into brownish, down-folded relics that happen to resemble dried hops. The leaves are pointed, and not chevron marked.

A smaller hop clover, *Trifolium procumbens,* runs along the ground rather than standing upright. Its leaf tips are blunt; the middle leaf is often notched, and it bears a short stalk, a feature not found in the leaves of the larger hop clover. The flowers are smaller in this variety, and the plant is fuzzier. An even lesser hop clover, *Trifolium dubium*, resembles the smaller hop clover, but the flowers are tiny, with only a dozen or fewer florets in the flowering head.

The two smaller forms are not found so often as the regular hop clover, and for this reason, as well as their fuzziness, they are seldom mentioned in literature about wild edibles. These smaller hop clovers might be confused with the somewhat similar wild indigo, *Baptista tinctoria*, a poisonous plant (page 9). The most important distinction between them is found in the flowers: The hop clovers have true clover flowers, whereas wild indigo has a flower stalk bearing spaced pea-like flowers. While the leaves of these plants are not much different, those of the wild indigo are stalkless and turn black upon drying, and—true to their name—produce blue coloring when steeped in water. It is definitely wise to wait until the blossoms appear before attempting to pick the leaves of the smaller hop clovers for table use. (Be sure to read the introduction to the clovers.)

BLACK MEDIK 

Medicago lupulina
Photo page #11

Also known as: Lucerne clover, yellow clover, nonesuch
Season: Summer
Habitat: Waste areas, lawns, roadsides, edges of parking lots and other rather dry wastelands

You might at first think this plant was a recumbent or slightly under-developed hop clover: The flowers are similar, though not quite as large. On closer inspection you would see that the clover-like leaves are neither as narrow nor so sharply pointed as those of the yellow hop clover; they are more roundly shaped, rather like soup spoons, with a tiny bristle at the apex. The dark bluish-green coloring of the leaves is broken by the herringbone pattern of the veins, and the outermost edges may be slightly toothed. The little yellow flowers and leaves are borne on stems that spread along the ground, rooting as they go, to a length of two or more feet.

The most distinctive trait, though, is the shape and color of the seed pods. Instead of the yellow-brown of the clover it resembles, black medik's seed pods at first turn soft green and then dull charcoal black. Each little black, spirally twisted pod contains one seed. The seeds may be collected and parched, and used as you would most other seeds or nuts. They are especially good when combined with other materials in granola or added to nuts in a homemade nut butter. If you can gather enough of them, you may grind the seeds into a nutritious flour to add, with wheat flour, to muffins, breads, and pancakes.

The plant belongs to the same genus as alfalfa, and has the same central taproot system, though it does not reach so deep as its well-known relative. Alfalfa's young sprouts are a well-known nutritious treat. These seeds should provide excellent sprouts, too.

Since black medik, like the clovers and other members of its family, is capable of supporting nitrogen-fixing bacteria, it is a welcome addition to poorer soils. Alfalfa is renowned as a heavyweight among the nutritious greens, and black medik is probably not far behind. (See the general introduction to the clover group.) It is not difficult to find patches of black medik large enough to make collecting the seeds worthwhile; the plant is easily enough identified that even little folks can help, but be sure to check their collections carefully.

WHITE SWEET CLOVER 

Melilotus alba
Photo page #17

(See the following description.)

YELLOW SWEET CLOVER

Melilotus officinalis
Photo page #17

Also known as: Melilot, white melilot, yellow melilot, vanilla clover, spike clover

Season: Early through late summer

Habitat: Fields, roadsides, waste places, open areas

THIS PLANT COULD BE HAZARDOUS IF EATEN WHEN SPOILED

Both of these sweet clovers are tall, branched plants with smooth, hairless stems. Their leaves grow in threes, and, crushed, give off a vanilla-like odor. On both plants, the leaves have stalks, and the spikes of the pea-like flowers top slender stalks that spring from the axils of the upper leaves. The only observable difference between the two varieties is the flower color—white or yellow. Neither of the sweet clovers is a native to this continent; though both were brought to this country from Europe, Western Asia and Northern Africa to be planted as fodder for domestic animals, these nutritious plants have long been used in the human diet, as well.

Before the flowers appear, the young leaves may be used in salads. (Early in the flowering time, nip the newly uncurled leaves to extend the salad season.) These fresh young leaves may be simmered for five to ten minutes and served as a pot herb or, better yet, as an accompaniment to other greens. The dried leaves, crushed, may be added to sweet or savory pastries to impart a vanilla-like flavoring. The seeds, which resemble peas, can be used as a flavoring in soups and stews. To store them for winter, simply wash them well, allow them to dry, and freeze in small batches. The seeds are reportedly rich in protein and other nutrients, so you'll be adding more than just flavor to a dish.

The flowers of these plants may be used like those of the other clovers in sachets, and at one time they were packed with winter clothes to discourage moths. Whether or not this was highly effective, the sweet scent of clover must certainly have been more pleasant than camphor. Though much of our knitted material today is moth-proof synthetic fiber, it is still a treat to bring out a vanilla-clover scented sweater for the first chill days of autumn. Medicinally, these clovers were long used in tonics, blood cleansers, and external washes for skin irritations and infections.

Years ago, it was noted that sheep, horses and cattle sometimes died from hemorrhages after eating clover that had been allowed to spoil in storage. Based on these unhappy observations, scientific investigations were begun to find out what was happening. It was discovered that these two clovers contained a chemical called **coumarin**. (Apparently it is coumarin which gives the vanilla scent to this plant.) As these plants ferment and spoil, a product known as **dicumarol** is formed. Dicumarol, taken into the body, acts as an anti-vitamin—that is, it blocks the ability of the body to utilize vitamin K, a substance vital in the formation of blood clots. When domestic animals absorbed large quantities of dicumarol from the spoiled clover, their blood was unable to clot, and hemorrhages took place in tiny blood vessels, leading ultimately to death.

This discovery led directly to the production of a very important medicine used in treating people whose blood, as a result of accident, surgery, fatty deposits, or hereditary disorder, tends to form misplaced (and dangerous) clots. The earlier anticoagulants used to dissolve these clots often caused severe side effects. Dicumarol, on the other hand, was found to be effective longer while causing far fewer reactions.

As an offshoot of these investigations, coumarin itself was synthesized and incorporated in perfumes as well as in foods as a flavoring agent. In 1953, however, it was banned by the United States for use in foods. (Possibly due to the chance that this substance might convert to dicumarol under such circumstances as long-term storage, spoilage, or an individual digestive reaction?)

With these potential risks in mind, I would recommend moderation in partaking of sweet clover leaves. Occasional use of them in salads, cooked dishes and teas shouldn't constitute a health hazard; cows, horses, and people have eaten and enjoyed these plants for centuries. Just make sure that the sweet clover you prepare for a meal is perfectly fresh. (For suggestion for harvesting and use, see the introduction to this group of plants.)

ALFALFA

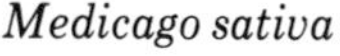

Medicago sativa

Also known as: Lucerne, buffalo herb, sweet lucerne
Season: Spring through fall
Habitat: Fields, roadsides; an escapee from cultivation

In areas outside the grain belt, alfalfa is often the top choice of plants for fattening cattle; it is also grown in otherwise fallow fields and plowed under for fertilizer. Since it is widely grown on farms, alfalfa has also escaped into surrounding zones. You will likely find it growing wild near a farm, and if you spot some in a tilled field and ask, the farmer will probably allow you to harvest several plants for kitchen use.

The plants look a little like clover. They have the three-leaf pattern of red clover and sweet clovers. Their leaves, not chevron-marked, are roundly lance-shaped and often toothed near the outer end. The leaves usually have the soft gray-green coloring of the red clover's, though plants growing in excessive moisture or insuffiicent sunlight may have more yellow-green leaves. The entire plant is free of hair or fuzz.

Alfalfa

Although alfalfa is a relative of black medik, the two plants share little family resemblance. Alfalfa is a tall plant, generally growing to a foot and a half in height. (In particularly rich areas, it may reach two to three feet.) It blooms from late spring through fall; the flowers, pea-like and violet, bluish, or purple, are held in clusters on stalks arising from the leaf axils. The flowers produce seed pods that are twisted into a spiral. (Black medik also forms twisted seed pods.) The seeds are edible, but are best used for sprouting. They may be collected and stored in dry containers for use throughout the year, or, come spring, to plant your own alfalfa patch.

If you decide to collect either leaves or seeds, be sure the alfalfa patch has not been sprayed with an insecticide or herbicide. Fields near large commercial gardens are sometimes the recipients of materials meant to protect the vegetables, for sprays may be carried by wind. If you should purchase alfalfa seeds for planting, be sure to use them only for this purpose—do not use them for sprouting unless you are certain they are untreated by any chemicals. You might as well collect your own from clean fields; untreated alfalfa seeds sold for sprouting and eating will grow in your backyard, too.

Alfalfa is believed to be a native of Asia. It has been cultivated in Europe since before the time of Christ, and migrated to South America with Spanish explorers. It wasn't until sometime in the middle of the nineteenth century that alfalfa became known in North America.

The plant is exceptionally vigorous! The roots of mature alfalfa plants may reach twenty, thirty or more feet into the ground, obtaining minerals that have leached out of the upper surface levels and are no longer available to any other crop plant. Needless to say, alfalfa is a superlative source of trace minerals.

The plant is also able to remove nitrogen from the air, and thus is high in nitrogen-containing products such as protein. It is also rich in vitamins A, D, and K. In the past, alfalfa was prescribed as a general tonic and was known as a natural cure for some forms of jaundice. It was also used as an antihemorrhagic in cases of peptic ulcers or other conditions characterized by an inability to clot blood due to an inadequate level of vitamin K. Vitamin D is necessary for many things, including the proper use of calcium within the body, and vitamin A helps to protect healthy skin, internal tissues and the body's immune response. The value of alfalfa has long been recognized, but little exploited. For such a highly nutritious plant, alfalfa is only beginning to find wider use as a popular foodstuff as well as a dietary supplement.

For people who need an extra dose of vitamin A and D, but who find it difficult to digest the fish oils that are better known as supplements, alfalfa can be a very important addition to the diet. Alfalfa leaves and sprouts leave neither the aftertaste nor the digestive upset that often linger after the oil-containing capsules—what's more, alfalfa is a pleasure to eat.

Most people have heard of alfalfa tea. You can make it for free from fresh or dried leaves and flowers, but it is not all that flavorful on its own. The addition of mint, orange or lemon peel, sorrel or even red clover will enhance the flavor, and with a dollop of honey you'll enjoy a warm, relaxing drink or an excellent iced tea.

The dried leaves may be added to cereals, stews and soups, even meatloaf. Fresh leaves may be chopped and added to salad, although, like clover, they may be a bit hard to digest. (They're so packed with goodness, a little will go a long way!) The young branches may be oiled and eaten as greens or added, chopped fine, to soups.

It is probably as lush, lacy sprouts that alfalfa is best known today. When a seed sprouts, the protein and vitamin content soar, and alfalfa sprouts are high quality food. While alfalfa seeds may be ground into a nutritious flour for use as a cereal or in breads, they become additionally wholesome, sweet and flavorful if allowed to sprout. If you do not have a special "sprouter," any large, clean wide-mouth jar will do. Another key component is a piece of covering for the jar, so that you may rinse the seeds without losing them down the drain. Fine netting, cheesecloth, even an ankle-high stocking may be fitted snugly over the mouth of the jar with a sturdy rubber band.

To begin the three-to-five day sprouting process, place three or four tablespoonsful of seeds in the bottom of the jar and add enough water to cover the seeds. Allow them to soak for a few hours or overnight, then attach your fabric or netting and strain off the water. Rotate the jar to distribute the seeds as evenly as possible, for they need space and air. Place the jar in a dark area at room temperature, and, each morning and evening, briefly rinse the seeds—just add enough fresh water through the cover to swirl them in, then pour it off again.

In about two days the seeds will have sprouted. When they are between a half inch and an inch long, you might wish to remove the seed hulls, although this isn't necessary. Just take the sprouts out of the jar and very gently "scrub" them between your hands in a large bowl of cold water, then skim off the brown hulls that will have risen to the surface. Return the sprouts to the jar and leave them in the sunlight for a few hours to fully develop chlorophyll and flavor. (Just don't let them bake in the hot sun or dry up.) The sprouts, crisp, sumptuous, and full of life, are delicious in salads, in or on top of sandwiches, even in cooked dishes like homemade egg foo yong or spring rolls. You won't get comments about "cow food" when you serve alfalfa sprouts—guaranteed!

FIREWEED

Epilobium angustifolium
Photo page #16

Also known as: Fireplant, willow herb, great willow herb
Season: Early summer through early fall
Habitat: Cleared areas, waste areas, burned-over areas, fields

Fireweed or willow herb is a very noticeable plant, with its spike of bright blossoms and its distinctive height—sometimes it will even outgrow a tall man! From midsummer through September, it bedecks fields and burned-over areas. Edible as well as lovely, this is a plant you might consider growing in your own yard: The young spring shoots are very good when served as asparagus, and the young leaves are fine as a cooked green. With the plant growing nearby, you'll be able to observe its complete growth cycle and, the next time around, recognize the young shoots afield.

The rosy coloring of the flowers will beckon from a distance, and even several feet away you can be fairly certain you've found fireweed by observing the unopened buds toward the top of the flowering spike. These will point downward; the flower stalk will gradually lift as the flowers bloom, and the open blossoms will point outward. Step a little closer and look for the four pink petals, large and showy, emphasized from the rear by four purplish bracts. (These usually fill the spaces between the petals like a background star.) Even the seed pods produced by these blooms will be ruddy; they are skinny and sausage-shaped, pointing upward. The seeds, released, are transported on the wind via their silky tufts. Collect a few of these for planting if you want your own patch.

This graceful, magenta-pink-flowered plant known most often as fireweed shares that name with another plant. Pilewort is also called fireweed and is usually found growing in the same areas as *Epilobium angustifolium*. Pilewort, however, produces white flowers and has coarsely toothed or lobed leaves.

The magenta fireweed may have received its other common name of willow herb from the shape of its leaves: they are long, alternately placed on the sturdy stalk, and usually toothless. The undersurfaces are usually paler, and the veins are more prominent underneath.

Once you have learned to recognize this plant in all its growth stages, harvest the young spring shoots and use them like asparagus. (Leave some to bloom, though, to ensure future seasons.) The tender young leaves may be cooked like lamb's quarters or dock; they are good whether on their own or combined with other wild greens. Though the older leaves become too strongly flavored to serve as a vegetable, they may be dried for use as a tea. To extend the fireweed's harvest season, can or freeze the shoots and young leaves.

This is a good beginner's plant, for it is found in abundance and is easy to harvest. However, this and other plants that help to reclaim damaged or burned areas are important for more than their food value. Leave plenty to continue regreening these hurt areas. If you find this plant in its seed-bearing stage, you might give a helping hand by spreading the ripe seeds around in any bare patches. There will be more fireweed plants there for you, too, the next year!

FOXGLOVE

Digitalis purpurea
Photo page #18

Also known as: Digitalis, purple foxglove, purple bells, bluebells
Season: Summer; blooms in summer
Habitat: Woodlands, shaded roadsides, meadow edges, gardens

THIS IS A POISONOUS PLANT

Foxglove is lovely, but deadly. Investigations following reports of its use in herbal medicine found the plant to contain several poisonous glycosides, among them **digitoxin**. This is a powerful heart stimulant which soon made its way into accepted medical use; it was later synthesized in the laboratory so that its purity and strength could more easily and accurately be determined.

All parts of this plant are poisonous. The plant produces two-chambered dry capsules that contain many seeds, and there is little danger of someone eating its unappetizing fruit. However, do not confuse its bell-shaped flowers with those of creeping bellflower! The foxglove flowers, too, range from blue-violet to white, but they are usually more pinkish-violet and have distinctive inner speckles of darker magenta or purple that beckon bees like landing pads. There are generally four scallops edging each open foxglove flower. Once the plant has flowered, you'll recognize it by its tall spike of pretty, colorful bells. But the flowers are not always present to serve as warning flags. The underground roots of this plant are toxic, as well as the flowers, and it is the leaves and seeds that are most harmful.

This biennial grows in two stages. During its first year, it produces a low rosette of leaves. During the second year, a flowering and leaf-bearing stalk will arise from this central rosette. These leaves are long, fat, oval, and pointed, with teeth along their margins. An incautious beginner might mistake them perhaps for those of the Jerusalem artichoke or another of the sunflowers. (It will be clear that this is not the artichoke, though, by the absence of any tuber.) If the toothing of the leaves is ignored, the leaves might seem to resemble those of a broad-leafed dock, but they haven't the papery sheaths that on the dock plant bind the leaf-stalks to the stem.

This foxglove is a garden escapee. The beautiful plants are often found growing wild, but are even more often found in flower gardens. Though decorative, they are dangerous to have in your yard if very young children are about.

The symptoms of poisoning by this plant may not develop for several hours after a part of this plant has been eaten. They may include nausea, dizziness and vomiting, rapid heart action and flushing. Call your poison control center right away if there is a question of poisoning: These symptoms call for immediate action, so do not linger or attempt to home-treat the person! The first procedure is usually to empty the person's stomach and administer medicines to counter-effect the plant's glycosides, so it is helpful for the doctor to know what part of the plant was eaten, when, and how much.

CREEPING BELLFLOWER

Campanula rapunculoides
Photo page #18

Also known as: Creeping bluebell, bluebell, European bellflower
Season: Summer; blooms in July
Habitat: Fields, roadsides, gardens, along rock walls, waste areas

DO NOT CONFUSE THIS PLANT WITH BLUEBELLS, FOXGLOVE OR LARKSPUR

It's a shame to bother these lovely plants for their nourishing and delectable underground stems. If you find a large enough patch, though, you might get enough thinnings to try them, for these runners, raw or cooked, are a fine food to remember in a time of need.

The creeping bellflower is an immigrant to this country. It is believed to have originated in Germany, and was likely brought along here for its beauty. The delicate blue-to-purple, five-pointed bells bloom on a tall stalk, the bottom-most buds opening first. All the bells usually hang from one side of the stalk; this sturdy stalk often reclines, and may root where it touches the ground. Though the stems are hairless, the flower petals may be a little fuzzy.

The leaves are arranged alternately. The lower leaves are heart-shaped and have stems, while the upper ones are more linear and lack petioles. All are toothed and sharply pointed at the ends. It is the flowers, though, that best announce the plant's identity. They bloom in July.

Although the flowers produce seeds, the plant has a second means of reproducing itself: underground runners creep from the established stands, engendering new plants as they spread. The underground branches that arise from these runners may be chopped and added to salads or boiled for fifteen to twenty minutes and served with butter, salt, and pepper. The milky juice of the plant seems to disappear in cooking, leaving no taste. The stems are starchy-sweet in flavor, and would go well in a stew or soup or in a mixed vegetable dish. If these plants weren't so pretty, we'd sample them more often!

POOR MAN'S PEPPER

Lepidium virginicum
Photo page #19

Also known as: Peppergrass, pepper weed, wild peppergrass
Season: Early to late summer
Habitat: Nearly any open area, waste places, roadside

Of the peppergrasses, this is the species most likely to be found by the city-dweller, for it thrives in the cracks next to buildings, in alleys, and along parking lots. It is probably better to avoid picking it in such areas, though, for the plants may have accumulated toxic materials from cars, sprays or industry. Once you get to know the poor man's pepper, search for it in uncontaminated territories.

The plant blooms in summer, with little four-petaled white flowers opening along the flower stems. The seed pods later form along these stems. Poor man's pepper seems to continue producing its flowers and seeds nearly forever, or at least until daunted by a deep summer drought or autumn's frost.

This bushy little plant usually grows not much taller than two feet. Its leaves are not so deeply notched as those of the dandelion, though they have much the same color and general appearance. Shepherd's purse, although its leaves are really more like those of the dandelion, may be confused with poor man's pepper by the beginner. Shepherd's purse produces heart-shaped seed pods, however, while those of poor man's pepper are more oval with a little depression at the top.

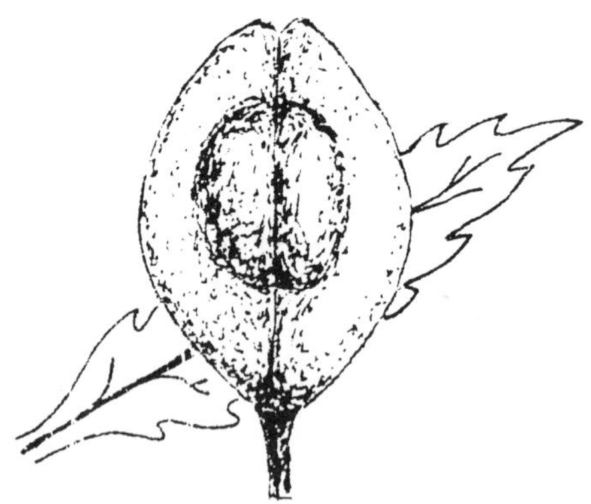

Poor Man's Pepper

It is the seed pods and the very young leaves of this plant which may be eaten. Add the leaves to salads or cook them with other vegetables. Slip them into soups, stews or chowders—they're very worthwhile, nutritionally. The seed pods serve as excellent seasoning for many dishes; they'll add zip to a salad dressing. Or, grind them when dry, and put them into a pepper shaker. This is a seasoning worthy of the table, just as the plant's name implies.

SHEPHERD'S PURSE 

Capsella bursa-pastoris

Also known as: Lady's purse, pickpocket, pepper heart, mother's heart, pepper and salt
Season: Summer
Habitat: Fields, gardens, lawns, city parks, vacant lots, disturbed ground

Once you have identified shepherd's purse, you'll see it everywhere! You might pick some from the school yard, the area around your place of employment, behind your favorite restaurant, or on the front lawn of the tire shop while waiting for your car.

The seed pods give this peppergrass away: they are little and heart-shaped (named for their shape's resemblance to the purses made by shepherds when male lambs were altered in the spring). The basal leaves of this plant resemble dandelion leaves; the upper leaves are toothed less strongly, and their bases clasp the flower stalk. When the plant blossoms, the whitish flowers will be in clusters at the top of the stalk, and the seeds will develop further down, branching at intervals on individual stems. The whole plant may be only six inches tall, especially when growing in a dry area or well-trimmed lawn, but it will grow as high as nearly two feet in suitable conditions. The seeds will mature earlier on plants growing in dry areas, though they may be a little smaller. Seeds found in moist areas will likely hold the greatest nutritive value—vitamins C and K, sodium, calcium, some protein, iron, and sulphur are among their contents. All seeds contain the materials necessary to sustain the growth of a new plant, so they will add vital materials as well as flavor to your menu.

Shepherd's Purse

The young leaves are good in salads. Chopped, they could be steeped in a vinegar and oil or other salad dressing to add some pep. Cook them as a pot herb with other greens or, if enough are available, by themselves. The seed pods are best early in the season; use the fully ripened seeds fresh, and dry or freeze some for winter use. They are wonderful in any recipe that needs interest and zip. The seeds may also be dried and ground for sprinkling on foods as a peppery-savory herb salt.

Shepherd's purse has been used in folk remedies as a cure for diarrhea and kidney disorders, and it is said to have a stimulating effect. It stimulates sluggish taste buds, for sure!

COW CRESS

Lepidium campestre

Also known as: Field peppergrass
Season: Spring through early summer
Habitat: Fields, waste places, gardens, roadsides, disturbed soil

Like the other peppergrasses, cow cress too bears tiny white four-petaled flowers on two, three, or more slender wands that project upward from the tops of the plants. The cow cress flowers grow along the stalks, though, rather than in clusters. In very dry locations, cow cress may only grow six or eight inches tall, and, if their leaves wither early, you'll hardly notice the plants unless they are right under your feet. In better conditions they may exceed fifteen inches.

It seems as though these plants have hardly begun to grow before their seeds have formed. The seed capsules of cow cress are almost squarish compared to those of the other peppergrasses. With two seeds contained in each, the capsules are held on small stalks away from the flower stems, angled almost like hands cupped to catch the rain.

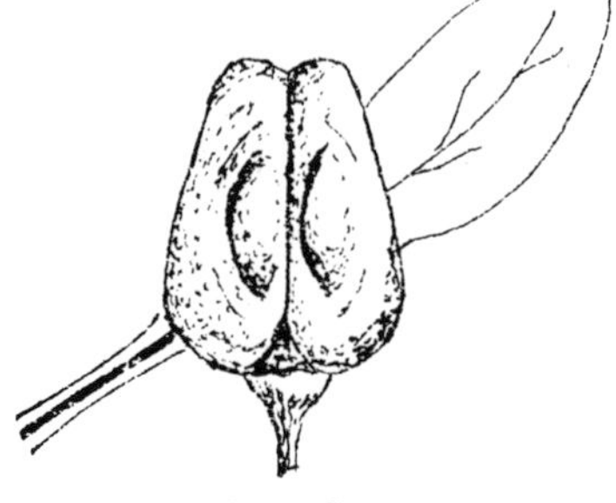

Cow Cress

At the base of the plant is a rosette of paddle-shaped, untoothed leaves. The more pointed leaves of the upright stem have basal lobes that clasp the stem; these upper leaves are slightly toothed.

The tender young leaves may be plucked and used raw as a spicy addition to green salads or cooked in stews or soups. They are tasty, too, as a pot herb, cooked with other greens. They will only need a few minutes' cooking if very young, fifteen or twenty minutes if a little older. Leave the mature leaves alone, though, for they become tough and quite hot. The green seed pods can be added to nearly any cooked dish for their peppery flavor and good nutrition; try adding some of them to an Italian-style salad dressing or vinegar and oil, for interest and sparkle.

Cow cress is reportedly high in protein and iron as well as the vitamins found in most greens, including A and C. Dried, the seeds seem to lose their zip, but frozen ones retain some flavor and can be kept for winter use. In times past, these seeds played an important part in keeping our ancestors scurvy-free during the winter months.

These plants often find their way into gardens, thanks to the birds who relish their seeds. Cow cress grows so early in the season, already producing seeds in midspring, you might just let the plants grow to maturity and consider them one of the early crops in your garden!

FIELD PENNYCRESS 

Thlaspi arvense
Photo page #19

Also known as: Field pennies, pepper pennies
Season: Summer
Habitat: Fields, gardens, near foundations, roadsides

This plant is easy to recognize. Its four-petaled white flowers are not showy, but the "pennies" borne on the flower stalk nearly immediately identify pennycress.

Overall, the plant may vary in height from a spindly six inches to around two feet. It rather resembles shepherd's purse, except for the absence of the toothed leaves that make the early shepherd's purse resemble a dandelion. Pennycress has toothed upper leaves; they are a little like holly leaves, and their bases clasp the flower stem.

The large seed pods develop on the lower portions of the flower stalks. On good-sized plants, these capsules, each bearing two seed chambers, may be nearly a half inch wide. They are quite round, and are deeply notched at the upper end.

The young leaves of this plant are good in salads. They may be added to other greens or, if plentiful enough, cooked as a pot herb by themselves. The seed pods provide good seasoning for soups and stews, and, when young and tender, are a fine addition to a salad dressing, though you may wish to chop them a bit.

These seed pods are worth drying for two reasons: Dried whole, the seed pods left intact, the stalks are attractive in dried flower arrangements. And, indeed, this is one way of storing seeds you intend to use on the table as a pepper-like seasoning! Just be sure to wash the stalks before drying them. When thoroughly dried, crush or grind the pods finely and keep them in a salt or pepper shaker. Pennycress is a nice change of pace!

GALINSOGA 

Galinsoga ciliata
Galinsoga parviflora
Photo page #19

Also known as: Gallengale, gallant soldiers, tiny daisy
Season: Early to late summer
Habitat: Lawns, fields, roadsides

This harmless little weed's life has probably been spared by a good many gardeners for its tiny daisy-like flowers. Little do many of them realize, though, that the galinsoga may be eaten.

These cheerful little plants were originally natives of tropical America. The two varieties differ very little, mainly in the amount of hair that coats their stems and leaves. Though they keep low where pruned by lawnmowers, they are capable of reaching up to two feet; most often, the plants range in the twelve to eighteen inch zone and are found near tree trunks, rocks and other structures that give them a little protection.

Their leaves are broad and oval, with a sharp tip and coarsely-toothed margins. The upper leaves have very short stalks, if at all, while the flower leaves have a proper petiole. You may not notice the flowers until you've nearly stepped on them or gripped them to wrest them from your garden or lawn. The insignificant daisy-like blooms are only about one quarter inch across. Each has a golden center surrounded by five tiny, white three-lobed petals. They bloom from May to frost.

Though the stems and leaves of the plant are velvety to somewhat hairy, this trait disappears in cooking. These parts make a good pot herb; we have prepared them with other summer pot herbs. If enough are harvested, they may be boiled for about a quarter of an hour, then served with butter or vinegar.

Land Plantains

It is said that several of the Indian tribes called land plantains "white man's foot" — perhaps these plants seemed to crop up wherever the settlers trod, for some varieties were brought to this country by European immigrants. Interestingly, the Latin root of the generic name, *planta*, also refers to a foot. This aptly describes the oval basal leaves that often lie close to the ground, like footprints.

Plantain, especially common plantain, seems to just love growing in lawns, and it's likely you'll not have to search far to sample your first leaves. You will even find these plants sticking out of cracks between sidewalks, next to steps, or in parking lots—they'll cling to life nearly anywhere a bit of soil might be found. They have a densely fibrous root system that enables them to find the smallest trace of moisture, but it is this very strength that makes these plants the bane of people who enjoy grass-only lawns. In some areas of the Orient, plantain is actually cultivated!

Some varieties of plantain are common to rocky areas, while others prefer ocean breezes and saline soil. Generally, the plantains grow best in soils that are not too rich; they cannot compete with the fast-growing plants that thrive in better soils. ***Don't confuse the edible land plantains, though, with the inedible water plantains*** of the *Alisma* species. Though the leaves are similar, the plants are not related. The habitat should be a solid clue to identity: *Alisma* grows in marshy areas only. The flowers of the two plants are completely different. (See Water Plantain.)

Of the more than twenty *Plantago* species, none have been reported inedible—that is, none are poisonous, though some may be so chewy that they are best used just as survival food. The toughness comes from strong fibers, found in the veins or "ribs" of the leaf; these may be stripped from the plant much as you'd de-string tough celery. The stringy fibers of the narrower leaves are closer together, and so you'd have little left if they were removed. If you don't mind chewing, it is far easier to leave these whole, or chop them cross-wise in larger leaves.

The narrower-leaved varieties have a stronger flavor. Chopped fine, the leaves may be added to a stew or soup. The longer cooking helps to tenderize them, but even then it is wise to cut closely across the grain of the ribs. The broader-leaved plantains may be plucked when quite young and used in salads; even these may be a little chewy, though, so the removal of the strings or fine chopping is recommended. When the leaves are a little larger they may be used as a pot herb, with the tough fibers removed. If the taste seems too strong, the addition of vinegar at the table will help to tame it. Plantain greens may also be cooked with a little honey or served with a cream sauce. Raw, they are bound to retain higher content of minerals and their significant amounts of vitamins A and C. Since it is not necessary to boil and reboil them, they are nutritionally worthwhile cooked, too, more so than certain other wild greens that need a change or two of cooking water.

As you would do when seeking a picking site for any wild plant, use discrimination: be sure the plantain leaves have neither been sprayed with herbicides or pesticides nor exposed to pollutants. If the summer has been hot and wet, be on the lookout for any grayish, powdery-looking patches on the leaves: these are evidence of a mildew that has rendered your wild "spinach" inedible. New leaves will appear later in the summer (mowing or clipping back seems to encourage new growth), and, if these are mildew-free, go ahead and pick. If you're not sure the fungus infection has gone, it's best to call it a season and await the new leaves' arrival the next spring.

Plantains produce a central, leafless stalk that bears inconspicuous flowers. These soon fade, leaving many kernel-like seeds. Although the seeds are eaten by birds and small animals, they are not really recommended as edible, although they have been sprouted or ground into flour.

The leaves have been used in tea, in the past, as an herbal medicine as well as a good drink. This tea, made from the leaves or roots, was purported to be effective in treating a wide range of ailments, including kidney and bladder troubles, syphilis and diarrhea. Fevers from colds and influenza were ameliorated with this same brew. Possibly the high amounts of vitamins A and C were responsible for plantain's beneficial reputation, for today these vitamins are known to be effective in treating many conditions.

COMMON PLANTAIN

Plantago major

Also known as: White man's foot, ribwort, broadleaf plantain, plantain, cuckoo's bread

Season: Spring through summer

Habitat: Lawns, roadsides, waste places

For most people, the broad-leaved plantains don't need any introduction: They're old regulars, no doubt, in your lawn. You probably know them by their low-lying, spoon-shaped leaves that grow in a basal rosette, each leaf with five to seven longitudinal veins. The leaves have long petioles, their lengths often exceeding the broadness of the leaves. The leaves are tough; their margins may be smooth and entire, wavy or toothed. One or both sides may feel rough due to hairs that are sometimes present. The petioles are greenish or whitish, blending into the light grass green of the leaves. In uninjured leaves, there are no reddish or purplish tints to the blades or the petioles; this will distinguish the common plantain from the blackseed plantain, which has red petioles. The petioles are grooved lengthwise. Though slender, these are very stringy, too tough to be eaten, but their length often allows the plant to cover up to two feet of ground space. It is its tendency to smother grass that makes this common plant unloved by most homeowners.

The leaves of common plantain, however, are the best of the edible plantains, so you might consider putting this lawn pest to good use in your menu. Suggestions for its preparation are given in the introduction to plantains.

Beginning in mid-spring, common plantain will grow a leafless, central, erect spike that bears tiny whitish flowers. On each plant there may be one or more of these spikes, and they may grow to a foot and a half tall. The small light brown seeds borne on the spikes are generally not to be eaten by humans, although they are enjoyed by numerous types of birds. For this reason, likely, is "cuckoo's bread" one of common plantain's names.

The ground-up seeds have been used in herbal medicine externally, as a poultice for sores, and some people stand by the leaves as a readily available treatment for insect bites or stings: the freshly picked leaf is rubbed on the afflicted area to soothe the inflammation or, chewed well, is patted on the skin.

ENGLISH PLANTAIN

Plantago lanceolata
Photo page #19

Also known as: Buckhorn plantain, narrow-leaved plantain
Season: Summer
Habitat: Lawns, meadows, waste places, urban nooks and crannies

The leaves of this narrow-leaved member of the plantain group are more erect than those of the common plantain. Springing from the same common basal portion, they are slender, each having three to five fibrous ribs. Each leaf tapers at either end, and has a short, grooved and tough petiole. The leaves and the stalk of the (usually single) flower spike are often coated with white hairs.

The flower stalk often reaches to just above the tips of the leaves, though it may be taller, and bears a short, dense spike of flowers. Usually some eight to fifteen inches above the ground, the floral head is brownish or bronze-toned when in bloom. The white stamens of the flowers contrast with these colors, and project like a halo around the one- to two-inch mass of blooms.

The leaves of this plant are edible, though strong in flavor unless very young, and require more cutting and cooking than those of common plantain. (See the general introduction to the land plantain for suggestions for preparation.)

BLACKSEED PLANTAIN

Plantago rugelii
Photo page #19

Also known as: Red-stemmed plantain, common plantain
Season: Summer
Habitat: Damp soils, roadsides, waste places, lawns

This species is easy to confuse with the common plantain; the leaves and basic plant structure of both plants are nearly identical. Blackseed plantain is just as edible, though, as common plantain, and may be prepared in the same ways. The leaves of the blackseed plantain may spread outward like those of the common plantain, or they may reach upwards. One outstanding difference is in the color of the petioles of the leaves: they are a purplish or reddish tone on this plantain, while they are green or whitish on the common plantain. Like the common plantain, this is believed to be a native of North America, but, unlike the common plantain, it is found mostly in the eastern half of our country.

The seeds of this plant, as the name implies, are a very dark brown or black. (Those of the common plantain tend to be a lighter brown.) This difference doesn't matter to the plant hunter as far as free vegetables for the table are concerned, but does help in telling one variety from the other. (See also the introduction preceding the land plantains.)

BURDOCK

Arctium lappa (Great Burdock)
Arctium minus (Common Burdock)
Photo page #19

Also known as: Great burdock, common burdock, cockle button, great dock, gobo, clotbur, beggar's buttons, bur weed, stick-button, hardock, bardane, hairy thistle

Season: Early through late summer

Habitat: Fields, clearings in woods, brushy areas, roadside, lawns

DO NOT CONFUSE WITH RHUBARB

This common plant, widely used as a food throughout the world, is well worth getting to know. Thanks to its prickly burs, burdock has been a world-wide traveller. It immigrated to this country with the early settlers, and was quickly adopted by the native citizens. Reportedly, it is still cultivated in Japan, where the roots and leaf stalks are eaten after their fibers have been tenderized by repeated boiling.

It is the young leaves and flowering stalks that you'll probably try first, unless you identified a group of the flowering plants late in the previous season and go to the same spot to gather some first year roots. Children and the uninitiated could easily confuse the first-year leaves of the burdock with those of the rhubarb: both are large and deep green. Since the rhubarb's leaves are poisonous, it is important to be able to distinguish them from those of the burdock. Burdock leaves have a net-like pattern that rhubarb lacks. Burdock leaves are also slightly woolly and rough, whereas those of rhubarb are very smooth and shiny. Burdock is a biennial, flowering only in its second year. During the first year, the long, deep taproots of burdock may be dug, and so it is best to learn to identify the plant by its leaves.

The plant is easy to spot flowering in its second year. It reaches three to seven feet in height, and its purple thistle-like flowers and brown burs are obvious against a background of other bushy plants. The round, fleshy stem is generally much branched, and these stalks bear large leaves, the lower ones often reaching eighteen inches in length and the upper ones usually four to eight inches.

The flowering stalks are delicious and easy to prepare. Cut some of them, and peel away the bitter green outer rind. Inside is a tasty, juicy, white pith that may be nibbled raw or sliced as a salad ingredient. The stalks are best cooked (peeled first) like asparagus. The young, tender leaves of the plant are also good to eat. Steam them for ten to twelve minutes and serve with butter and vinegar or lemon juice. (Their fuzziness disappears in cooking.) Even the leaf stems may be peeled and eaten raw with a little salt, or cooked as you would the young leaves. To store the stems or young leaves, blanch them and freeze until needed. They may also be canned. This plant is a worthy item to add to your wild grocery list.

When you go after the roots, attempting to pull them from the ground will result in little more than an aching back and a severed plant. A shovel is needed! Once you have them, scrub the roots thoroughly and boil in two changes of water. (A pinch of bicarbonate of soda added to the first boiling is reported to assist in breaking down the fibers.) Peeled and sliced, the cooked roots may be served just like carrots.

These roots were believed to have blood purifying properties, and were held as especially effective in treatment of kidney ailments. In the first half of this century, collectors dug the large, fleshy first year's roots and sold them for their alleged medicinal properties. It was *Arctium lappa*, the great burdock, that was particularly sought for medicinal purposes. (The great burdock differs from the common burdock, having larger flowers, longer stems, and lower leaves with grooves along their upper edges.) Farmers were generally happy to be rid of this plant, and gladly allowed collectors to haul baskets of it away. No more would a farmer have to put up with burs clinging to his clothing, ruining his wool, and distressing his favorite hound! No doubt, the collectors used other parts of the plant in their own kitchens. The roots, also, were long used for other than their curative powers; dried, they were often added to soups and stews. This is something we may easily do today—burdock roots are easily dried for storage, and may be used as a nourishing ingredient all winter long.

HORSERADISH

Armoracea lapathifolia
Photo page #20

Also known as: Wild horseradish, stingnose, pepper radish
Season: Early through late summer
Habitat: Around old cellar holes, fields, roadsides

Many people know the horseradish, at least in the bottle if not in the flesh. The wild horseradish makes an excellent condiment, unexcelled by the grocery store variety, and you can vary the amount of its root gratings to suit your taste.

The wild horseradish is usually a garden escapee. Likely places to investigate are vacant farms where there aren't any "no trespassing" signs, fields near farms, and any area where a house has burned or been torn down.

In a fertile location, these big plants may reach four or more feet toward the sky. The flowers are white and four-petaled, borne at the tops of flower spikes. At the base of the plant you'll find large, deep green leaves. These have stalks, are wavy-toothed, and at first they may appear to belong to a separate, adjacent plant. The upper leaves are narrower, almost like a supple, wide leaf of grass; these, also, are somewhat toothed. The seed pods are held out from the flower stalk like those of shepherd's purse or pennycress, but they are quite small and rounded, and generally less numerous. Small as they are, each of the pods holds several seeds.

Unless you have planted these in your garden, you may have difficulty being sure these plants are horseradish until the flowers and seeds appear. At this time, only the very youngest upper leaves are really usable. When you know the plant and its location, you'll be able to get the earlier, tender young leaves. These are tasty raw, added to salad, or cooked and served simply with a pat of butter. The leaves are not what it's all about, though; it is the root of the plant that is its real gift. Late in the summer or in the fall you can dig the large, fleshy roots from the ground and wash and peel them as you would potatoes. The root is thoroughly white inside. If you take a tiny taste, its immediate bite will assure you that you have a good horseradish root. The root, ground fresh, may be used to form the basis of a zesty sauce.

Don't grind too much at any one time, though; even stored in the refrigerator, the sauce will lose its flavor over a period of several weeks.

In some areas of the northeast, the horseradish is a perennial, but in the more northerly range it may act as an annual. You may want to try collecting some of the seeds to start your own plants near the time the groundhog thinks about showing his nose. Reportedly, though, the horseradish spreads more readily by means of its roots, so it is best grown from a root cutting. If the cutting is placed in poor soil, the root that eventually develops will be crooked and hard to deal with; rich organic materials will allow the root to grow large and straight. Allow the plant to grow throughout the summer, with the exception of what leaves you pop into your saucepan, and harvest the roots late in the season, saving some of the roots to plant next year. Plant them as early as possible; February or March is not too early if the ground is free of snow and you can get your spade into it. A lazier gardener might harvest only some of the root material from each plant, leaving the remainder in the soil. If you do so, be sure to mulch the roots left in the garden, especially if you live in the more northerly states. Inside, store the roots in sand or even sawdust in an area that remains cool but not freezing, and they will keep well, ready for your kitchen or garden. If they are buried beneath a foot or more of sand, they will often survive all but the coldest winters outdoors.

Besides serving as the main feature of horseradish sauce, a few gratings of the roots may be added to a salad dressing or barbecue sauce or an egg or potato salad, for pizzazz. You don't need much; in a dressing, allow it and the horseradish to keep company awhile so that the tang may spread throughout.

Horseradish root will add more than flavor to a meal: It contains such nutrients as protein, calcium, phosphorus, iron, sodium, and some vitamins, including vitamin C. (The amounts would vary according to the soil, as would the trace mineral content.) But since few people would be inclined to eat enough horseradish to take in significant amounts of these, its greatest value is probably as an appetite stimulant, adding interest to those foods vital to our good health. Prepared in our own homes, it is a condiment lacking the additives, coloring agents and preservatives of many food enhancers found on store shelves.

MUSTARDS

Brassica species:
Brassica rapa (Field Mustard)
Brassica nigra (Black Mustard)
Photo page #20

Also known as: Wild mustard, charlock, other names for various other species
Season: Early spring to early fall
Habitat: Fields, waste places, roadsides, gardens

The mustards of the genus *Brassica* are an easily recognized group, though it is not so easy to tell one from the other. All species are reportedly edible, though the degree of mustardy zip varies, so just knowing that you have a mustard is certainty enough.

When you are first hunting these plants, the thing to look for is a cluster of spaced yellow flowers atop a tall spike. The flowers, usually a half-inch or less in diameter, may be pale to bright yellow; they always have four petals. There are other plants with four-petaled yellow flowers, though, so to be on the safe side do not pick any part of the plant until some of the flowers have formed the characteristic mustard seed pods. You'll not have to wait long, for as the flowering stalk continues to stretch upwards, the lower flowers will already be producing their pods — often the half-dead petals will be found still clinging to an already enlarged seed case.

The small round seeds contained in the pods may be ground into a fine homemade mustard condiment. You may wish to add spices, white wine, whatever you see listed in your favorite store-bought mustard or country cookbook, to vary the strength and flavor to your own taste. The seeds may also be dried and ground into powder for use in sauces and seasoned dishes. Keep in mind, though, that the seeds of all mustards and their relatives contain potentially harmful materials. It is best not to over-indulge in uncooked mustard seeds, regardless of their degree of domestication.

There is much more to mustard than its nippy seeds! The young leaves may be cooked as a pot herb. The addition of salt pork or bacon to the cooking water does help to mellow the sharper varieties. Let the young leaves lend their flavor to blander cooked greens, or throw them, finely chopped, into a salad for some excitement. Another delightful use for the wild mustards is to serve as a cooked vegetable the heads of the unopened flower buds. Boiled briefly, their taste is much like that of broccoli, a close relative.

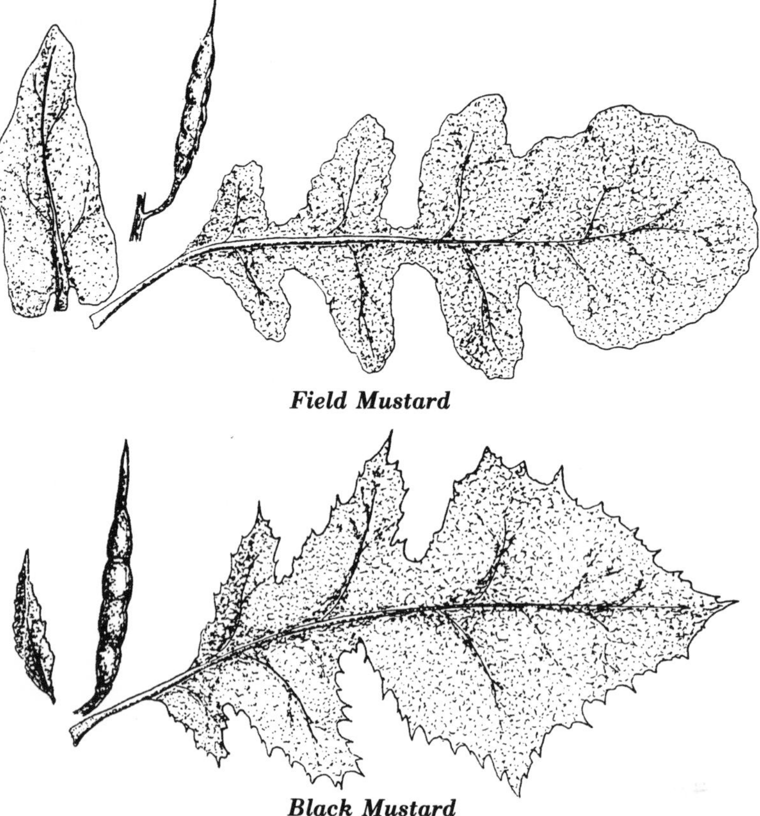

Field Mustard

Black Mustard

The upper leaves of the mustard plants are often not much at all like the lower leaves. The upper leaves of the field mustard tend to have a rounded arrowhead shape; those of the black mustard will be far narrower and smaller, tapering to a point, with irregularly toothed edges. The much larger lower leaves of the black mustard have two sets of deep indentations and are coarsely toothed; those of the field mustard are broadly lobed and more roundly toothed. Sometimes the lower leaves of the wild mustards have such extreme indentations, there seem to be smaller leaflets near the leafstalk.

On some members of the mustard family, the stems and leaves may have bristles. The lower leaves of the black mustard are bristly, while those of the field mustard are smoother and more succulent. Mustard leaves are usually deep to gray-green, and those of the field mustard even appear to be dusted with talcum powder! The leaves of the field mustard clasp the stem, whereas those of the black mustard have short petioles.

With such great variation in stems and leaves among these and other kinds of mustards, it is the flowers, petioles and seed pods that will help you to surely identify a mustard. Each flower is attached by its own petiole to the flower spike; the seed pods are held in a distinctly upright position, like candles in holders on a wall, each with a pointed "wick," the remnant style and stigma of the flower. On a closer look, though, the comparison to candles ends, for the pods, when filled out with mature seeds, will be decidedly lumpy.

Mustards vary in height, depending upon the type of soil they've chosen to grow in, the amount of rainfall and other general conditions, and their inherent traits. Some may be only about a foot tall, while others will be tall enough that you won't need to stoop to examine their flowers.

If your homesite has room for more wild young things, do not grind all the mustard seeds you collect — rather, plant some so that you may enjoy the very earliest, tenderest, and least bitter leaves the next spring.

GROUND CHERRIES

Physalis heterophylla (Clammy Ground Cherry)
Physalis pruinosa (Strawberry Tomato)
Photo page #20

Also known as: Husk tomatoes, lantern plants
Season: Mid- to late summer
Habitat: Waste areas, dry grounds, fields, open woods, gardens

CAUTION — DO NOT EAT UNRIPE FRUIT. DO NOT CONFUSE WITH THE HOUSE PLANT *SOLANUM PSEUDOCAPSICUM*, "JERUSALUM CHERRY," OR BELLADONNA OR MATRIMONY VINE, ALL POISONOUS

There are several species of *Physalis* plants, all with similar fruits. One, the Chinese lantern plant, also known as the winter cherry, is cultivated for its fruits but not for eating, and is probably the best known *Physalis*. The husks that surround the berries of this plant turn a golden orange as they dry; the "lantern"-bearing stalks are cut and allowed to dry for decorative arrangements in the home.

Many of the ground cherries or husk tomatoes are native to North America. Most have bell-like flowers, yellowish with dark centers, that arise singly from the axils of the leaves. The amount of toothing and hairiness of their leaves varies as to species.

Low, sprawling plants, they are often found in waste areas such as the rear of parking lots and junk yards, where you'd least expect them, or cultivated into rich greenery in gardens. Some are sold commercially for garden harvesting, and many of our older citizens may recall planting them years ago in their gardens. At that time they were most frequently called husk tomatoes, regardless of species.

All the ground cherries produce a cherry-like fruit enclosed in a papery husk. The husk drys and splits as the fruit matures; the husk photographed was prematurely opened to show its fruit within. This berry, when ripe, may be red or yellow, depending on variety. It is this berry that is the ground cherry's edible portion, but ***it must not be eaten until fully ripe — the berries are considered poisonous in their unripe condition. The leaves, like those of potato and garden tomato plants, are poisonous.*** Wait until the husk has split naturally and the fruit has attained its ripe color before picking. Don't be concerned if the husks and fruit have fallen to the ground before ripening; this is natural in some of the plants. You can store them in a cool, dry place until they ripen, or leave them where they are if they won't be bothered by chipmunks, squirrels, and mice.

The cooked ripe berries of the strawberry tomato are sweet, and make delicious pies and jams. Properly cooked, they may be used as tomatoes, too. They lack enough pectin to make a good jam on their own, so add pectin or a fruit high in this setting material.

The strawberry tomato has hairy, coarsely toothed leaves. The clammy ground cherry has fewer teeth, but is also hairy. The flowers resemble those shown, and may be lighter yellow or greenish. The husks and cherries look basically the same, varying only in their colors when ripe. Belladonna's flowers are normally purplish, tinged with yellow; those of the matrimony vine are typically purple to violet. Belladonna's berry becomes ***black*** at maturity. ***Belladonna is very poisonous!***

Most varieties of these plants bloom around mid-summer and produce their fruit late in the summer. The fruits may not fully ripen until very late summer or on into the fall. If you cannot find wild ones around you, look into your plant and seed catalogs, obtain some plants suitable to your climate and let them go wild! They're tasty, and well worth the expense for years of enjoyment.

CARRION FLOWER 

Smilax herbacea
Photo page #24

Also known as: Carrion brier, naked brier
Season: Shoots and leaves, early spring
Habitat: Meadows, moist roadsides, ditches, low woods, river banks

DO NOT CONFUSE WITH DEADLY NIGHTSHADE, POISON IVY, OR BANEBERRY

What an unattractive name! Still, it warns you not to pick these flowers for table posies; to attract certain insects needed for pollination, they happen to smell like decaying flesh. Hold your nose, though, for the shoots and young leaves are a good addition to your grocery list of wild collectables.

This plant belongs to the same genus as does the prickly greenbrier (see Greenbrier); their leaves are very similar. This plant's leaves vary from one to four inches long. They are grassy green, paler underneath, and generally have five to seven nearly parallel veins. Their bases are rounded or heart-shaped, and the side edges often curl inward, making the leaf look a little like a wide hourglass. The leaves may be coated with a grayish waxy substance that rubs off.

In late spring and early summer, flower clusters resembling those of the wild sarsaparilla will spring from long stalks that arise from the leaf axils. There are generally anywhere from eight to twenty-five yellowish-green, six-petaled flowers in each ball of flowers. Male flowers will appear on one plant, females on another. Late in the summer and on into early fall, the female flowers will produce red berries. (They later turn a deep blue-black. These are inedible.)

The stems of the plant, round and green in color, are neither hairy nor woody. This climbing vine-like plant branches and puts forth curling tendrils; the first time we spied these plants, my husband called them "tentacle plants," for they looked like some otherworldly creatures springing upward, reaching four to six feet, with clinging tendrils seemingly everywhere. If, however, the tendrils have found nothing to twine around for support as the leaves and flowers develop, the stems may sprawl along the ground.

Once you know what you're looking for, it's easy to spot the tender young plants early in the spring. When hunting this plant, look for the young tendrils on the shoots. The best use for this plant is to cook the young shoots and little leaves as a pot herb. They require only fifteen to twenty minutes' boiling; your fork will tell you when the stems are tender. If you haven't enough for a bowlful, snip them into a stew or soup.

JAPANESE KNOTWEED

Polygonum cuspidatum
Photo page #26

Also known as: Japanese bamboo, American Bamboo, wild bamboo, giant knotweed, wild rhubarb

Season: Young shoots in spring

Habitat: Waste areas, gardens, fields, roadsides, thickets; nearly anywhere it can find room, though it prefers a moderate supply of water

DO NOT CONFUSE WITH DOGBANE

If you're tempted to transplant a wild edible to your own patch of land and are looking for a variety that will beautify your property, grow quickly, provide shade, and produce copious food, this is it! Japanese knotweed spreads and grows quickly; it is this spreading nature, though, that some people consider its greatest drawback.

This plant was originally imported from Japan as an ornamental. As summer climaxes in the heat of the dog days, this tall individual will be seen growing in shady thickets, adorned by vast numbers of tiny greenish-white flowers borne on fragile fingers. The stems of this plant are gaudy: the thin, uppermost leaf and flower-bearing stalks are red, and the bamboo-like main stems below are greenish, mottled with red and purple, and dusted with a powdery bloom. Though this plant has an alien look about it, it has made itself quite at home throughout the North American continent. Japanese knotweed is an aggressive plant, growing up to eight or ten feet each year, and thrives as well in your garden as it will along a railroad track or competing with willows along a brook. They spread not only by seed, but by their underground rhizomes.

Their young shoots are edible, and the plants will rebound after each harvest with new growth. The delicious baby shoots are most easily identified by the presence nearby of the old gray hollow, bamboo-like stalks that remain from the previous season. Until the first leaves unfurl these might be mistaken for milkweed or poke shoots, though the knotweed shoots are generally the heaviest of the three. ***Since exceptionally strong dogbane growth might be confused with these by a novice hunter—with dire results—it is wisest to wait until a few leaves unfurl when you're picking for the first time.*** Knotweed leaves look triangular, not at all like the paddle-shaped leaves of the other plants, and they are a bright, shiny green. The young shoots may be cut up to about a foot in height, and, with their leaves removed, cooked briefly like asparagus. They will not, however, taste anything like this look-alike; related to the docks, sorrels, and smartweeds, they have the lemony-acid tang that allows them to be used like rhubarb. If they're too tart a vegetable for your taste, a touch of sugar or honey will improve the flavor. These young stems are generally fork-tender in about four or five minutes' boiling time, and need only a crown of butter in the serving dish.

The shoots you've missed or allowed to continue growing will form hollow, curving branches that bear pointed leaves three to six inches long, with square or heart-shaped bases. The bamboo-like stalks have knobby joints every six to eight inches, and are sheathed in a papery material. The mature plant is easily recognized by its many sprigs of flowers, its large, triangular leaves, and the dusty green, purple-mottled rind of the stalks. During warm weather or periods of dryness, the leaves will often develop red edges.

The older stalks may still be salvaged for food. Both young and old tissue will freeze well after cooking or simply blanching, so don't be afraid to harvest more than you'll need for a single meal. Cut the older stalk into sections, eliminating the joints, then carefully peel or strip off the outermost spotted rind. The rind is bitter. The skinned stalks will be green and hollow, and may be sliced into thin rings to be served cooked as a vegetable. The young shoots, too, could be cut into rings and added raw to a salad, for zip. The older stalks, however, are better cooked. You could chill these and use them in a gelatin salad or aspic. We like these green rings best in a cream of onion and sorrel soup, though they'll go along with nearly any kind of soup or stew. With the addition of sugar, this versatile vegetable will also make a flavorful jam or "rhubarb" pie!

No nutritional information seems to be available on this plant, but since it is related to the power-packed dock and domestic buckwheat, there is every reason to assume it is full of nutrients.

If you have invited uninitiated guests to your home for dinner or a cookout, there's nothing quite like the look on their faces when they see you calmly stride to what appears to be a thicket of weeds, cut an armload, and return to your kitchen to prepare a delightful dish. Many people who favor garden shrubbery that is more delicate (and less useful) and have cursed the Japanese knotweed for its stealthy, relentless incursions would be amazed to learn that they could keep this invader in check by eating it!

POKEWEED

Phytolacca americana
Photo page #26

Also known as: Pokeberry, poke, inkberry, pigeonberry, garget, poke salad

Season: Shoots and young leaves, spring through summer

Habitat: Wood edges, fields, waste places, around buildings and parking lots

SOME PARTS OF THIS PLANT ARE POISONOUS

This is one of those plants that inspires wonder as to how its edibility was determined. Pokeweed reportedly contains not only a saponin-like material but an alkaloid known as **phytolaccine.** ***These poisonous materials are present in the roots, mature leaves and stems, and very likely in the fruits and seeds; cases of poisoning have been recorded, and it would be advisable to avoid these portions of the pokeweed.*** Yet, these plants have been cultivated in areas of the world for centuries for their delectable young shoots. Canneries in the southern United States offer these shoots for grocery store sale, and some people make an excellent part-time income collecting these each spring from their area's weed patches.

If you are stalking the wild places in the spring, pokeweed shoots are definitely a vegetable you should consider. If you are a beginner at identifying plants, though, first observe the plant through a full growth cycle, and then harvest some of the succulent greens the following spring. Many authorities advise gathering them when they are up to six inches in height, but the commercial product is apparently prepared from shoots up to a foot tall, so the picking time for these shoots is somewhat generous. A mature plant in its second or third year of growth can withstand two or three cuttings, so don't give up when you've harvested your first crop of the terrific greens: this is a vegetable you can gather throughout the spring and on into the early summer.

This branching, weedy plant, when mature, looks like a bush. In a sheltered area it may reach six to eight or more feet in height, and, an attractive plant, it would make a good privacy blind or short wind screen around a lawn. The broadly lance-shaped, wavy-edged leaves are colorful against the reddish stems. White flowers are produced on sturdy, fleshy-looking stalks, and blue-black berries are soon to follow. During lean times, the juice of these berries was used as an ink, thus earning this plant one of its common names, "inkberry." Children who discover this wild ink often present their mothers with blueberry-red stains that are difficult to remove. Be sure to tell your young ones ***not to eat these berries, though—they are harmful.***

Once the stalks of this plant take on their purplish-red hues, leave them alone, regardless of size. The berries, unless you want to use some of them to plant a poke patch close to home, should be left on the stems; while they are not suitable as human food, they are important in the diets of many little animals and birds.

Pick nothing but the tender young shoots and leaves. The baby leaves make an outstanding vegetable, served like spinach, by themselves or mixed with dock, sorrel, or mustard leaves. For variety, cook a little bacon or salt pork with them, or add them chopped to a soufflé. The young leafy tips are very good. The stalks may be lightly skinned and cooked as asparagus. The young shoots are good with butter, salt, and pepper, and excellent with a cream or cheese sauce. These greens will need at least a half hour's cooking, especially if the stems are not first peeled.

If you've the room, and turn into a real poke lover, bring some of the roots, in flats, inside to winter in your cellar or spare room. Kept moist, they will root into their fresh bed of soil and supply you with springtime greens when all the world's winter gray outside. ***Just be sure never to include any portion of the roots in with your picking!***

If you don't have room for a winter crop, you can still enjoy poke shoots all winter long. The abundant stems and young leaves you gather in the spring may be parboiled for ten to fifteen minutes and then frozen like any other vegetable. Can them if you prefer, first cooking them for a full half hour. You'll be glad to have this nutritious wild vegetable to remind you of summer!

VIII

Trees, Shrubs and Woody Plants

MOUNTAIN ASH 

Pyrus (Sorbus) americana
Pyrus (Sorbus) decora
Photo page #21

Also known as: Rowantree, mountain sumac, winetree, missy-moosey, Indian mozemize, peruve
Season: Berries ripe in early to mid-fall
Habitat: Open woods, along wet areas, parks, lawns, around homes and public buildings where planted for their decorative values

Though the orange-red berries of this graceful little tree will never be number one on anyone's jelly or wine-making list, they are found so often today, and are so totally ignored, it seems worthwhile to include them here. Mountain ash will produce attractive, flat clusters of white flowers in the spring, and lush bunches of fruit during the summer. While found scattered in the wild, they have been rather extensively used as plantings in parks, around homes and public buildings, so you usually needn't safari far to find them? Be cautious of sprays when picking in civilized areas, though, and always wash the berries well.

The underripe fruits are very bitter. Waiting is the name of the game! Autumn is the time of harvest, when summer's berries and most fruit you'd use for desserts and jellies are but a warm memory. After a few good frosts, these fruits will fully ripen and lose their unpleasant taste. The cherry-like fruits never really become sweet; they have a somewhat sour flavor that demands the addition of honey or sugar. Their flavor blends well with that of wild cherries, and neither will suffer from the necessary cooking and sweetening. Use them in jellies, fruit sauces, pies, breads, and desserts. They'll also make a zippy wine!

There are two species of mountain ash: *Pyrus americana*, the American mountain ash, and *Pyrus decora*, the northern mountain ash. They differ little, the main variation being in the shape of their leaflets. Both have pinnately compound leaves, like those of a sumac or ashes, with usually nine to seventeen leaflets. On the American mountain ash the leaflets are narrower and more pointed than those of the northern mountain ash (shown in the photograph).

The fruits of the American mountain ash are about a quarter-inch in diameter, while those of its northern cousin tend to be a bit larger. Their leaves turn a bright gold in the fall, contrasting with the reddish berries and outdoing their earlier holiday colors of red and green.

THE OAKS

Quercus species
Photo page #21

Also known as: (various names)
Season: Nuts ripe in autumn (some take two years to mature)
Habitat: Most prefer somewhat dry, rich soil, but some will live in moister zones

There are many different oaks, and the beginner may have difficulty in telling some of them apart. Several species are pictured here, but this does not nearly begin to clarify the problem! Fortunately, the most usable oak, the white oak, is one of the easiest to identify.

Oaks are divided into two groups: the red oaks and the white oaks. The red oaks have leaves with sharp-pointed lobes, while those of the white oak group have rounded lobes. The acorns of *Quercus alba,* the white oak, are smaller than those of some of the other oaks, but they are the ones we may most easily use.

The acorns of the red oaks have very high levels of tannic acid, a material that can harm the digestive system by acting as a strong binding agent. The American Indians early discovered the nutritive value of acorns, and they found several methods to leach out the tannin so as to use the nutmeats for food or flour; the black bread made of acorn flour was a real staff of life for many tribes, and the work involved in gathering and storing the nuts and preparing them as foodstuffs was a focus of much community activity.

To render high-tannin acorns edible, the Indians would bury them in the ground or suspend them in streams for months, allowing the rain or stream water to leach the tannic acid from the soft, swollen nuts. They would look, too, for collections of acorns buried and forgotten by animals. After they have been leached in the ground or in running water, the hulls look black and very unattractive, but the nutmeats inside are more appetizing. If you're ever lost in the woods, remember that black acorns, leached over a long period of time, are ready to eat; they might even be a lifesaver!

The leached nuts were sun-dried for storage. Once the nuts were shucked and pounded into meal, the flour thus produced was rinsed with warm water to remove any remaining bitterness and then dried for use. This process would seem a real undertaking to we who have other flours that are far easier to prepare. Still, acorn flour might serve well in times of food scarcity or emergency, and has done so in Europe.

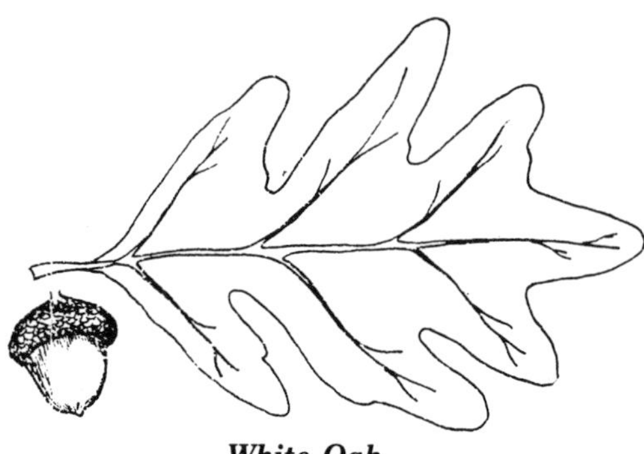

White Oak

The acorns of the white oaks need less elaborate preparation than those of the red oak species. Indeed, some white oak trees will produce sweet acorns with very little tannic acid. A small taste will tell you whether you've been fortunate enough to find one of these, for any bitterness indicates the presence of tannic acid. Since the white oaks are lower in tannic acid content, boiling their acorns in several changes of water until the water is no longer discolored is usually all that is needed to render them sweet and palatable. They may then be roasted or used as any other nut. Roasted and ground, they may even be used to stretch and mellow coffee.

The white oak is widespread throughout the northeast, and its acorns are easily collected on a fall foliage hike. The nuts are tasty, nourishing, and well worth trying. If you've a white oak tree on your property that seems tardy in producing its acorns, just wait until the next season: the acorns of the white oak take two years, generally, to mature.

The Hickories

You should get to know the hickories: most species can provide you with delicious, sweet nuts to use in baked goods, candies, or snacks. Hickory nuts are excellent raw, containing quality food energy (plus phosphorus and iron) within their golden hides, and they are a fine survival food or trail snack. The U.S.D.A. Handbook No. 8 tells us that a 100-gram edible portion of hickory nuts will yield 673 calories, 13.2 g protein, 68.7 g fat, 12.8 g carbohydrate (including 1.9 g fiber), 360 mg phosphorus, and 2.4 mg iron.

These nutritious nuts, packed with the best the deep-rooted hickory has to offer, are easily collected and stored. Gather them when fall winds shake them loose along with their dull golden leaves. Be careful, though — ***not all hickory nuts are good to eat.*** (See the individual species for their distinctive characteristics.)

These trees have long been held in high esteem for the quality of their wood. When General Andrew Jackson refused orders to disband his troops far from their homes and marched back with them through thick and thin, he was given the name "Old Hickory" to commemorate his toughness and steadfastness; his grave is sheltered by six massive shagbark hickories. Hickory wood is heavy, hard, strong, and tough, and is said to be weight for weight stronger than steel. As firewood, hickory yields more heat than most other woods; a cord of hickory is considered almost equal in heating ability to a ton of anthracite coal! Hickory, though, is perhaps best known not as a fuel, but as a strong, resilient hardwood. Once used for wagon parts, hickory was — and still is — a prime wood for tool handles, archery bows, racing sulkies, and skis.

Though industry has primarily chosen other materials to serve us, the usefulness of hickory is something we can rediscover, both in the workshop and in the kitchen. Hams smoked over green hickory wood are well-known flavor gems; try smoking fish over some pruned hickory boughs! These trees, tapped, will even yield sugar and syrup. Best of all, gather the ripe nuts and bring them out to brighten winter evenings: enlist folks to shell them for your holiday kitchen (hammers will be helpful), and pay them with some of the golden hickory nuggets!

SHAGBARK HICKORY

Carya ovata
Photo page #21

Also known as: Shellbark hickory, scaly-barked hickory, upland hickory
Season: Nuts ripe by fall
Habitat: Prefers rich well-drained loamy soil; often found on rocky hillsides as well as in city parks

This tree is often confused with the true shellbark, but this presents no problem: the nuts of both varieties are equally good to eat.

The shagbark hickory received its name from its bark, which will often have shaggy patches. Wide strips of the smoky gray bark loosen in vertical patches, their ends curving away from the trunk. While they look fragile, these shreds are difficult to pull away. They fall away, though, as the tree grows in diameter, and these shards of bark may pile up at the foot of each strong trunk. These trees are tall, often growing to one hundred or more feet.

The young twigs are usually reddish brown, becoming darker and darker gray as they develop. From these stout twigs grow alternately-placed compound leaves. The entire leaf, usually from eight to fourteen inches in length, is comprised of five to seven leaflets, five most frequently. The three largest leaflets are usually about five inches long. Two pairs of leaflets will lie parallel to each other, while the odd man forms the tip. Each leaflet is oval and lance-shaped, with a sharp ending point. The edges are finely and sharply toothed. The leaves are dark grass green in color, and are paler and sometimes downy on their undersurfaces. The leafstalks may or may not have a coating of velvet, and are often subject to insect invasion (evidenced by lumps on the surface).

Toward the end of summer, the large, greenish nuts of the shagbark will be seen hanging in pairs or singly from the branches. As the nuts mature, their husks will turn a rich brown and then nearly black. When the leaves become golden and are whisked from their branches by fall winds, the nuts too will fall. Whether these fruits dry outdoors, on the ground, or in your home, the husks will split along four seams and will reveal a nearly white nut covered by a thin shell. You'll need to pry or smash the husk open to get at this delicious, sweet nut. The shagbark hickory is of the same genus as the pecan, and you'll taste the family resemblance. (See the introduction to the hickories for suggestions for use.)

Occasionally shagbark hickories are found that are identical to the regular shagbark in all but one feature: their bark is not shaggy. Though lumbermen term these "bastard hickories," their nuts and wood are identical with those of the more easily identified shagbarks.

SHELLBARK HICKORY

Carya laciniosa

Also known as: True shellbark hickory, hickory, bigleaf hickory, big shellbark, bottom hickory, kingnut hickory
Season: Nuts in autumn
Habitat: Prefers wetter areas and bottomlands, though it may grow on

slopes; its range is more southern than shagbark's, and is the most limited in range of all the hickories of the northeast

This tree seldom reaches the height of the shagbark hickory. Still, it is similar enough to the shagbark that the two might be confused. Close attention to differences in color and size will help in telling the two apart. Both are known for their fine nuts and hardwood.

The true shellbark has leaves much like those of the shagbark, though they are larger, often reaching two feet in length. They are usually comprised of seven leaflets, though there may be from five to nine in number. Like the leaflets of the shagbark, these do not have petioles. The leaves and nuts of this tree are the largest of the hickory group. On top, the leaves are dark green and shiny, while underneath they are a yellowish green and often densely velvety. The velvet may extend onto the leafstalk.

The gray bark divides to form long, thin, curved plates, and these give the tree trunk the shaggy appearance that most leads to the confusion between this and the true shagbark. This tree, though, has very dark brown twigs, and the nuts are large (one to two inches long), with chestnut-colored or orange-brown husks. Inside each is a nutlet covered by a thick shell. These sweet kernels are excellent, and the wood of the tree is interchangeable with that of the shagbark. (See the introductory information about the hickories, their common traits and uses, and study the illustration on page 166.)

MOCKERNUT HICKORY 

Carya tomentosa

Also known as: Mockernut, whiteheart hickory, bullnut, hognut, white hickory, bugbud hickory

Season: Nuts in autumn

Habitat: Grows nearly anywhere except the very northernmost portions of New England

This sturdy hickory may grow a hundred or more feet tall, with a trunk diameter of up to three feet. Its gray bark is not shaggy, but is furrowed into shallow, flat ridges; the twigs may be woolly. The shiny, dark grass-green leaves are quite large; made up of five to seven stalkless leaflets, they may reach fifteen inches in length. Each lance-shaped leaflet has a broad mid-section, and the outermost leaflets will be broader towards their tips. The leaflets are finely toothed, pale, and densely hairy underneath. The foliage, like that of many of the hickories, is pleasantly fragrant.

In the fall, the nearly spherical nuts, measuring up to two inches, will turn a dark red-brown just before they fall. Each hard-shelled nut contains a reddish-brown, tough-skinned sweet kernel. These nuts are a tasty treat once you've shelled them! Their hard shells are such a job to remove, most people ignore them, but if you have a strong hammer and lots of patience, they'll provide a tasty diversion on a cold winter's night.

The wood of this tree is very strong, and this is considered one of the best of the hickory trees for hardwood. (See the introduction that precedes this group of trees, and look at the illustration on page 166.)

RED HICKORY

Carya ovalis

Also known as: Hickory, oval pignut hickory, pignut hickory, pignut

Season: Nuts in autumn

Habitat: Grows nearly anywhere except along the coast and in the northernmost portions of New England

This variety is a fine stand-in for the shagbark hickory: its wood and fruits are quite good. The small plate-like scales of its pale gray, furrowed bark as well as the appearance of its leaf will tell you of its kinship with the rest of the hickories. The leaves usually have seven leaflets, though there may be only five. One distinctive feature of the red hickory is the stalk on its end leaflet; all hickory leaflets, as a rule, have no petioles. The entire leaf usually ranges from one half to one full foot in length. The finely toothed, lance-shaped leaflets are hairy when young, but become smooth as they mature. The sweet, inch to inch-and-a-half nuts are edible and delicious. (See the introduction to the hickories for suggestions for use.)

PIGNUT HICKORY

Carya glabra

Also known as: Sweet hickory, pignut, hickory, black hickory, bitter nut hickory, broom hickory

Season: Nuts in autumn

Habitat: Found in southern and western areas of New England

BITTER — NOT EDIBLE

This is the tree whose wood our early settlers shaved into shape for broom and brush handles. Equal in ruggedness to that of the shagbark, the wood of this large tree was also used for plow handles, wagons, and other working implements. It also fueled the pioneer's woodstove and kept his cabin warm. Probably it was chosen to serve these purposes because, while it supplied the typically good wood of the hickories, it could not supply a good food: the nut is usually too bitter to eat.

The bark of this tree, gray in color, is marked with low grooves and branching ridges. Never truly shaggy, it sometimes bears platelike scales. The light green twigs bear compound leaves that may reach a foot in length. The stalkless leaflets may vary from three to seven in number; there are usually five. The leaflets may be long and oval or lance-shaped. They have finely toothed edges with in-curving teeth and lack hair, except in the axils of the veins on the undersurfaces.

The bitter nuts are easily spotted. They are shaped like upside-down pears, with the broadest area nearest the twig. Their bitterness, probably due to tannin, renders them inedible for all practical purposes. (See illustration, page 22.)

BITTERNUT HICKORY

Carya cordiformis

Also known as: Swamp hickory, pig hickory, pig walnut, bitter walnut, bitter pecan tree

Season: Nuts in autumn
Habitat: Prefers bottomlands, wet areas, rich or sandy soils

THESE NUTS ARE NOT EDIBLE

It's just as well that this tree is not immediately recognizable as a hickory, for the nuts are so very bitter that even animals usually leave them alone. The tree is not shaggy at all. The bark is light green with reddish or brownish overtones, cut by shallow furrows. The twigs at first are a bright green, but they later turn gray and may appear to be rough, with corky growths and many leaf scars marring their surfaces when mature. The leaflets of the long, compound leaves are narrower than those of most hickories, and greater in number: usually each six to ten inch leaf bears from seven to eleven leaflets. The dark grass-green upper surfaces of the leaflets flip up to reveal paler, hairy undersides.

Like the pignut, the bitternut hickory bears easily recognizable nuts. These are shaped rather like flat-bellied cones: though nearly round at one end, each has a pointed tip. The thin husk splits along four seams to reveal a nutlet that may be warm brown to gray. The wood of the tree is good, and the bitternut, as an asset to your property, is perhaps the most attractive of the hickories in general outline.

Short-lived among the hickories, these large trees may reach the two century mark. The wood provides excellent heat with little residue, and the early settlers obtained medicinal and burnable oil from this tree. As hardwood for tools and equipment, this hickory is a little inferior to the others. (See the general introduction to the hickories, and study the illustration on page 166.)

BLACK WALNUT

Juglans nigra
Photo page #21

Also known as: Eastern black walnut, American walnut
Season: Nuts in mid-autumn
Habitat: Rich bottomlands, gentle hills, but not swampy or excessively cold areas; seldom north of Massachusetts or Connecticut
SEE ALSO BUTTERNUT

As the days grow nippy and golden with the glow of autumn leaves, this beautiful native tree yields its bounty of sweet, edible nuts. The black walnut usually lives upwards of seventy-five years, and may reach a height of sixty to seventy or more feet. While not a giant among trees, it will grow straight and tall in cool, moist, forested areas, but spreads to provide inviting shade when it is given plenty of room on lawns. You'll seldom find the black walnut planted near walkways, though. Like the butternut, its fruit, leaves and inner bark contain enough tannic acid to stain hands and clothing.

The virgin forests of this country once produced walnut trees up to six feet in diameter. This wood was close-grained and dark as the corridors of the forest. The fine wood that left the sawmill was used for cabinetry, furniture, gunstocks and cradles, for its satiny finish would irritate neither a baby's skin nor a hunter's hand. Yet this lovely tree was once so commonplace that it was even used for such lowly purposes as railroad ties and fences!

Today, the large trunk sizes are the exception, and these trees are nearly worth their weight in gold. Black walnut has a reputation for being exceptionally light and resilient in proportion to its strength and for never warping or shrinking or splintering. Black walnut is still used for gunstocks, for it is said to be elastic to the recoil of a weapon. The wood is used primarily for fine, expensive veneers. With sharp blades peeling very thin, continuous sheets of the lighter-fleshed modern tree's wood, one tree may be worth many thousands of dollars!

Black walnuts grow slowly. If we are to have any left for future generations, they need to be replanted and cherished for their beauty and nuts instead of their flesh. If you wish to help, collect some of the nuts, hull and all, when they have fallen during mid-autumn. Find a suitable spot for the growth of your tree-to-be, for the black walnut puts down a strong taproot and does not transplant easily. Blanket the nuts with about four inches of soil.

You'll have to wait awhile for the harvest, but you'll see the promise when a young, sumac-leaved shoot appears the following spring. Gradually, as the young tree grows, its bark will become deeply lacerated and dark brown to blackish in color. Narrow, forking, dark or reddish ridges will develop, and by adolescence the bark will probably begin to show some thick scales. It will never become shaggy, though. The limbs and twigs will be stout and strong. At first the twigs will be covered with pale and light rust-colored hairs; these will deepen to rusty-brown with age, and are spotted with orange lenticels (pores that look like specks against the darker skin of the twig). As on the butternut, the twigs are scarred with large brands left when the leaves depart each fall; these brands give the older twigs a rough appearance.

In the fall, graceful leaves up to two feet long will cascade from the crown. Each bears fifteen to twenty-three stalkless, long oval leaflets that are finely toothed and sharply tipped. They resemble those of the butternut in coloration, but lack, for the most part, any hairy stickiness. The lower, pale surface may be velvety near the veins. Look at the ends of these long compound leaves to quickly determine whether you've spotted a walnut or a butternut: The walnut often lacks the odd-numbered terminal leaflet.

The nuts of the black walnut and its cousin the butternut ripen at the same time, during October. Greenish-brown balls, two to three inches in diameter, they hang singly or in pairs among the fall colored leaves. Wait until they fall to the ground to collect them, and wear gloves — the husks are covered with sticky, staining hairs. Spreading your collection to dry for awhile in a cool, dry area will hasten their coming to full maturity, as well as make husking them a bit easier; just be sure the nuts are resting on something you don't mind having covered with brown stains. Keep your gloves on as you remove the husks from the good-sized nuts with their typical walnut shells; the husks are fleshy but resistant.

The U.S.D.A. Handbook No. 8 tells us that the nutmeats are good food, high in food energy as well as phosphorus, iron, sodium, potassium, and vitamin A. They are also equal to or higher than many of the green vegetables in thiamine, riboflavin and niacin (key B vitamins).

While black walnuts are fine as they are for snacking or including in cakes, muffins and candies, you might try making a nut butter from them if you have a plentiful harvest and a food mill or blender. Black walnut butter is a flavorful change of pace from peanut butter! Refrigerate this taste treat to keep the sweet oils from going rancid.

BUTTERNUT 

Juglans cinerea
Photo page #22

Also known as: White walnut, oilnut
Season: Nuts in mid-autumn
Habitat: Prefers moist, rich soils

The branches of the butternut tree are no cloud sweepers. They seldom reach beyond fifty feet into the air. The butternut's a graceful tree, though. It has at maturity a trunk that may reach up to three feet in diameter, and is a nice tree to have around for its tasty nuts as well as its beauty and shade.

The bark of this tree varies from light brown to gray. It is usually quite smooth on the young tree; as the tree passes into middle age, the bark gradually darkens and becomes rougher with valleys and entwined, flat, light gray ridges. Beneath their fuzzy mantle of orange-brown sticky velvet, the young twigs are bright green. With age, they too gray and roughen. When the leaves depart in the fall, they leave U-shaped scars edged with velvet. Both the butternut and the walnut trees, close relatives that they are, have brown pith at the center of the twigs. This pith is divided into chambers in both trees; in the butternut the pith is dark brown, while in the walnut it is a lighter shade.

Since both the butternut and the walnut bear edible fruits, it doesn't matter which nuts you have picked for eating purposes. However, there are several distinguishing characteristics which help to set the butternut apart. Its leaves may be twenty-five or more inches long, and are comprised of eleven to nineteen finely toothed, lance-shaped leaflets. These leaflets, yellowish-green with paler undersides, are three to four inches in length and hairy and sticky to the touch. The central leafstalk, too, is covered with this tacky fuzz. The butternut's compound leaf nearly always has a final, odd leaflet at its tip, whereas the black walnut usually lacks this leaflet.

While you're busy relaxing at the beach, the butternut tree will be ripening its nuts. They are enclosed in a thin, hard, sticky-hairy outer husk. Beneath the rind of this husk is the thick-walled nut that resembles a walnut. You'll know you have gathered butternuts or walnuts when you look at your fingers: either will leave you with stubborn brown stains. The butternut bears its fruits in clusters of two to five, each nut being around two inches in diameter and roughly egg-shaped. They usually have ripened by the time these hardwood trees have reached their full autumn glory, and will fall soon after with the leaves. If you would like to try a popular old pickle recipe, and have found some immature nuts, simmer the shelled nuts that have been pared until the white center appears. Then pickle the drained nuts in spices and hot vinegar.

You'll have to work to get the husks off, but the sweet, oily kernels are a real treat! If you can get your husk crackers to stop nibbling long enough, chop some of the nuts to use in cooking. They may be included in any muffin, granola or cookie recipe calling for walnuts, filberts or pecans. Refrigeration will help to prevent rancidity in warm weather, but you cannot wait too long. Just like butter, the fresher they are, the better.

Butternuts are not only good, they're good for you. The U.S.D.A. (Handbook

No. 8) has determined that a one-hundred-gram edible portion will yield 629 calories of food energy, 23.7 g protein, 61.2 g fat, 8.4 g carbohydrate, and 6.8 mg iron.

CHESTNUT

Castanea dentata
Photo page #22

Also known as: American chestnut, edible chestnut
Season: Nuts in autumn
Habitat: Woodlands with good drainage, parks, lawns

DO NOT CONFUSE THIS WITH THE HORSE CHESTNUT

In the early 1900's a blight attacked many of our chestnut trees. Though in many cases the stumps continue to try to grow, these shoots do not usually reach full size. Occasionally you will find trees that escaped the damage, either through luck or resistance. The lovely nuts are still on our list of wild edibles, though they are not available in the numbers of long ago. The sprouting stumps may live long enough to bear nuts, but they seldom fully mature before they are attacked by fungus.

Do not confuse this tree with the horse chestnut, whose fruit is poisonous. (See Horse Chestnut, which follows.) There is also a "chestnut oak" that bears leaves shaped like those of the chestnut, but, true to its genus, it produces acorns.

The leaves of the American chestnut are long and coarsely toothed, the sharp teeth tending to curve toward the leaf. Each has a central mid-vein and secondary veins branching from this; these smaller veins are nearly parallel to each other. The leaves are borne alternately on the twigs, unlike those of the horse chestnut whose leaflets are palmately arranged. The leaves are quite large and hairless; the twigs are brown and also hairless. Cut through a twig to view the central pith: this will be not round, but five-sided. The bark of the tree is dark brown with wide, flat plateaus between the shallow valleys.

The husk that holds the nuts is easily detected by eyes or bare feet! It's a spiny, round husk, dark brown when mature, usually about two inches in diameter, and its extreme spininess will distinguish its fruit from that of the horse chestnut. (The single large brown nut of the horse chestnut is within a large, fleshy greenish spherical husk that is heavily thorny.) Inside each husk you'll find two or three edible nuts encased against a pale, silken inner lining. The nuts are a shining brown, stoutly heart-shaped, somewhat flattened on one side, and usually have a bit of fuzz near their tops. Each will have a definite point at the end.

If you can find enough American chestnut husks to gather, let them ripen on the ground until frost splits the husks open, or carry them home and store them in your garage where cold can reach them, and remove the husks when they become loose. Occasionally you will find a nut that is wormy or moldy; chuck those with obvious flaws, and avoid eating any discolored portion of the nut once roasted—it will be foul-tasting.

Chestnuts may be used in a variety of ways (even as an elegant pudding!), and you'll find many old recipes for them, especially in English and European cookbooks. These are the nuts of which bards sang! They are terrific simply "roasted on an open fire"; just cut an X in the shiny brown shell on the upper (round) side so that they won't explode, and keep them away from too hot flames or coals, or they will scorch. Chestnuts may also be roasted in the oven for 15-20 minutes at 400° F. Once roasted, the outer shell and bitter inner husk become brittle and are easily peeled off with the fingers. The nutmeats, sweet and mealy, are delicious and filling. Add them to a vegetable dish, pilaf, or casserole. Perhaps the nicest way to enjoy sweet chestnuts, though, is just as they are, straight from the fireplace, with family and friends.

HORSE CHESTNUT

Aesculus hippocastanum

Also known as: Common horse chestnut, buckeye
Season: Nuts in autumn
Habitat: Mainly around habitation, but may escape into woodlands

THIS IS A POISONOUS PLANT

This alien, lovely in its own right as a stalwart, decorative tree, produces large, inedible nuts. The shiny brown chestnut color of the nuts is really the only way in which the horse chestnut resembles the American chestnut. The leaves are not individual as on the chestnut; they are arranged like fingers on your hand (palmately) in groups of five to seven leaflets. In the spring, this large tree bears cone-shaped groups of lovely pink and white flowers. These flowers give rise to the fleshy, globular fruits, each husk containing one nut. The husks are thorny, not covered with spines as are the husks of the chestnut. Those of the horse chestnut split into three parts to reveal the large, round, warm-brown shiny nut that children love to gather. At one time these were worn around the neck or carried in the pocket to ward off arthritis, but that is about all they are good for; they contain a poisonous resin which cannot be removed by boiling, though it is reported that some tribes of Indians leached the harmful material from the starchy nutmeats by certain methods, some similar to those used to leach tannin from acorns.

For all practical purposes, this is a tree which we may enjoy with our eyes, but not as food. The wood, however, is good for carving, and the tree is lovely in a landscaped yard, though the nuts must first be removed before you mow your lawn late in the season. (NOTE: See the illustration on page 166.)

The Birches

There are six species of birch trees, not including three shrub-like *Betula* species, native to the eastern United States. Beautiful and graceful, they contain large amounts of sap, and this makes them vulnerable to snapping and splitting under prolonged, deep cold. It is for their fine hardwood that some varieties have been heavily cut. But the birches are useful to us, too, for their sap and fragrant leaves as well as their wood. The extract of the leaves of certain species is used in shampoo and scented body oil, even tea, and the sap may be drunk as a beverage, boiled down for syrup or sugar, or used to make a refreshing beer. (See individual species.)

The bark of the birch is thin, compared to that of most trees, and ranges in color from rich mahogany brown to purest white. Birches typically have alternate, simple, double-toothed leaves which spring from slender twigs. Often these leaves are found in pairs on short spur branches. The openings in the bark of the stems and trunks of trees, **lenticels**, are very noticeable on birches; those on the trunks are generally horizontal, dark, and quite large.

The flowers of the birches proclaim the advent of spring before the leaves unfurl. The male flowers are inconspicuous fuzzy catkins which look rather like oversized pussy willow flowers. The female flowers are smaller, but will later develop into little cone-like structures called **strobiles**. Birches are very successful in distributing their winged seeds, and some species, especially the yellow birch, are often the first of the deciduous trees to develop in an idle meadow or burned-over area. If you are pollen sensitive, you may first realize the birches have blossomed when you experience the sniffles of early season hay fever, for the birches produce copious amounts of pollen. (This, along with the pollen of other early-flowering trees, will coat windows and turn sluggish streams yellow in the northern states.)

PAPER BIRCH 

Betula papyrifera
Photo page #22

Also known as: Canoe birch, white birch, silver birch
Season: Sap in earliest spring
Habitat: Roadsides, lawns, parks, riverside, open woods

This lovely tree may grow as high as fifty to seventy-five feet. A quick-growing tree, the paper birch will live up to eighty years in the woods, but beautifies the landscape for a lesser time if planted on a lawn. It likes moist soils, and you'll find it growing along the edges of brooks and rivers. It doesn't mind having acidy evergreens for neighbors, and these trees are often found together.

You may have chewed upon birch wood in a toothpick or watched thread spin off a birch spool on a sewing machine. It provides delightful Christmas logs, and you may have burned it in your fireplace. Birch, though, is generally more decorative and aromatic than it is heat-efficient. The pliable wood of the paper birch was even fashioned into snowshoe frames by settlers as well as Indians.

The American Indian used the bark of this tree to make everything from canoes to wigwams, including kitchen articles such as cups, dishes, and containers for heating water. Their birch bark canoes, now copied in fiberglass and aluminum, are yet unequalled for lightness and speed. They were made of carefully cut and stripped sections of white birch bark sewed together over a frame of white cedar or arbor vitae, and caulked with the resin of neighboring evergreens. The bark also became teepee covers, fire kindler, and, when burned as punk, an effective insect repellent.

With its white bark peeling naturally from the trunk, the paper birch is easy to recognize. The inner bark thus bared is pinkish-orange to orange-brown in color. The twigs, however, are not white like the trunk. Beginning as greenish shoots, they later turn dark orange-brown with scattered orange-colored lenticels and mature to a blackish tone. Dark also are the lenticel scars that stripe the trunk. Wherever bark has been removed from the satiny trunk, black scars record the event; they never rewhiten. (The bark should not be peeled from living trees; this is a good way to kill a tree. Strip dead trees for birch bark.)

The ovate, nearly triangular leaves are dark green above and paler beneath. Averaging about two to three inches in length, they are usually rounded at the base.

Their edges are sharply and doubly toothed, with a sharp point at the tip.

Great stands of these trees are found throughout the northeast. Paper birches flag their snow-white bark against a backdrop of green leaves and blue sky around many lakes, along forest-tunneling New England roads, and from rocky pinnacles cleft by highways. Thousands are raised by nurseries and sold to homeowners who want beautiful lawn accents for years to come.

Of the birch's many uses, the clear sap is perhaps the most enjoyable. This may be taken as beverage straight from the tapped trunk or chilled. The sap may be boiled down to a delicious reddish syrup or sugar; this is not so flavorful as the sap of the black birch or as rich in sugar as the slower-flowing sugar maple serum, but it will nevertheless make a good birch beer or wine; use it in much the same way as the sap of the black birch. (Also see the preceding introduction to the birches.)

The sap was once believed to have curative properties. Sip a glass of the first fast spoutings of this tree in the crisp early spring, and you won't be concerned with any medicinal values! When I do this, surrounded by the bare remnants of winter, I can feel the glow of the season's re-creation of life flow through me. That's real medicine! Perhaps you'll experience the same reverent appreciation of these gifts—a feeling of oneness with the other life of this world.

YELLOW BIRCH

Betula lutea, Betula allegheniensis
Photo page #22

Also known as: Bitter birch, silver birch, gray birch, (do not confuse with *Betula populifolia*), swamp birch

Season: Sap in early spring

Habitat: Cool, mountainous areas; will live in dry or moist areas

Neither the yellow nor the black birch is thought of by most people as a birch tree. These species, with their neutral-toned bark, tend to fade into the background in a forest, not commanding the eye's attention like their more striking relatives, the white birch and the gray birch. Though the yellow birch is sometimes called "gray birch," the true gray birch is a distinct species. This smallish tree is dark gray or black as a sapling, but as it reaches into adolescence its non-peeling bark will turn a dingy white. The young yellow birch, on the other hand, has bark that is bright silvery-gray, sometimes with tones of orange. Like its cousin the white birch, the yellow birch has bark that peels naturally, but in thin, curly, translucent strips rather than the large swaths of the white birch's bark. On a snowy day, the peeling strips on the trunk of the yellow birch will glisten with gold and silver highlights.

The yellow birch has the horizontal lenticel markings of the others in the genus. The bole may reach a diameter of two to as much as four feet, while the crown may top out at nearly a hundred feet. This is the tallest of the birches. It grows to a larger diameter than most other birches, too.

The dull, dark green leaves are generally between three and four and a half inches long. They're a little more coarsely double-toothed than those of the black birch, and come to a sharp end point. The young twigs that hold the leaves are light orange-brown and covered with hair; later they bald and darken. When broken, these twigs give off a light wintergreen aroma, the confirmation that you have found a yellow birch.

This tree was first described by the early explorers of the northeast, but it wasn't until the early 19th century that it was scientifically described and named. It grows not only in the north, but in the cool swamps and mountain coves of the more southern Atlantic states. Stronger than many of its kin, it is recommended by the U.S. Department of Agriculture for planting in dry areas.

Not many yellow birches of giant stature remain today, for this species is the birch most valued for its timber and was widely used in the past two centuries. The sapwood is nearly white, and beautiful rolled and curved patterns are found in the grain of some trees. The shipbuilders of Nova Scotia and Maine sought this wood to use for the parts of boats which would constantly be under water. In lumber camps it was used for oxen yokes, the frames of the snow sledges for hauling lumber, and the frames of snowshoes. With the bark still on, this wood was used to build log cabin bunkhouses for the workmen. Carriage manufacturers coveted yellow birch, for hubs made from it would not lose their grip on the wheel spokes, nor easily crack. Today it is used for interior finish, cabinets and furniture.

A light-flavored tea can be made from the leaves and young twigs. Though its sap is neither as strongly flavored nor as sweet as that of the black birch, this tree will provide the makings for a good birch beer.

In a time of emergency, the inner bark could be dried and ground into flour or finely cut and boiled in a stew. Unless it is a life or death situation, though, use only the limbs or trees you intend to remove, for stripping off the bark, if it does not kill the tree, renders it defenseless to the invasion of insects or fungi. (See also the introduction to the birches.)

BLACK BIRCH

Betula lenta
Photo page #22

Also known as: Sweet birch, cherry birch, mahogany birch, mountain mahogany tree, wintergreen birch

Season: Sap in March and April

Habitat: Mountainous areas, young forests, wood edges, cleared or burned-over and uncut fields; prefers moist, cool, rich soils

DO NOT CONFUSE WITH CHERRY TREES OR THE MOUNTAIN MAHOGANY BUSH (*CERCOCARPUS* SPECIES)

South of the middle Atlantic states grows another tree, *Betula nigra*, that is more rightfully called the black birch. Preferring wet soils, this southern variety has reddish-brown to silvery-gray bark that separates into papery scales as the tree ages. While it possibly may produce an edible sap, it is not as useful as *Betula lenta*, the black birch discussed here.

This, along with the yellow birch, is one of the sturdier birches. Sometimes reaching a height of fifty to sixty feet, it has a respectable two to three foot trunk diameter. This "black" birch is easily recognized by its smooth, very dark red-brown to red-black bark which somewhat resembles the poisonous bark of many cherry trees. Throughout the year, the bark and broken twigs have the odor of wintergreen. During the summer, even the leaves will give this same scent when bruised. This trait allows immediate identification.

The dark green leaves, which are a yellowish green on their undersurfaces, are oval in shape, rounded or heart-shaped at the base, and have fine sharp-pointed teeth on their edges.

The oil of wintergreen produced by this tree is chemically identical to that made by the checkerberry plant which often carpets the woodland floor at its feet. This same substance is produced synthetically today in laboratories as a flavoring agent and for use in muscle rubs and linaments, but oil of wintergreen may be obtained by distillation from the twigs, bark, wood and even the leaves of this tree.

A hundred or more youthful trees are required to produce a single quart of natural wintergreen oil. The black birch all but disappeared when it was found that it would yield far more oil of wintergreen than harvests of checkerberry plants could provide. (This was before scientists learned to synthesize oil of wintergreen from wood alcohol and salicylic acid.) The black birch was also in great demand as a counterfeit mahogany; while it is actually stronger than and as hard as mahogany and cherry, it never gained real fame in its own right. Rather, touched up with fillers and stains, it was sold under the name of "mountain mahogany," which gave it a more glamorous image and a higher price tag. With the sapling trees going toward the production of wintergreen oil and the mature trees going beneath the saw for lumber and manufacturing, it is no surprise that large stands of these lovely woodland inhabitants disappeared.

If you are fortunate enough to have black birch trees accessible to you or on your own property, you may wish to tap them for pure enjoyment. They should be at least six inches in diameter, and the tapping is best done in March and April. The birches are so exuberant in this first flush of spring that you can hold a pail beneath a spigot bored into the tree and wait while the sap gushes it full! Place the taps on the sunnier side of the tree, just as is done for the sugar maple. Be sure to wood-plug the holes afterward. It will be a time before the flowing sap ceases, even with a carefully placed plug. Drink the sap fresh from the tree or chilled for a short time in the refrigerator; make a syrup or sugar from it by boiling it down, or produce a birch beer or wine for later enjoyment.

This birch reportedly yields good amounts of vitamins A, C, E, B^1 and B^2, as well as many minerals absorbed from the rich forest floor. An excellent way to capture the nutritious essence of this tree is to prepare a tea: First chop some leaves, twigs or inner bark (preferably from a root or branch you wanted to prune). Since boiling liquid will destroy not only the delicious wintergreen flavor but the vitamin content as well, heat water or sap to just under boiling. Steep the chopped solids in the hot liquid for about ten minutes, strain and sweeten with honey. Some people like milk or cream added to this brew, while other prefer a few drops of lemon. Many like it just as it is.

There are many family recipes which have been passed down through the ages for preparing birch beers and wines. In Europe, the wine was apparently the favored drink. There seems to be little difference between the beer and wine recipes except in the time the brew is allowed to "work" before capping. (See the introduction to the birches.)

AMERICAN HAZELNUT

Corylus americana

(See the following description.)

BEAKED HAZELNUT

Corylus cornuta
Photo page #22

Also known as: Hazelnut, sweet hazelnut, little hazelnut, filbert
Season: Nuts in late summer and early fall
Habitat: Roadsides, wood edges, open woods, thickets

These two shrubs or small trees are very similar, differing only in the shape of the covering of the nuts, the hairiness of the twigs, and details of nut structure. Their fruits are delightful, if you get a chance to sample them. The little animals and birds usually know just where to find them, and usually beat all but the wise foragers to them!

The hazelnut shrub has an almost heart-shaped leaf, with small teeth upon the larger teeth (doubly toothed). On the American hazelnut, the twigs are stiffly hairy, as are the leafstalks, while those of the beaked hazelnut usually lack hair. Both shrubs produce birch-like catkins in the spring that are followed by the fruits often called filberts in this country. The American hazelnut's nut, encased in a toothed husk, looks like it is covered by two small leaves that enveloped it, with broad ruffled edges at the outermost end. The beaked hazelnut's nut covering looks more like a bird's head, fibrous-feathery over the head, with a long "beak" at the outermost end. Both shrubs are found throughout a wide range, but you've got to look for them. In the early fall, look for green leaves outlined by margins of yellow.

When the nuts are firm and full, but before the wild harvesters have really robbed the shrub for their winter pantries, harvest the nuts and let them mature fully in a cool, dry place. They're not terribly large, but are a sweet, nicely-flavored nut of many uses, raw or lightly roasted.

SWEETFERN

Comptonia peregrina (Myrica peregrina)
Photo page #28

Also known as: Sweetgale bush, wild tea, sweet fern bush
Season: Leaves in summer, nutlets in early fall
Habitat: Dry woods edges, clearings, waste places, cleared or burned fields

Sweetfern is neither a fiddlehead fern nor one of the sweetgales. It is a fernlike bushy plant with, as its name suggests, aromatic leaves. Though limited in use, it can be easily recognized by the novice forager. Once you become acquainted with this plant, you'll find it growing nearly everywhere, from the banks along railroad tracks to unnoticed niches in your own backyard.

The mature plant appears to be a little bush with reddish stems. Sweetfern will lose its leaves in the winter, if the wild animals do not forage from it first. The leaves are what have earned it the "fern" portion of its name, for they resemble the individual divisions of the fronds of some of the ferns. Each leaf is cut nearly to its middle by a series of rounded lobes along its sides. Crush one of these leaves, and you'll sniff the unmistakable fragrance that is an immediate identification of the sweetfern.

It hasn't showy flowers. The blooms look rather like spiny sea urchins. Although this plant belongs to the same group as the bayberries, the little nuts produced by the flowers are not at all waxy. These nutlets may be ground and used as a seasoning on meats. Or, try mixing them with some of the peppergrasses' seeds for a surprising seasoning in a barbecue sauce or gravy. The nutlets, young and tender, may reportedly be eaten, and the leaves, fresh or dried, make an excellent tea. It's best unboiled; just steep the leaves in hot water to desired strength, and remove the leaves before reheating to the desired temperature. Sweetfern is a fine tea on its own, though you'll probably wish to sweeten it, or in a combination wild tea: it will perk up the flavor of less robust plants. Mint is a wonderful partner for these leaves!

SHRUBBY CINQUEFOIL 

Potentilla fruticosa
Photo page #23

Also known as: Bushy cinquefoil, woody cinquefoil, fruiting cinquefoil, five finger, golden hardtack

Season: Summer

Habitat: Pastures, meadows, roadsides, waste places, beaches and shorelines

There are several other cinquefoils, all of the *Potentilla* genus. Part of the rose family, they generally share at least two common traits: all have five-petaled yellow flowers and arrangements of usually five leaves or leaflets (hence the name cinquefoil, which derives from the French words meaning "five leaves"). Most species are herbaceous (non-woody), in contrast to the shrubby cinquefoil. In some species, the leaves may be comprised of palmate leaflets or lobes and may be toothed. The shrubby cinquefoil, however, has toothless leaves arranged along a leafstalk. Shrubby cinquefoil is really the only cinquefoil recommended for kitchen use, and its several unique characteristics will easily set it apart from its kin.

As its name implies, shrubby conquefoil is distinctly shrubby. A compact, neat little bush, it usually remains at a level of one to three feet. It has reddish-brown woody stems with thin, loose bark peeling off in shreds, and is the only cinquefoil to have such stems. Yellow, inch-wide buttercup-like blossoms twinkle among its many branches in mid-summer and may continue their cheerful show until the early frosts. Even without its flowers, the shrubby cinquefoil is a nice-looking bush, and will enhance any lawn. (Transplant a small bush, having first asked the landowner's permission, or start it from seed.)

The leaves are divided into five, sometimes seven, slender oval leaflets lacking leafstalks. They have fairly sharp tips. The edges are untoothed but often roll under, especially in dry weather. Measuring about an inch long, the leaves are olive-green and silky on their upper surfaces, pale green and downy underneath. The young stems may show some velvet also before the bark begins to develop.

The cinquefoil will produce a small, dry fruit that is at first green and later turns brown. It's very hairy.

Snip off some of the healthy young leaves. They may be dried, then steeped for a few minutes and served as a tea. Their taste is somewhat astringent, and they are better when mellowed with other tea herbs, in my estimation. Cinquefoil has been used by herbalists for mouthwash and for relief of sore throats and colds.

JUNEBERRIES 

Amelanchier species
Photo page #23

Also known as: Shadbush, sarvisberries, tall blueberries, serviceberries
Season: Berries late June to September, depending on the species
Habitat: Woodlands, hillsides, road edges, streambanks; gravelly soil, moist areas; habitat usually varies with species

These plants are medium to high shrubs, though some might be classified as small trees. Their flowers, white with five petals like those of the strawberry or blackberry, bloom at about the same time as shad swim upstream to spawn, hence one of this plant's common names, "shadbush." It will bear blueberry-like fruits that are purple to blackish, once they ripen. American Indian tribes apparently preferred these to blueberries, but these excellent fruits are all too often ignored in present times. The berries are delicious uncooked, and make lovely jelly, jam, preserves or pies. Their sweetness is an identifying feature, but be sure you've checked the other characteristics first.

Their leaves are oval in shape, pointed, with shallow teeth along their edges. Depending on the species, the toothing may be just on the upper portion of the leaf or may cover the entire margin. The leaves of all the common species are smooth on their upper surfaces; a few varieties have leaves that may be a little downy underneath.

The bark of these bushes is grayish in tone and tight, never shaggy. The flowers have slender, often drooping, petals. While the flowers may actually be seen before the leaves, the clusters of berries are the final identifying feature: They bear a five-pointed crown like that on a blueberry or huckleberry, right down to the crown at each berry's tip. The immature berries may be nearly fuchsia in color and some may be clouded with brown hues, but the ripe ones will resemble nothing so much as a blueberry or huckleberry, right down to the crown at each berry's tip. These shrubs are easily spotted when in flower; mark the spot and wait for the berries to ripen.

BARBERRIES 

Berberis canadensis (American barberry)
Berberis vulgaris (Common barberry)
Photo page #23

Also known as: Sourberry
Season: Berries in late summer, throughout winter
Habitat: Open dry woods, thickets, roadsides, edges of fields

EDIBILITY OF IMPORTED, SMALL-LEAF BARBERRIES UNKNOWN

The American barberry and common barberry differ but little botanically, and their uses are the same. You'll know when you've run into either of them, for they're thorny bushes! Their blood-letting thorns are usually found in groups of three, pointing in three different directions, with one longer than the others. The thorns arise at the nodes of the slender, arching stems. If you need a barricade hedge, you might consider barberries, for they can be pruned, supply you with edible fruit, and still keep out people and pets. They might well be named for their resemblance to barbed wire!

Once summer begins to be really warm, the branches will bear clusters of fragrant yellow flowers. The green leaves arise in whorls just above the thorns. Each approximately inch-long leaf is closely toothed, rounded at the end, and generally somewhat wider above its middle; wedge-shaped at the base, it gradually narrows to combine with the leaf petiole. If you cut through the dark brown, warty stems and branches, you'll find the inner bark and wood to be yellow in color.

As the leaves begin to turn, the berries of this plant will have ripened to their brilliant red tones. (Those shown in the photograph are not yet ripe.) Clusters of the oval, beadlike scarlet fruits will remain on the bush the better part of the winter if they are not harvested by you or little animals. They are very tart (the Indians called them "sour berries"), but make excellent, flavorful jams and jellies; they are best simmered awhile with other fruits in a compote or fruit pie filling. Since they are high in pectin, they will assist in jelly making when added to fruits which lack this setting material. They may be cooled slightly and added to muffins or coffee cake, but you'll need to add a bit more sweetening to compensate for their sourness. Barberries ripen around the time when a tart fruit sauce would go well with hearty autumn dishes, and you can make a condiment that is very like cranberry sauce. Barberries may also be simmered and squashed to serve as the base for a really good summer cold drink, the juice will need to be diluted and sweetened.

FLOWERING QUINCE 

Chaenomeles japonica and others

Also known as: Japanese quince, Chinese quince, quince, pink-flowering quince, scarlet quince, apple quince

Season: Fruit ripe in late summer, early fall

Habitat: Hedges or on lawns; escaped to roadsides, pasture edges

These lovely Japanese imports may not generally be considered wild plants, but a few have escaped, and even those growing close to people are frequently overlooked.

There are several varieties of these decorative, man-high shrubs, but only one or two are really hardy in the northern states. Most bear pinkish-red flowers, usually in clusters of two to six blooms, but in some varieties they may be light pink or white. The blossoms usually appear before the leaves are mature. On most, the blooms are so large and gaudy, the leaves are overshadowed.

Flowering Quince

The leaves alternate on the spiny branches; they are rounded in outline and usually coarsely toothed. Many reach a length of two and a half to three inches at maturity. The quince shrubs bloom in early spring, and by late summer most seem to have lost half their leaves, but this lets you more easily see the excellent fruit being produced.

The fruits look like small greenish or yellowish apples, but don't bite them — they'll bite back! Wait until they turn a ripe yellow before picking. They must be sweetened and cooked, but then their flavor is lip-smacking good. Try them stewed or in a jam. They mix well in preserves or blend with other simmered fruits. Don't just let them sit on a lawn and look pretty — use them!

SUMACS 

Rhus glabra (Smooth Sumac)
Rhus typhina (Staghorn Sumac)
Photo page #24

Also known as: Lemonade tree, vinegar tree, smooth sumac, staghorn sumac, red sumac

Season: Fruits, late summer

Habitat: Waste areas, roadsides, dry soils

These lovely shrubs or little trees with their bright cone-shaped flower heads are able to grow nearly anywhere, and are frequently seen in dry waste areas unsuitable for other trees. Their pinnately compound leaves have an almost tropical lushness, and turn glorious hues of red, yellow and violet in autumn. Sumac will serve well as a privacy screen, and may be trimmed as a hedge. There are other species than the two described here. ***Do not confuse these plants with their harmful relative***, the poison sumac (*Rhus vernix*). The habitat of the harmful species helps to set it apart from the edible varieties — it prefers wetlands. Its leaves are not toothed, whereas those of most of the other sumacs are singly toothed, and it has white, not red, berries.

The two most commonly found sumacs of our area are the smooth sumac, *Rhus glabra*, and the staghorn sumac, *Rhus typhina*. The latter species is most often encountered; it is named for its fuzzy stems that resemble the antlers of the male deer before they've shed their velvet. There are usually fifteen, seventeen, or more leaflets on the graceful leaf of either species.

The flower heads begin to bloom in mid-summer, and by the end of the summer, purplish-red berries will have developed on each greenish-white head. The berries of the staghorn sumac are hairier and generally more sour than those of the smooth sumac, but those of both are very usable. Collect them, as entire clusters, when the berries begin to ripen to red tones.

After bruising the newly-ripe berries by rubbing gently, soak the fruit cluster for a short time in cold water, until the liquid has turned a rosy pink. Remove the cluster and strain off any hairs, add a little sweetening, and you'll have a refreshing "pink lemonade" for a summer afternoon. The fruits may also be mashed with a fork; steep about a quarter cupful of these in three cups of hot water to make a very nice sweet-sour beverage; a little honey will complement the lemony flavor. (More sweetening will be needed for the fruits of the sourer fuzzy staghorn sumac.) Reportedly, some of the Indians gathered sumac heads and soaked the berries in maple syrup before using them to make a tea.

The fruits of these bushes may also be dried for storage to bring summer's flavor to your winter diet. Served either hot or cold, sumac lemonade was long reputed to be an especially good drink for people suffering from colds or flu. Sumac berries very likely contain high amounts of vitamins, especially vitamin C.

Look, then, for these short trees with their fifteen to thirty toothed leaflets and cones of reddish fruits: they will provide you with flavorful, nutritious drinks for summer or winter, while you chuckle at your neighbors who spend their good money on imitation beverages.

CHOKECHERRY 

Prunus virginiana
Photo page #24

Also known as: Sour black cherry
Season: Fruit ripe in late summer
Habitat: Open areas such as unused fields, roadsides, waste places; sometimes open woods

SOME PARTS OF THIS PLANT MAY BE POISONOUS

Related to the plums and peaches, cherry trees come in a variety of shapes, sizes and fruit types. Not all are sweet. Besides the truly wild cherries, domesticated varieties often escape into pastures and roadsides, providing exceptionally nice, free harvests. Next to trees that bear larger, sweeter fruits, the smallish chokecherry tree is not of prime interest; still, the fruits are edible and abundant and many people use them to make delicious jellies and wines.

Often not more than a shrub in size, the chokecherry produces small red fruits that darken to purplish-red or almost black when mature. These diminutive cherries hang in long strands like those of the wild black cherry, but a tiny nibble will immediately tell you the difference: you'll quickly pucker up from their strongly astringent, acidy juice. Chokecherries are well named!

The leaves of all types of cherry trees share a strong resemblance, and these are no exception. Their shape is usually oval, or an elongated oval, with a sharply pointed tip. Tiny sharp teeth line the margins of these two- to four-inch leaves. They are hairless on both surfaces, dark green above and lighter beneath. Look at the leafstalks for a quick identification test: where the short petiole joins the leaf you'll see, nearby, a pair of dark, raised lumps. These are glands.

The thin, usually smooth bark of these trees is grayish-brown, and, like that of most other cherry trees, horizontally marked with lighter lenticels (openings in the bark). The broken bark and stems have a strong, bad odor; the hydrocyanic acid present in the bark and twigs (as well as the leaves and pits) is held responsible for the smell. Hydrocyanic acid contains cyanide, and these plant materials can poison people, cattle, horses or pets. Consequently, ***all but the fleshy part of the fruit must be avoided.***

If you can find enough of the fruits, which are usually ripe in July and August, cooking and sweetening will tame them into good jams, jellies and pies. They will need considerable sweetening, though! Some varieties of the chokecherry have been cultivated, especially in Canada, and their fruits are far less tart.

The spikes of white spring flowers make this tree an attractive species for edge plantings or privacy screens. They grow with little care and make the birds happy, too. They'll also provide a dry cherry wine to ease winter's chill.

WILD BLACK CHERRY 

Prunus serotina

Also known as: Bitter black cherry, rum cherry, whiskey cherry
Season: Fruits in late summer
Habitat: Woodlands, unused fields, roadsides

SOME PARTS OF THIS PLANT MAY BE POISONOUS

It's no accident that so many cough syrups and cough drops are flavored with cherry. Some of these flavorings are synthetically manufactured, while others ring true, having been derived from the bark of this tree. Known for centuries for its sedative properties, wild cherry bark was used by the Indians to relieve pain of childbirth, digestive complaints, colds, and hemorrhoids, and became a common ingredient in commercial cough remedies. The young bark was collected in the fall when it contained the greatest amount of hydrocyanic (prussic) acid, its effective ingredient. This powerful chemical can act as a poison as well as a medicine, however, and is best treated with respect.

The dark, reddish-brown bark is bitter to the taste and may remind you of the scent of almonds when freshly broken. The leaves, too, contain hydrocyanic acid, and farmers remove these trees from their pastures because ***the bark and leaves, if eaten in quantity, can be lethal***. Hydrocyanic acid is found in the pits of the fruits, too, but is reported to be destroyed by heating. Consequently, it is not necessary to remove them until after cooking when you make cherry jelly. It is still not wise to let the children eat the pits of any of the cherries.

The tree is easily recognized as a cherry. Like its cousins, its close-grained, richly-colored wood is used for veneers and other wood products. Black cherry has the toothed, lustrous green leaves common to this group; they are, however, longer and narrower than those of the chokecherry. They are paler below, and the middle, main vein is edged on this undersurface with hairs, often cinnamon-colored. Though the fruit of this cherry becomes darker than that of the chokecherry, it is borne in the same manner.

While wild black cherries are usually not very sweet, they never have the acrid taste of the fruit of the chokecherry tree. The black, shiny globes will swell to about a half inch in diameter, and though their taste may be slightly bitter, they are thin-skinned and juicy. Bears and children love them, even if they're not sweet. They make excellent jellies and wines.

You'll find the fruit ripening from about mid-July through fall, but you'll have to beat the birds and other animals to them! Chipmunks and squirrels store the pits against winter famine, and we've spied our bluejays tucking them away for later snacks. Covering one or two of the small trees with cheesecloth will help to thwart these wild cherry fanciers, and you can collect as many as you can use. The wild black cherries may be frozen, canned, or dried for future use.

WILD RED CHERRY

Prunus pennsylvanica
Photo page #24

Also known as: Bird cherry, pin cherry, red cherry, fire cherry
Season: Fruits in late summer
Habitat: Burned-over areas, unused fields, roadsides

SOME PARTS OF THIS PLANT MAY BE POISONOUS

Lumbermen and farmers don't think much of this little tree: its soft wood is of little value, although it can be formed into small items. Still, when lumbering operations or fires cut swaths through the pines and spruces of our forests, it is this tree that often takes their place. Consequently, in the past century or so, its range has been ever-widening.

The cherries are produced on individual stems, like those of the cultivated red cherry tree and unlike those of the black cherry and chokecherry trees, although several may spring from the same point on the branch. They are bright red, thick-skinned, and sour-fleshed. There is little fruit wrapped around the pit, but these wild cherries do make a nice jelly or wine. You'll have to pick a fair number of them, though, unless you only intend them to flavor other, fleshier fruits—each cherry is only about a quarter of an inch in diameter.

The bark on this tree is thicker than that of most of the other cherries, and is dark reddish-black in color, marked with orangy-brown lenticels. As these lenticels mature into their second and third years they become raised, lighter, and often appear greenish because the bark has peeled away from them to reveal the inner layers. ***The same cautions about the leaves, bark and pits of other cherries apply equally to this tree.***

The lance-shaped leaves are narrow, oval, and toothed along their margins. The leaf petioles often bear glands near the base of the leaf. Usually the leaves are a bright, shining green above and a lighter tone below, and are not as firm in texture as those of the wild black cherry.

Look for the fruits of this tree when you're searching for the more useful black cherry. Their flavors blend well, and they are ripe during the same season. All the cherries are quite high in vitamin A, good in vitamin C content, and are worthwhile for their other nutrients.

COMMON ELDERBERRY

Sambucus canadensis
Photo page #23

Also known as: Elderberry bush, American elder, Canadian elder
Season: Blossoms in late spring, fruits in late summer
Habitat: Rich, moist hillsides and ditches, roadsides and clearings, waste places and idle fields

(See the following description.)

RED ELDERBERRY 

Sambucus pubens
Photo page #28

Also known as: Poison elder, poison red elder, red elder, hairy elder
Season and Habitat: Same as common elderberry

DO NOT CONFUSE THIS POISONOUS PLANT WITH THE EDIBLE COMMON ELDERBERRY

These two plants, though closely related, are not too much alike. Still, an overly enthusiastic plant hunter might rush to the conclusion that if one type of elderberry is edible, then the other must be too. Not so! Once you have learned to tell the two species apart, though, you'll have a delicious wild berry to add to your repertoire.

The common elderberry, whose products are so fine in pancakes, muffins, jelly, jam, and wine, produces in springtime a platter-like cluster of tiny whitish flowers. By the end of summer, these will have been replaced by flat, wide clusters of tiny black berries with purple overtones. The clusters are often quite wide, sometimes spreading to a foot or more. ***The poisonous red elder, on the other hand, produces roundish or pyrimidal clusters of white flowers that are followed by tiny red berries in the same overall formation.*** These berries usually have developed by mid- or late July, whereas those of the dark-fruited elderberry will mature considerably later.

Both shrubs have pinnately compound leaves, paired opposite on the stems. The common elderberry typically has three to five pairs of leaflets, with an odd one at the tip; the red elderberry generally has two or three pairs of leaflets with an odd one at the apex. The leaflets of both species are toothed. The common elderberry, however, oftentimes has an extra little thumb-like lobe on the lowermost leaflets of each leaf. The red elderberry's leaves are velvety when young, and even at maturity the undersides of the leafstalks will usually show this hairiness; the leafstalks and young twigs will often have a reddish tone.

The flowers of the common elderberry have long been used in making fritters and pancakes. The flower heads are briefly rinsed, drained, and their blossoms then plucked from their stems. To make sumptuous elderflower pancakes or fritters, add a healthy handful to batter for three or four people. Top them with elderberry syrup made from the previous season's harvest, and you've a real feast! These same flowers, fresh or dried, have long been used for tea: simply steep them in water, and sweeten if desired. Early settlers gave elderflower tea to their children to quiet upset stomachs and relieve gas. It is reported that some of the Indians used this tea to reduce fever.

The fresh berries are not sweet, nor do they even smell good. When cooked, however, they become very tasty. They are reportedly high in certain vitamins and minerals, as you'd expect from a fruit, and for their usefulness alone they are worth collecting. Elderberries are usually found in great enough numbers so that, even though they are small, they are not too difficult to gather.

Air or oven drying not only removes the rank odor and bad taste of the raw berries, but is a good way to store them. Just reconstitute them with hot water and add to your recipe. Elderberries may also be frozen, but are best cooked a bit first.

It takes but little simmering to tame the smell and flavor of the fruits, and the less they are cooked, the higher their vitamin content will be. Elderberries may be made into jams and jellies, but will need the assistance of commercial pectin or a fruit that is naturally high in pectin.

This common, yet overlooked, fruit is easy to harvest, for you can spot either the flat flower or fruit clusters from quite a distance. Still, to be absolutely certain that you have the common elderberry, even if all other traits seem to coincide, cut through a branch: the central area will be filled with a firm, white pith. Finding this, go ahead and pick.

GREENBRIER

Smilax rotundifolia
Photo page #24

Also known as: Common greenbrier, cat brier
Season: Shoots and leaves, early spring
Habitat: Woodlands, roadsides, clearings in woods

DO NOT CONFUSE WITH DEADLY NIGHTSHADE, POISON IVY OR THE SARSAPARILLAS

When stalking this plant, look for wide, rounded leaves with heart-shaped bases and parallel veins. The tip of each broad leaf comes to a point. At nearly every leaf axil you'll find a pair of tendrils by which the rather weak-stemmed plant holds itself erect, climbing over other plants and up tree trunks. If you cut through the stem you'll find the interior tissue to be all the same, with no tough, stringy pith. These green stems are armed with thorns, and provide protective hiding places for rabbits and other small animals.

The greenbrier is most easily recognized at maturity, when the leaves and tendrils are fully developed. Once you have identified some of these plants, mark their location and, next spring, look for their young shoots — they'll look much like the young shoots of their cousin, the carrion flower. These make a good "asparagus," cooked briefly to tenderness. The young parts of the plant may also be chopped and added to mixed vegetable dishes, soups, and stews. You can cut these tender portions throughout the early growing season.

As summer progresses, yellowish-green flowers, borne in clusters like those of the carrion flower, are produced at the leaf axils. These will mature into bluish-black berries. They're not known to be edible by us, although many of the wild creatures find them good.

There are several other species of greenbrier, the bristly greenbrier being the closest in leaf shape. Common greenbrier usually has five veins in each leaf, and its thorns are well spaced, as on many of the garden rose bushes; the bristly cousin's leaves usually have seven main veins, and its thorns, as the name implies, are thinner and more densely placed along the stem.

HOBBLEBUSH

Viburnum alnifolium
Photo page #23

Also known as: Wild raisin, raisin viburnum
Season: Berries, late summer to early fall

Habitat: Woods edges, roadsides in shaded area, openings in woods

This is a little, straggly bush that usually looks half-starved. Often the supple branches will loop downward to the ground, causing the woods hiker to trip — perhaps this is how the plant gets its name "hobblebush"! The branches often root where they touch the ground, and the hobblebush produces new plants this way as well as by seed.

The leaves of the hobblebush are wide, pointed and oval, with tiny teeth along the leaf margins. Since the plant grows primarily in the shade, the leaves may reach to six or eight inches in length so as to best capture whatever light is available. Like other members of the *Viburnum* genus, the hobblebush bears its leaves in pairs, opposite each other on the branches. The ends of the twigs, the leafstalks, and the undersurfaces of the leaves are velvety with rust-colored hairs.

This is one of the first bushes to blossom in the woods, and the early warmth of May generally produces flat-topped white clusters on these bushes. They are composed of many flowers, but the flowers in the outermost circle ringing each cluster are the only ones to have large petals. These are actually sterile flowers; the central, smaller ones are the berry producers. This characteristic serves to separate the viburnums.

Late in summer you'll find that these little bushes have replaced their snowy crowns with bunches of bluish-black berries. When they're fully ripe, they'll have the sweetness of raisins; indeed, these plants are also known as wild raisins. The sweetness of the berries will help to distinguish the hobblebush from other similar bushes, for the characteristic rusty hairs of this plant may not be so apparent late in the season. It is best to stake out these bushes when they are in flower, and use the flavor as a double-check. (NOTE: See the illustration on page 22.)

Each berry contains one large seed. Though you'll want to remove the seeds by straining the berries through a mesh, the fruits are excellent in jams, jellies, pies, sauces, fruit syrups and fruit leathers. Don't pass them up! On the trail, they're a sweet nibble, though you'll be spitting seeds frequently. But that's just returning one good deed with another, for you'll be spreading this good-natured little bush in thanks for its tasty fruit.

WILD RAISIN

Viburnum cassinoides
Photo page #25

Also known as: Northern wild raisin, northern witherod, raisin bush
Season: Berries, late summer through early fall
Habitat: Likes cool, moist, rocky woods, woodland clearings, roadsides where there's adequate moisture, marsh edges

Since there are several plants besides this one that share the common name of "wild raisin," there may be some confusion. The hobblebush is one of them, and another is a southern cousin, very similar in appearance to the northern wild raisin, that seldom extends north of the middle Atlantic states. These all produce edible berries.

In May and early June there are many white-flowered bushes in our woodlands, and I highly recommend identifying those growing nearby. This way, you can watch each variety throughout its growing season. The wild raisin is a common and often overlooked member of this group, and is well worth getting to know.

Usually these shrubs do not grow higher than seven to eight feet. Like most of the *Viburnums*, their branches are usually quite supple, and the leaves are carried in opposite pairs on the branches. The leaves of this species are long, oval, and pointed. The bases, too, are usually pointed. The flowers, generally produced in clusters at the ends of the branches, are like those of their cousin the hobblebush in overall shape and form, but they are all the same size on the wild raisin. Each flower cluster has its own distinct stalk, subdivided into many separate stalks that bear the flowers.

The leaf margins are most often smooth or slightly wavy, though some leaves may have broad, barely distinguishable, toothing. Sometimes cinnamon-colored fuzz may be seen on the midrib's surface beneath the leaf, as on the hobblebush leaf.

From late in the summer into fall, look for the clusters of edible berries that will have replaced the springtime flowers. The berries are more oval than round, and each usually bears a little tip that is a remnant of the female flower parts. The berries are blue-black, often hazed with a whitish bloom as is found on many of the blueberries. Each berry is a little over a quarter of an inch long, but usually many will be found on each bush. A nibble will confirm that your identification's correct, for the berry will taste very much like a raisin.

These berries may be eaten raw, but each has a large, flat seed. If you don't like spitting out seeds, simmer the berries and then strain out the seeds. De-seeded wild raisins mix well with other stewed fruits, blend readily into jellies and preserves, and are very nice in mincemeat or pies. Their sweetness will tame some of the tarter wild berries. They may also be used to flavor and sweeten a pancake syrup or some of the blander teas, but are best crushed first to release their juices.

Wild Raisin

GUELDER ROSE

Viburnum opulus
Photo page #25

(See the following description)

HIGHBUSH CRANBERRY

Viburnum trilobum

Also known as: Cranberry viburnum
Season: Fruit, fall through winter
Habitat: Thickets, road edges, old garden sites, thin woods

These two closely related bushes look very much alike. The guelder rose, however, is not recommended as an edible, for its fruits are bitter. This European ornamental was likely brought to the colonies both for its beauty and its bark's medicinal values. To avoid "bitter" disappointment in an intended highbush cranberry sauce, note the guelder rose's distinctive traits: Its lobed leaves are less long/pointed than those of the highbush cranberry, and the glands on the leafstalk of the guelder rose have concave surfaces, whereas those of the highbush cranberry have rounded surfaces.

The highbush cranberry is not of the same genus as the true cranberries. Its fruits, however, may be used as you would any cranberry, or in combination with the low cranberries. Look for eye-level or higher shrubs that have leaves similar to those of the red maple, borne in pairs (opposite) on the twigs, with three lobes and coarsely toothed margins. The leaves are usually about three or four inches in length. At the base of each leaf you'll find several glands, each raised well above the surface, with rounded tops. Two smaller leaf-like structures may be found where the leafstalk joins the twig.

Throughout the spring and early summer, these bushes bear two- to three-inch clusters of white flowers near the ends of the branches. It will look as though not all of the flowers have bloomed, for the outermost halo of the cluster will be made up of larger-petaled flowers, as on the hobblebush (also of the genus *Viburnum*). These outer flowers are actually sterile, and are there to attract the insects necessary to seed production. The actual fruit-producing blooms are the smaller ones that fill the central area of the cluster. By early fall and throughout Indian summer, these clusters will have ripened their red berries, which closely resemble those shown in the picture of the guelder rose. Split one open, and look closely at the seed within for a last identification trait: the seed will be smooth and ungrooved.

The berries are rather too tart to be eaten raw, but for a delicious cooked fruit sauce they are worth seeking. Just simmer them with a little water and lemon or orange peel, strain off the seeds, and add sugar or honey. Many times the harvest from one or two bushes will be far more plentiful than that of a whole morning's work at a true cranberry patch.

Though they are probably most outstanding as a cranberry sauce, highbush cranberries may also be simmered and crushed to give up their juice. Strain, sweeten, and dilute this to make a refreshing drink. These fruits may also be combined with other fruits in jellies, preserves, and pie fillings.

Blackberries and Raspberries

Worldwide, there are many species of the genus *Rubus*, possibly several thousand! Nearly all of them are shrubby plants, although some of them are small and herbaceous. The stems are usually armed with thorns or bristles, and many are long, trailing, thicket-forming—and blood-letting! Several dozen varieties are commonly found in New England in a wide range of areas, from swamps to wooden glades to sunny meadows, from coastline to alpine habitats. Most people quickly learn to identify the brambles, as the group is generally called, and to avoid the skin-tearing thorns in order to reach the delicious and nutritious fruits that can be used in so many ways. They are so plentiful, you can eat all you can hold as you pick, and still bring home enough to preserve, can, or freeze. Serve them fresh on cereal, or use them in shortcakes and in pies.

This large genus of plants is subdivided into two major groups, the blackberries and the raspberries, and several smaller ones. (Purple-flowering raspberry and cloudberry, for example, fall into two of the smaller subgenera.) The portion of a flower that supports, but does not actually produce the fruit, is called the receptacle, and in brambles this generally occurs as a whitish, cone-shaped structure. This receptacle will mark the most obvious distinction between raspberries and blackberries: When you pick a ripe raspberry the receptacle remains behind on the plant; when you pick a juicy blackberry, you eat the whole thing, receptacle and all.

The flowers of all the brambles look like strawberry or wild rose flowers, each having five petals and many stamens. In the center of each flower there are multiple pistils (the female portions), each of which will form a small cherry-like fruit. All these little drupelets together become the berry. The brambles are actually close cousins of the roses, even though their fruits are so different. (The rose produces a single tomato-like fruit.) The berries of the various brambles ripen at overlapping times throughout the summer, and the picking season of the whole group is long enough to keep you busy all summer. The raspberries generally ripen first, soon followed by the blackberries, though there will be late harvests of both types.

Horticulturists and nature are both constantly striving to produce new varieties of these plants, and the selection of commonly found wild brambles will very likely be different in future years. The following are some of the berries you may expect to find most often when foraging in New England; when you discover a typical bramble berry that almost but not quite fits the description for one of these species, and assume it is an edible variation on a delicious theme, check shrub books.

Do observe this one caution, however, when picking any bramble berries, especially those species that prefer moist areas: There is one plant that produces a berry similar to a raspberry — golden seal, whose root is used medicinally. The berry, which has black seeds, contains several dangerous alkaloids, and ***must be considered non-edible and possibly poisonous***. Due to its resemblance to several members of the *Rubus* group, golden seal is described in this section of the book for purposes of identification.

The brambles have other uses. Their leaves may be dried and brewed for a robust tea — collect them before or while the plants flower. All parts of these plants, however, except for the fruits, are high in tannic acid, a very effective internal and external tightener, and herbalists who have recommended them have had to be careful not to overdose: ***in large enough, or concentrated enough, doses, tannic acid can be dangerous and actually harmful***.

The berries freeze or can easily and keep well. Years ago, many people dried them for later incorporation in recipes. The fruits may also be mashed and dried into an outstandingly flavorful fruit bark.

Blackberries are not only tasty, but they are very high in nutritional value. The U.S.D.A. Handbook No. 8 lists these contents for a one hundred gram serving of the raw berries: 58 calories, 1.2 g protein, 0.9 g fat, 12.9 g total carbohydrates including 4.1 g fiber, 32 mg calcium, 19 mg phosphorus, 0.9 mg iron, 1 mg sodium, 170 mg potassium, 200 I.U. vitamin A, measurable amounts of several B vitamins, and 21 mg vitamin C. Unfortunately, the usual mineral content of these berries is not itemized, but it is likely that the wild ones, especially, would be a worthy addition to your diet for their trace minerals, too.

HIGH BLACKBERRY

Rubus villosus

Habitat: Woods edges, fence rows, roadsides

This bramble has a hairy, prickly stem, and its three- or five-lobed leaves are hairy on both sides and toothed on their edges. Even the leafstalks are prickly. The stems are tall, slender, branching, often recurved at the top, and will extend three to six feet high. The leaves are 2½-4 inches long; the terminal leaf has a petiole, while the side leaves in each group have either short stalks or none at all. The flower stalk is about an inch long, and the flower petals are white. Each fruit is composed of about twenty black, shining, fleshy globes. These blackberries, excellent in flavor and low in acid content, are ripe in August or September. Look for them in sunny thickets. (See the preceding introductory material for suggestions for use.)

DWARF BLACKBERRY

Rubus pubescens

Habitat: Along rivers, ponds, ditches

DO NOT CONFUSE WITH GOLDEN SEAL

As its name indicates, this is a rather smallish bramble, reaching generally to about eighteen inches in height. It has creeping stems. Erect leafy branches bear several leaves and flowers. The leaves are composed of three leaflets, and the flowers may be white or pink. This variety is generally found on damp slopes or shores. The berries are about a half inch in diameter, sweet, and good. (See the introduction to the brambles.)

RUNNING SWAMP BLACKBERRY

Rubus hispidus
Photo page #28

Habitat: Damp areas

DO NOT CONFUSE WITH GOLDEN SEAL

The branches of this plant are slender, arising from a creeping, woody stem that runs along or curves over the ground. The stems are hairy-bristly, with backward-pointing bristles. The leaves usually have three leaflets, although sometimes there are five, and are smooth and green on both sides, coarsely toothed, and thickish. They measure an inch or two long, have barely any leafstalk, and will remain on the bush for a long time, sometimes throughout the winter. The white flowers and fruit of this variety are both small. The fruit is reddish, ripening to dusky purple; it may have a whitish bloom, and is rather sour. This blackberry ripens early. (See the introduction that precedes the brambles for general information and uses.)

NORTHERN DEWBERRY

Rubus canadensis
Photo page #25

Habitat: Thickets, road edges, fence rows

This plant is characterized by its low, trailing stems. The stems are a little prickly. The relatively short (1-1½ inch) leaves generally have three leaflets, but some may have five. Their shape is an ellipse or a flat-sided oval, and they are light green, thin, unevenly toothed, and stalkless. The flowers are large, the petals white and twice as long as the sepals, and they occur individually on long stems. The very sweet, juicy black berry is large, with a diameter ranging from a half to a full inch. This bramble flowers in May and produces its fruit from July through August. (See the hints for preparation given in the introduction to the brambles.)

CLOUDBERRY

Rubus chamaemorus

Also known as: Bake-apple, baked-apple berry
Habitat: Mountain areas; high, moist areas

DO NOT MISTAKE THIS PLANT FOR GOLDEN SEAL

This herbaceous alpine plant has erect, unarmed stems, and there are usually only two leaves and one flower. The leaves have five rounded lobes and are rough-surfaced and toothed. The flower has five white petals and a center cluster of yellow stamens, and produces a large yellow or amber berry that is sweet and juicy. The plant flowers in June, and the berry ripens by September.

There is only one word of caution regarding this plant: ***Its two maple-like leaves closely resemble those of golden seal.*** Though the golden seal has roots long valued by herbalists, its raspberry-like fruits must be considered non-edible, possibly poisonous. Golden seal, however, grows usually in a different habitat than cloudberry does. Golden seal will be found in rich woods, whereas cloudberry will be found in wet, sphagnum bogs and woods.

Cloudberry reaches its southern limit in New England. Though it occurs in large numbers where it is found, it grows only in certain areas, so be careful not to overpick. (NOTE: See the illustration on page 10.)

GOLDEN SEAL

Hydrastis canadensis

Also known as: Turmeric plant
Habitat: Rich, moist woods

NOT A BRAMBLE — POISONOUS

This herbaceous plant ranges from portions of New England (mainly Vermont) to the Carolinas. It prefers rich, moist, usually deciduous woods. It grows six to twelve inches high, and has stems that may become purplish and hairy at the upper ends. There are usually only two leaves on the stem, placed in alternate fashion near the top. There may be a separate lower leaf. The maple-like shape of these three- to five-lobed leaves causes the plant to look very much like the cloudberry. This too is a single-flowered plant. However, the three sepals, which look like petals, are greenish-white or reddish-white and are soon lost. There are many stamens, and the flower produces a red, juicy raspberry-like fruit with dark, nearly black seeds that normally ripen in mid-summer. This fruit is ***not edible***, for the plant reportedly contains three dangerous alkaloids — berberine, canadine, and hydrastine. As two of its common names imply, its root contains a rich golden pigment that stains effectively and may be used for a yellow or orange dye. (See also the introductory description of the bramble group, and study the illustration on page 10.)

GARDEN RASPBERRY

Rubus idaeus

Habitat: Meadow or woods edges, roadsides, meadows, backyards, farms

This is the raspberry often sold for planting in gardens and on farms, and it may be found in old fields and thickets as an escapee. It has bristly, recurved prickles. The leaf is divided pinnately into three or five leaflets, each a broad oval and unevenly, sharply toothed. The leaves are hairy beneath, smooth above, and attached directly to the leafstalk, except for the leaflet at the end. The white flowers are borne in clusters, with petals shorter than their hairy sepals. Many variations of this prolific plant have been developed and cultivated for canning, freezing, and commercial use. Generally growing to about five feet, the plants produce large, sweet fruits varying in hue, as they ripen, from white to rose to red. (See the introduction to this section on brambles for more complete suggestions for use.)

WILD RED RASPBERRY 

Rubus strigosus
Photo page #25

Habitat: Meadow or woods edges, roadsides, backyards, some shady coastal areas

The stems of this bramble bush are loaded with bristles and spines! Otherwise, this plant is much like the garden raspberry. The wild red raspberry's leaflets are coarsely toothed and blunt at their bases. Each leaflet is around two inches long, and the terminal one has a distinct leafstalk. The flower is white, with petals about the same length as the sepals, and yields a hemispherical, light red berry with a wonderfully rich flavor. The plant flowers in May, and the fruit will be ready for picking beginning in late June. Though the berries are most abundant through July, the picking season often extends to late August. (See the introduction to the brambles.)

BLACK RASPBERRY 

Rubus occidentalis
Photo page #25

Also known as: Blackcap
Habitat: Thickets, rocky fields, farm edges

The recurved stems of this plant are slightly hairy and armed with sharp prickles. The long-stalked leaves have three leaflets, each of which is 2-3 inches long, ovate, and sharply and doubly toothed or nearly lobed. They are hairy beneath. The two lateral leaflets are stalkless, and the terminal leaflet has a stalk. The white flowers are borne in the axils of the leaves and in terminal groups. This bramble is usually slender, growing four to eight feet tall, with recurved stems that often reach the ground and root at the touching ends. It flowers in May, and the berries are ripe in July. These fruits are roundish, black with purple hues, often with a whitish waxy or powdery bloom on their surface, and have a lively, agreeable taste. (See the introduction that precedes the brambles for suggestions for use.)

PURPLE-FLOWERING RASPBERRY

Rubus odoratus
Photo page #28

Also known as: Scented raspberry
Habitat: Rocky open areas, mountains, high woodlands

This doesn't look like a raspberry bush until the fruits are formed, and even then you'd have second thoughts! This straggling shrub has palmately lobed leaves, resembling a maple's, each with three to five lobes. The middle lobe of the leaf is the longest, and the margin is unequally toothed. This plant has no thorns; the stems, sepals, and flower stalks are covered, though, with reddish hairs. The entire plant usually does not exceed six feet in height, and the terminal groups of flowers are likely to be the features that draw your attention. The flowers are rose-purple, between one and two inches in diameter. The edible berry that forms is red, shallow and thin. It may be somewhat dry, and the flavor varies from tart to sweet. These raspberries may be used cooked or raw. (See the introduction to the brambles for general hints for use.)

Blueberries, Huckleberries and Bilberries

The many berry bushes of the genuses *Vaccinium* and *Gaylussicia* all have several features in common, including the production of edible, nutritious fruit. Some of the berries require a bit of cooking or the addition of a sweetener before they taste really good, but most of them are so nice to eat right out of hand that you'll likely come back from your picking sprees with a bluish-purple tongue!

The most immediate feature to look for when hunting any of these berries is the characteristic crown at the base of each blue or black globe: the remains of the calyx which enveloped the developing ovary will be seen at the base of the berry as a circle of five sharp points. Another trait shared by all species of these bushes is that ***they do not have thorns***, prickles, or thorn-like branches of any sort. There are a few other types of berry bushes in the same family (the Heath family) that, when bearing berries, might be taken for blueberries or huckleberries — the bearberry, dogwood, buckthorn, or even one of the shrubby honeysuckles. The flowers, however, will generally set the blueberries and huckleberries apart from the others: their blooms are white to pink and have narrow bell shapes. After careful checking, a novice may feel secure in picking any of the varieties described here, as long as the bush has traits common to all members of this group.

While there are several differences between the huckleberries and blueberries, the characteristics of both will often intermingle, and both naturally-occurring and man-created hybrids are regularly found growing wild. Blueberries aren't always blue, and some huckleberries are identical to the typical blueberry that we see in our market. The berries of the huckleberry, though, normally contain ten large, hard seeds, whereas the fruits of the true blueberry contain many little seeds. The leaves of all these plants follow a common pattern with only minor variations: They are small, usually elliptical shape, and have short petioles. Most huckleberry leaves are toothless and spotted with shiny, small golden resin dots. Blueberries and bilberries generally have minutely toothed or leathery leaves. All these bushes have slender green, yellow-green or reddish twigs that may or may not be fuzzy. One feature that sets the true blueberry apart from all the rest, though, is the tendency of the twigs to be covered with fine, warty lenticels.

Between all the varieties, you can be picking berries over quite a season! The delicious fruits that you don't eat raw can be included in muffins, pancakes, cakes and pies, or made into mouth-watering jams, jellies, and sauces. To bring the flavor of summer into winter, they may be easily canned or frozen. Nutritionally, these wild berries will be valuable in your diet, for they contain vitamin A, vitamin C, calcium, phosphorus, potassium, and some of the B vitamins.

DWARF HUCKLEBERRY

Gaylussacia dumosa
Photo page #27

Also known as: Spreading huckleberry, hairy huckleberry
Habitat: Sandy woods, woods edges

This little bush generally doesn't grow over a couple of feet high; it may be as low as six inches. The one or two inch leaves are not toothed. They are shaped rather like an oar, blunt-tipped, with a little bristle at the end. The leaf base is wedge-shaped, and the zig-zagging branchlets that bear these leaves are often fuzzy. Even the leaf surfaces may be a little hairy, but the clincher will be the presence of minute resin dots, found especially on the lower surface. A hand lens will help you to see them clearly. On fresh leaves, they will glimmer in the sunlight. The bush flowers in spring; the groups of white or pinkish blooms are followed by black berries that ripen from June through early fall. These have the five-pointed crown typical of this group. Though the fruits may be somewhat hairy, they are perfectly edible. (See the introduction to this group of related plants.)

TALL HUCKLEBERRY

Gaylussacia frondosa

Also known as: Dangleberry, woolly dangleberry, blue tangle, blue huckleberry
Habitat: Rocky or sandy woodlands and wet areas

This two- to four-foot shrub is very much like the dwarf huckleberry. Its leaves, though, are covered with whitish hairs; they are also more oval in shape, and have resin dots on their lower surfaces only. The cluster of bell-like pink flowers droop from the branchlets in late spring or early summer, and are replaced by berries that look very much like typical blueberries. The berries even have the whitish powdery bloom usually associated with blueberries, and are quite sweet. They'll be ripe from mid- to late summer. (See the introduction for suggestions for use.)

BLACK HUCKLEBERRY

Gaylussacia baccata

Also known as: Common huckleberry
Habitat: Moist wood edges, roadsides

Perhaps this species received its Latin name from the fact that it was the best known of the huckleberries for its berries — *baccate* means "to bear berries." (Bacchus, of course, was the Greek god of wine!) This small huckleberry bush may at first look very much like the dwarf huckleberry. Its leaves may be oval or oar-shaped and, like those of the other huckleberries, they are untoothed. If you peek below them, though, they will usually have a more yellowish tone. Both surfaces of the leaf, and oftentimes all new-grown areas, will be thickly spotted with resin dots; the leaves and erect young twigs may feel sticky from them. The small groups of greenish-pink to greenish-red flower bells appear anywhere from April to June. These bushes may be side by side with the tall huckleberry, growing in the same areas, but their berries will be a little later in developing, sometimes still ripening on into September. Keep picking, for these are the most commonly found and best of the huckleberries! (See the introduction to the blueberries and their relatives.)

VELVET LEAF BLUEBERRY

Vaccinium myrtilloides

Also known as: Myrtle blueberry, Canada blueberry, sourtop
Habitat: Cool woods, wet areas

This well-branched shrub is distinguished by its velvety, whitened branches. The branchlets have the typical warty appearance of the blueberry group, though on young shoots you may have to look closely to note this trait — they will be covered with fuzz. The oval leaves range in size from three-fourths of an inch to a couple of inches and are pointed on both ends. These are the only blueberries with leaves not at all toothed. The leaves are fuzzy on both surfaces, especially the lower. The whitish or pinkish bell-shaped blooms of early summer yield, in August, blue berries covered with a white powdery haze. These are somewhat sour, and will need sweetening to make a good jam. (See the introduction that precedes this group of related plants.)

LATE LOW BLUEBERRY

Vaccinium angustifolium

Also known as: Common low blueberry, small-leaved blueberry
Habitat: Nearly any open, rocky pasture, road or wood edge

The late low blueberry is probably the most familiar species of blueberry in New England. Finely bristle-toothed leaves are one hallmark of this well-branched, small shrub. It is, however, a confusing plant: some varieties will bear blue berries with a whitish bloom, but others will bear shiny black berries. The leaves measure under two inches. Pointed on both ends, they have an elliptical or a narrow diamond shape, and are attached to the stem with a short stalk. Bright green above and lighter below, the leaves may be hairy underneath. The young twigs, too, may be hairy. White to pink urn-shaped flowers of spring will give rise to the berries from late summer through early fall. They're sweet picking if you can beat the chipmunks and squirrels to them. (See the introduction to the blueberries, huckleberries, and bilberries.)

EARLY LOW BLUEBERRY

Vaccinium vacillans

Also known as: Early low creeping blueberry, mountain blueberry
Habitat: Rocky and sandy areas in partial shade

While the late low blueberry sometimes may be a bit hairy, this shrub seldom shows any sign of hairs. The long oval leaves are not so shiny as those of some of the blueberries, but are usually whitish beneath. They may tend to become thicker and more leathery in the heat and dryness of summer. These leaves vary in length from very short to two inches long; they may lack teeth entirely or have just a few. The flowers, which may appear as early as March and continue blooming into early summer, are usually whitish, but may be tinged with pink. Later in the summer, many dark blue berries will develop. These will be hazed with a white bloom, and they are sweet and delicious. As the last flowers fade, the first berries are generally ready; September usually sees the end of the crop. (See the introduction to the blueberries for suggestions for use.)

HIGHBUSH BLUEBERRY 

Vaccinium corymbosum
Photo page #27

Also known as: Common highbush blueberry, garden blueberry
Habitat: Wet areas and moist, cool rocky woodlands

This was the parent strain of many of our cultivated blueberries and is a good producer in its own right as a wild plant. While it is commonly found in New England and the Canadian maritime provinces, it is most comfortable from lower Massachusetts southward. This shrub may grow to ten or twelve feet high. Its yellowish- or reddish-green branchlets are warty, and may have hairs. The leaves are toothless, generally, and green underneath. They are elliptical in shape, and if they bear any fuzz at all it is only a slight amount. The urn-shaped whitish to pinkish flowers that burst forth in May or June produce blue to blue-black berries that ripen later in the summer. If you wait until after July or August to go after them, though, you'll have missed them. The berries have the whitish bloom that immediately tells you you've found a typical blueberry, and they are sweet and delicious. (See the instruction to the blueberries.)

BOG BILBERRY 

Vaccinium uliginosum

Also known as: Tundra bilberry
Habitat: Tundras, mountaintops, shorelines, cold wet meadows and bogs

A well-branched, spreading, often leaning shrub, it seldom exceeds one foot in height. The leaves are nearly stalkless, untoothed, and often leathery. They're smaller than most of the leaves of these related plants, generally never reaching an inch in length, and are oval in shape, sometimes broadest above the midpoint, and pointed at the ends. Their undersurfaces are paler and sometimes a bit downy. Small groups of two to four flowers arise among the leaves during the early summer months. These little bells are white or (more often) pink, and they later produce a very sweet and edible berry. Look for these tiny blue-black fruits with a white bloom late in the summer and on into September. You'll have to do a lot of bending to get them, but their flavor is well worth it! (See the introduction to this group of related plants.)

DWARF BILBERRY

Vaccinium caespitosum

Also known as: Early bilberry
Habitat: Moist, rocky woodlands, along shady shorelines

This low shrub grows less than a foot high, yet produces sweet and well-flavored fruit. You may well find these shrubs in little groups near your favorite swimming spot, but be advised to pick their berries bending over rather than sitting down — ant hills are often found around them. Dwarf bilberry bushes have shiny toothed leaves that are long, oval, and pointed on both ends. They are larger than those of the bog bilberry, but usually do not exceed an inch and a half in length. They're often broadest above the middle. Spot these plants early in the summer when their white or pink bell-shaped flowers appear, alone in the leaf axils, and then look for the light blue fruits during the hot days of late July and August. They resemble blueberries, and have the same whitish bloom. (See the suggestions for use in the introduction to this section.)

DEERBERRY

Vaccinium stamineum

Also known as: Squaw huckleberry, northern deerberry
Habitat: Dry, open woods and thickets

Deerberries look somewhat like large blueberries, but the shrubs that produce them look different enough to give a beginning edibles hunter second thoughts. These rather tall bushes are generally between knee-high and ten feet tall. The leaves, alternate and untoothed, are not leathery, and are usually covered underneath with whitish velvet. The branches are darker in color than those of the blueberries; they're most often a purplish tone, and lack the warts of the blueberries' branches. The thinner branchlets often bear a whitish fuzz, and produce smaller leaves and clusters of greenish or purplish-white flowers in spring. The fruits, each of which has a small blueberry-like crown, have the same green or purple color as the flowers, and often have a hazy whitish bloom. These light-toned, often sour fruits are usually a half-inch or more in diameter, and hang individually like Christmas tree ornaments from the fruit-bearing branchlets. They ripen from late summer to early or mid-fall. Though they're not too pleasant eaten out of hand, they are edible and nutritious, and are better when stewed briefly and sweetened. They're quite good company for other fruits in conserves or jams, and their large size makes for worthwhile picking. (See the introduction for further suggestions.)

JUNIPER

Juniperus communis
Photo page #26

Also known as: Dwarf juniper, fairy ring juniper, gin bush, creeping juniper
Season: Fruits, summer through winter

Habitat: Open areas, roadsides, dry rocky hillsides, mountainous areas; landscaped areas, especially where there are sandy soils

While it can grow as high as a small bush or tree, the common juniper is most often found sprawling; you'll easily recognize this unbalanced but appealing evergreen bush. Many birds and animals find safe shelter under the juniper's low, prickly branches, and you'll see why when you attempt to walk through or sit upon these evergreens.

The juniper has needle-like, hollow and sharply pointed leaves growing in whorls of three around its branches. Each leaf is usually about a half-inch long, three-sided, and marked with an identifying broad white band on its upper surface. This band, running the length of the rigid leaf, shows the location of the pores, or **stomata**, of the leaf. If you are careful, you may be able to harvest the berry-like fruit without gloves, but it takes patience and determination. Don't dive straight in; work up from the lower part of the branch.

Juniper bushes are separately sexed. The female bush produces small, hard, berry-like cones. These look very much like blueberries, but they lack the crowns of blueberries and are not at all juicy. Each will have a whitish bloom on its deep blue-gray surface. The seeds contained in juniper berries will not germinate for two to three years, but, if you'd like to raise your own bushes, dipping the berries very briefly in boiling water will reportedly shorten this time. Starting juniper bushes from seed will be certainly easier than digging their widespread, very intertwined roots. It is this interlocked root system that makes them so valuable for holding soil on hillsides.

Juniper berries are used to give gin its flavor, and may have given gin it's name as well: The French word for juniper is "genévrier," and gin is called "genièvre." In years past, these berries were known for their ability to combat scurvy; undoubtedly, they are high in vitamin C. They were also known for their diuretic effects, so to be on the safe side, ***do not eat too many of them.*** (Juniper berries are used only as distinctive flavoring agents, so you'd be unlikely to use them every day.)

To make a juniper beverage, brew a few of the young sprigs and berries for five to ten minutes in hot water. Strain and sweeten with a little honey, and you'll have a soothing tea that is very good for sore throats. I've also found it nice occasionally on those hot "dog days" of summer when, through overindulgence in liquids or whatever, the body seems to bloat and retain extra liquids; the slight diuretic effect of juniper tea seems to help.

The berries have their own indescribable flavor, and lend a very nice piquancy when roasted with meats like veal, lamb, or venison. Crush the berries first, and remove them before serving the meat or gravy. Add a few to an herb vinegar, or plunk three or four into a pot of chowder. (Again, remove before serving, for these are not chewable berries.)

A very good selling point for juniper berries is, they do not need to be stored. In fact, if you can find a juniper with its nose above the snow in the winter, the frozen berries, preserved naturally, can be plucked for wintertime use. That's the time we're most apt to be brewing tea for wintertime sniffles, and when those berries seem to flavor a venison roast just right!

AMERICAN YEW

Taxus canadensis
Photo page #26

Also known as: Ground hemlock, red-berried hemlock, red-berried yew
Habitat: Moist woods and road edges

THIS IS A POISONOUS PLANT

This evergreen, too small to be called a tree, is attractive to many people as a holiday decoration. Its red berries may also be tempting to children or a stranded hiker or hunter, but ***they should not be risked — the seeds are very poisonous.***

A relative of this plant, the Japanese yew *(Taxus cuspidata)*, has been used heavily for landscaping around homes and public buildings. It, also, is poisonous.

Both of these species contain a material known as **taxine**, which slows or stops heart action. ***All parts of the yews are poisonous.***

The needles are flat and pointed. In some species of yew, the needles are a glossy dark green on the upper surface and yellowish on the underside. On the American variety, they are green on both surfaces, and each needle has a short stalk that leaves no bump on the stem when it parts from it. Overall, the plant resembles a balsam fir, but grows as a low straggling shrub rather than as a tree. (Cultivated shrubs are taller and more well-kempt.)

Pick these plants for decorations or plant them around your home, but be wary. If you have children playing in your yard or animals in pastures, you might decide to remove any yew plants from those areas.

ROSES

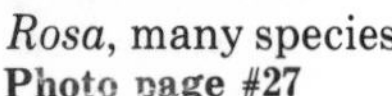

Rosa, many species
Photo page #27

Also known as: (many specific names)
Season: Flowers, summer; hips, late summer through winter
Habitat: Gardens, road edges, shorelines, pastures, nearly any open or semi-open area

How many people delight in the fragrance and beauty of the rose, yet think that only the wild rose can supply them with vitamin C-packed rose hips! Nature and rose specialists alike have contrived to interbreed the roses and create new forms, and there are many varieties of common and uncommon roses. Take note: the pampered hybrid rose's hips are just as usable as those on the stalwart, prickly wild rose. There is, however, one factor that detracts from the garden rose's usability — that is, the use of sprays to control insects. You don't need spray residue in your tea or jam!

Rose hips can be collected nearly year-round; you may even find some naturally frozen ones in mid-winter. Whenever you gather them, be sure to inspect every rose hip for insect invasion — holes or discolorations are a giveaway. It's easy to collect enough rose hips to provide valuable summertime vitamins throughout the stormy season.

You may dry the rose hips (whole or with the seeds removed from the outer pulp) for future use, or process the fresh ones to make jams, jellies, teas, syrups, purees, fruit barks, even soup. Some recipes recommended stewing the washed hips whole, after removing the withered calyx, then straining out the seeds. You may also peel the outer skin and fruit from the seedy core, and stew or soak to make a jam, adding sweetening as desired. (Barberries could be added to the rose hips in a jam, to provide natural pectin; apples serve the same purpose.)

Rose hips are a delicious trail nibble, and may be added fresh to a fruit or gelatin salad. Rose hips are highly respected for their soaring vitamin C content, and are used as the basis for most natural vitamin C diet supplements. It has been found that they are far superior in vitamin C content to citrus fruits. Wild rose hips have provided needed vitamin C in shortages of other vitamin-C-rich foods. Outdoor people would do well to become familiar with these fruits, for the dried, frozen, puckered-up tomato-like hips could be an important source of food for someone lost. (The prickles of the stems will be a significant identification feature in winter.)

Considering that rose hips are a ready standby rich in important nutrients, local and free for the price of gathering and processing them, it seems utterly impractical to rely (as many of us do) on tropical imports, often treated and transported at great cost, for our vitamin C!

REDBUD

Cercis canadensis
Photo page #27

Also known as: Judastree
Season: Flowers in early spring, pods in early summer
Habitat: Lawn ornamentals, woodlands

The redbud is easy to spot in the spring. The pea-like flowers appear before the leaves, and are a beautiful sight as they outline the branches of this tree in soft violet-pink tones. The heart-shaped, smooth-edged leaves that later appear generally range from four to five inches broad, and are pointed.

Most trees will still be leafless when the redbud puts on its show. Gather some of the flowers and flowerbuds — they may be added fresh to a salad or fried, plain or in batter. They are delicious served stir-fried with other tender vegetables; their relationship to peas will be sensed in their flavor.

The multiple flowers develop edible pods two to three inches in length and a half-inch or so in width. At first green, they'll later darken to deep rose browns, dusky echoes of the flowers' hues. The young pods, too, sauteed for a short time in butter, are an excellent vegetable. Catch the pods when they're very young, and cook them together with some of the late flowers. (The older pods are not used.) ***Be certain of identification,*** though, before you pick the redbud pods—several other trees manufacture similar structures.

This is a wonderful tree to consider for landscape planting. Not only will it grace your home with its lovely blossoms, gild itself in final beauty in the fall, but also add a new delicacy to your menu.

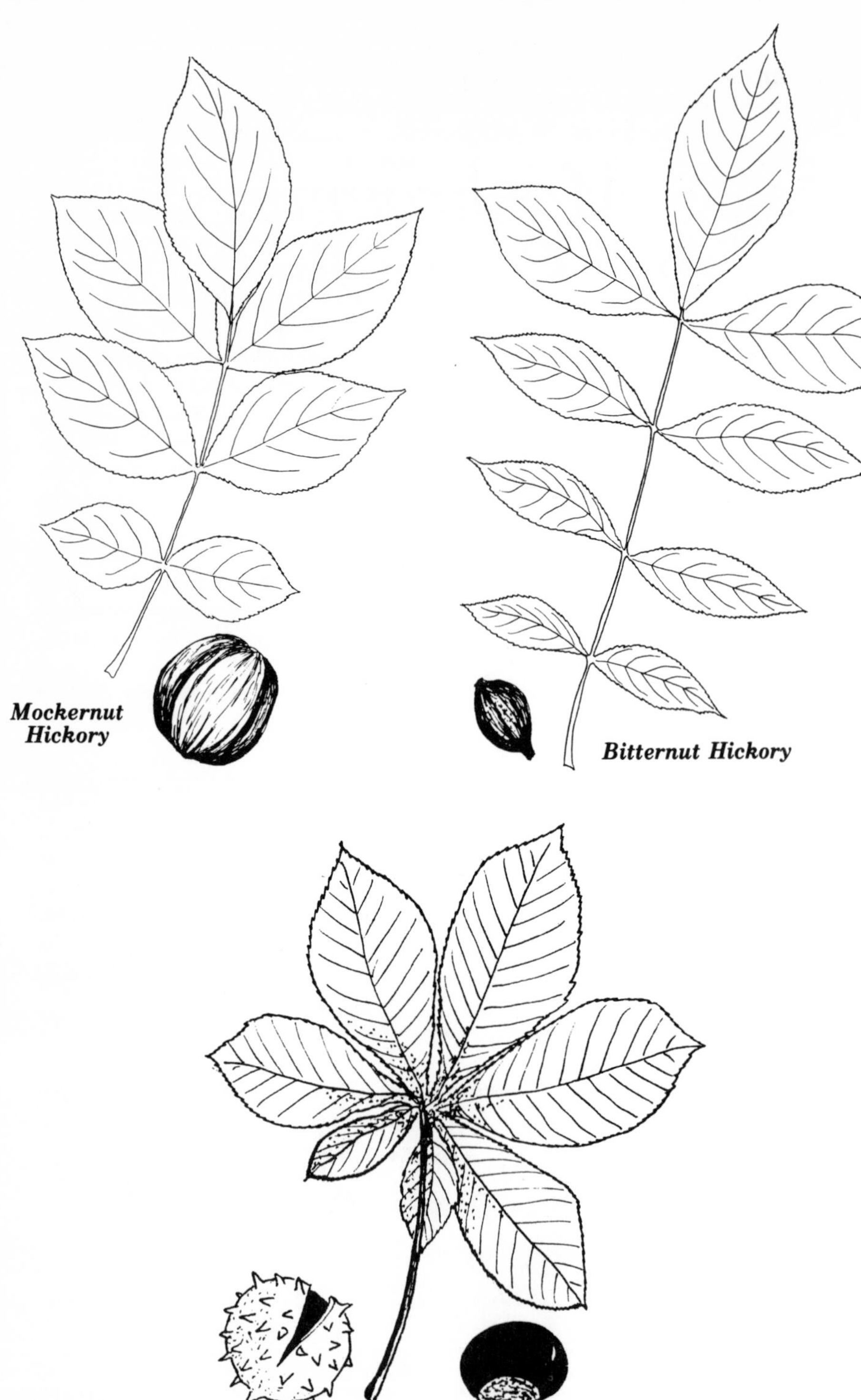
Mockernut
Hickory
Bitternut Hickory
Horse Chestnut

IX

Mushrooms and Other Fungi

Mushrooms can be delicious or deadly, and there is little room for experimentation. The many edible mushrooms are certainly identifiable, but lack of due caution could lead to a harmful or even fatal mistake. If you have small children, it is wise to become familiar with the poisonous species (such as the amanita family) which are commonly found, even if you never choose to hunt mushrooms for the table. If you do intend to sample the edible varieties of free, wild fungi, be sure to commit the traits of the amanita mushroom to memory.

Some of the poisons possessed by "toadstools," as so many people call them, are discussed under plant poisons in the introduction of this book. The spores of these fungi may be high in poison content. The spores are small, invisible on the hands, under fingernails, or on the surfaces of your collecting container or knife. The spores, of course, are not the only poisonous tissues in these fungi.

"Keep your hands out of your mouth!" "Don't eat until you've washed!" These are orders which seem to automatically spout from parents' mouths, but they are crucial commands if unfamiliar mushrooms have been handled.

It is vital to keep different kinds of mushrooms separate as you collect. Many times we've neither the time nor the inclination to certainly identify species in the field, so we pick first and test later (often making spore prints when we get home). We make sure to take along several paper bags for collection, and, if the weather is warm and sunny, our cooler comes too. The bags serve to adequately separate species, and are ***never*** reused. Closing the bags while they are stored in a larger container helps to prevent the spread of potentially dangerous spores. Mushrooms spoil quickly, just like fresh meat. The cooler helps to prevent this. An otherwise edible mushroom, if allowed to decompose, could make you very ill.

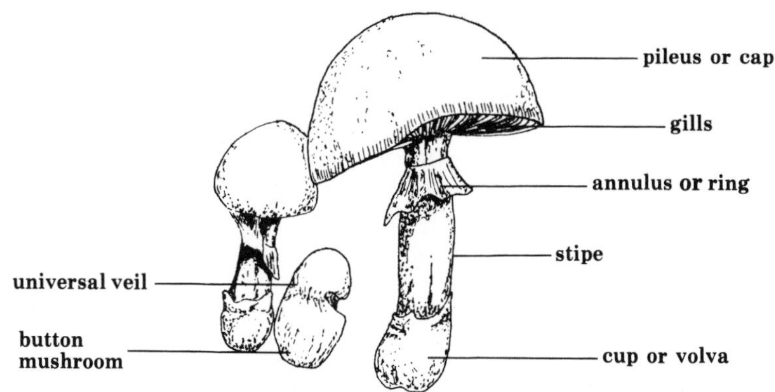

Parts of a Mushroom

In identifying the mushrooms you have gathered it is often important to make a spore print. This will help you to determine the color of the reproductive cells, or spores, produced by the gills. Often the spore color is one of the really distinctive traits of a type of mushroom, and a spore print may provide conclusive evidence that what you have is or is not edible!

A spore print is best made at home, where the caps can be left undisturbed for several hours or overnight. Use both dark and light paper of at least the thickness of standard typewriter paper — the mushrooms will usually give off some moisture. Gently remove each stem from its cap and place the cap undersurface-down on the paper. If you invert a cup or small bowl over each cap to keep breezes from disturbing the pattern made as the spores drift down from the gills, you will have a beautiful mandala made by nature which you can spray-fix and mount.

The Amanitas

The amanitas are, as a group, beautiful to behold. Most of them look large, colorful, and eminently edible. But — don't! While there are a few nonpoisonous amanitas, the group contains some of the deadliest plants known. There are reports of hybrids between the good and bad amanitas, with varying amounts of poisons found in the confusing halfbreeds. I'd advise anyone to leave this group entirely alone.

Below is a list of characteristics which should serve as warning flags. Not all amanitas possess each of the traits listed. Often good mushrooms may have some of these features. At the start of your hunting career, it is better to throw out the baby with the bath water and avoid any mushroom that has any of these characteristics unless you are certain it is not an amanita.

1) When the young amanita develops, the baby mushroom is entirely covered by a membrane called the **universal veil**. The developing button pushes through its surrounding veil. The remnants of this tissue often appear as scattered flakes or rough patches on the mature cap. In some amanitas this veil is so tough that it simply splits, and flakes do not form. The veil remnants may also be washed off by rain. Be sure to look at both young and old mushrooms when checking for these, and keep recent weather in mind.

   At the base of the mushroom, the lower portion of the veil may form a loose or girdle-like cup. It often fits the base snugly, like a sock fits your foot. Again, like a sock, it may sag and wrinkle. In most amanitas, this lower cup or **volva** makes the base look swollen. Collars or ridges at the top of this enlarged base are additional clues. Some have a loose-fitting volva which may break away in the soil if you simply pull the plant from the ground, and others appear to have no cup at all but just a very fat bottom. For this reason, always carefully dig out the base of all collected mushrooms and examine them critically.

2) The **gills** of the amanitas are most frequently white or an off-white tone. Turning the mushroom bottom-side up, or cutting down its length, you'll find that the gills seldom reach all the way to the stalk. They are free from the stem, or narrow to just arrive at it. The gills of the amanitas produce **white spores**.

3) In many mushrooms, a thin membrane connects the young, down-folded cap with the stem. In most, but not all amanitas, this will tear loose at the expanding cap's edge, and remain hanging as an encircling skirt-like ring around the middle to upper part of the stalk. This ring, or **annulus**, is most often white, but may bear hints of the cap's coloration.

FLY AMANITA 

Amanita muscaria
Photo page #29

Also known as: Orange amanita, red amanita, orange or red toadstool, fly poison toadstool, fly agaric

Season: Early and late summer

Habitat: Generally acid soils in evergreen or mixed woodlands, shaded lawns, pastures, roadsides

THESE ARE POISONOUS PLANTS

It is said that, years ago, people who knew the dangerous abilities of this mushroom found it useful in killing insects in their attics, barns, and basements. That's how it got its name: They would take a cap and place it in a saucer of milk or other liquid to attract the bugs whose demise they desired. Apparently, the insects would ingest the poisonous spores along with the liquid. Of course, this primitive insect trap had to be kept out of the way of pets, livestock, and people.

The fly amanita seems to be one of the most prolific and widespread of the amanitas in our area. You can expect an early crop after the first warm summer rains. Unless humidity remains high and regular showers intervene, the very hot days of midsummer will restrict their growth to cool, moist, wooded areas. They'll reappear on a wider scale as cooler evenings and dew return later in the summer.

Some of the fly amanitas are all white, beautiful in their chalkiness. They glow like summer snowballs. More common in the middle and southern states are the reddish-orange varieties. The yellow ones seem to grow nearly anywhere, as do the tan varieties. The tan ones, not of this species, closely resemble the fly amanita, and should be treated accordingly.

You cannot fully rely upon cap color for positive identification. The amount of moisture and sunlight, degree of maturity, and type of soil will cause color variations between the button and adult stages as well as between groups growing at different locations.

Their caps generally range from three to eight inches in diameter. Normally, tannish, yellowish or white flakes are found on the cap. (These may wash away in a downpour.) The upper, outer edge of the cap often bears little lines, called striations, which run in the same direction as the gills. The caps are dome-shaped when young; as their bloom matures, the caps become flat to even concave with upturned edges. The outer tissue of the cap may be any shade from pure white through red.

Cutting through or breaking the cap reveals white flesh. There may be a bleeding of cap pigment into the zone just beneath the upper skin. The gills also are white, though they may become creamy in age. (Rain may spread the cap pigments to them.) The edges of the gills frequently bear minute hairs, but you may need a hand lens to see this.

The slender, firm stem ranges through the same tones as the gills, or may even be tannish. It generally bears a ring which is white to cream in color. This thin-textured ring is just a short distance down from where the gills and cap are found. If you split the stem of the mature mushroom lengthwise, it will usually be hollow, or partly so. At the base of the stem is generally a bulbous bottom. Remains of the volva are apparent as rings or scales just above this base.

The fly amanitas are extremely dangerous, regardless of color, and should be removed from where children play. Small bodies or circulatory systems already weakened by age or disease are probably most vulnerable to the poisons in these mushrooms. Adults in good health who have eaten these mushrooms in small quantities often survive, though they may well wish they were dead while enduring the miseries of amanita poisoning!

Ignorant or thoughtless are the manufacturers and artists who allow illustrations or models of these pretty-looking, lethal mushrooms to appear in childrens' wallpapers, books, lamps, or other articles designed for their use. A child might read of a fairy tale character nibbling from a "magic" red mushroom with white polka dots, or associate the white flecked mushroom on his lamp with home's safety.

The amanitas generally like the soil beneath evergreens. Don't let this fact relieve you, however, if you have a treeless lawn or one hosting only hardwood trees. The spores of these or any other mushrooms are carried by breezes, birds, animals, insects, and even ourselves. They may take hold and sprout anywhere if the conditions happen to suit them. Though it is never found growing on wood, the fly amanita may find a house-shaded patch of lawn just as suitable as the soil under a pine tree. People sometimes have topsoil imported, from sites unknown to them, for improving lawns and gardens. Rich forest loams may support not only excellent turf, but uninvited mushroom spores as well. You may suddenly find an unexpected crop of amanitas where nary a mushroom appeared before.

Reports indicate that extracts of this mushroom are used in isolated areas of the world as an hallucinogen. Some people feel proper preparation renders it edible. Since individual mushrooms, and mushrooms growing in different areas, vary in their amounts of toxin, I sincerely feel it is extremely dangerous to experiment with these mushrooms in any manner.

Specimens of the fly amanita contain varying amounts of the poison known as **muscarine**, sources say. This acts on the parasympathetic nerves. Apparently, the blood vessels dilate, and this causes an extreme drop in blood pressure. The skin flushes, the pupils of the eyes constrict, and the pulse slows. Muscarine is reported to be found in several other related and unrelated species, as well.

Various reports indicate that the fly amanita also contains **muscimol, ibotenic acid**, and other hallucinogenic compounds. These act directly on the central nervous system. The presence of these poisons cannot be detected in the flavor of the mushroom; your tongue cannot tell you that you are poisoning yourself.

If you suspect that someone has eaten a possibly poisonous mushroom, it is important to recover any eaten or non-eaten evidence of what has been consumed in order that proper medical treatment may be given. Quickly contact your local hospital or poison control center. They will tell you what to do, but any evidence you can provide will make their assistance swifter and more certain. **Atropine** is sometimes used as a counter-drug.

These are lovely mushrooms, beautiful to behold and photograph. They serve a function in their ecological niches, helping to decompose organic materials in the soil. They're common. Unfortunately, they're just not for us.

YELLOW AMANITA

Amanita flavocina
Photo page #29

Also known as: Orange amanita, yellow bottom
Season: Spring through fall
Habitat: May be found under evergreens, in mixed woodlands, under hardwoods, along the roadside or on lawns

THIS IS A POISONOUS PLANT

This mushroom is easily confused with the orange-toned muscarias. Its edibility is in question; most authorities consider it poisonous. It's mentioned here because it may be found under the hardwood trees on your lawn. Also, it might lose its flakes to heavy rains and be mistaken for the edible *Amanita caesarea* of historical fame.

This bright yellow to light orange amanita is usually smaller than most of the muscaria tribe, with caps normally in the one-to-four-inch range. The cap bears flakes, often large, and may have a lightly striated margin. In wet weather the cap is often sticky or slimy.

Below the cap, the gills are white to yellowish. Within, the flesh of the cap is usually white, with yellowish to cream tones just beneath the cap's cuticle.

Supporting the cap is a firm, thin stem, decorated above with a thin, yellowish toned or edged ring that is often ripped and sometimes absent. The whitish or yellowish stem widens at the base to form a fat bulb which usually bears the bright yellow powdery remains of the volva.

THE BLUSHER

Amanita rubescens
Photo page #29

Also known as: Red-staining amanita
Season: Spring through fall
Habitat: Woodlands, roadsides, often blooming in great quantities

NOT RECOMMENDED — THERE MAY BE DEADLY HYBRIDS

This amanita is reported to be edible, but I wouldn't consider picking it for multiple reasons. There are many creamy to tannish-toned deadly amanitas. If the spores of one of these tannish, poisonous amanitas developed in the same plot of ground as a group of blushers, it would be very difficult to be sure it was not a blusher. There is also the possibility of a hybrid with the appearance of a rubescens, but the chemical make-up of one of the dangerous varieties. The chance of even one deadly mushroom winding up at the dinner table is just too serious.

The blushers' caps, ranging in size from three to six inches in diameter, are supported by a stem whose length is usually from four to seven inches. The caps range from white or nearly white to shades of reddish brown. The gills are white. Where cap or stem are wounded, generally the injured tissue displays reddish hues, the basis for this mushroom's name. There is a fat base on the stem.

PANTHER AMANITA

Amanita pantherina
Photo page #29

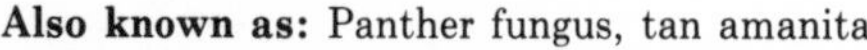

Also known as: Panther fungus, tan amanita
Season: Late summer and fall
Habitat: Woods, pastures

THIS IS A POISONOUS PLANT

This deadly amanita with its three- to five- inch caps *looks* innocent enough. With its flakes washed away, one might mistake it for an edible tan mushroom. The cap's color varies from a deep, dull brown through cinnamon tones to a muted light yellowish tan, or even a dingy white. The pigments of the cap's edge may fade with age and showers to nearly gray or white. The cap bears light-colored pointed flakes, and the margin is generally marked with striations.

Beneath the skin, the flesh is white, just like the gills. The solid stem usually at least equals the cap's diameter in its length. Normally, the large bulbous base of the stem bears a couple of ridges just above the bulb. The large white ring is usually found about midway along the stem, its outermost margin thickened and often grooved.

DESTROYING ANGEL

Amanita virosa
Photo page #29

(See the following description)

SPRING AMANITA

Amanita verna

Also known as: Death cap, white angel, white devil, poison toadstool
Season: Spring through fall
Habitat: Woodlands or edges of woods

THESE ARE DEADLY PLANTS

Pure white, like specters beckoning from the grave, these two mushrooms may be confused with some of the harmless species such as *Agaricus* or *Lepiota* by an avid, incautious mushroom hunter. Early in our days as fungus fanciers, we had such a misadventure. We had picked *Lepiota naucinoides*, an all-white mushroom. My father brought in what he thought was another *Lepiota*. Fortunately, before I cut this button to have it join the rest, something told me to double-check its identity. It's likely I would never have had the opportunity to tell this tale if it wasn't for that second thought; five people might have died shortly after eating that batch of mushrooms. The memory still sends shivers down my spine.

Even a small quantity, a nibble, may be deadly. These are the mushrooms I consider to be the very ultimate of the dangerous ones. Both species look innocently beautiful, resembling each other closely. Their pure white caps may become stained by soil contents, but normally are a glistening snow white, and are without flakes, warts or striations. Usually the entire mushroom is an unchanging white, firm and delicious-looking.

The high-up ring is large, white, and usually does not wash or break away. The sac-like volva which surrounds the enlarged base sticks closely to the bulbous bottom of the spring amanita, and is more loose and evident in the angel.

What makes this pair of closely related beauties all the more sinister is that symptoms of poisoning from them may be hours or even days in appearing, far too late to remove them from the digestive tract. There are no bad odors or tastes (which would be extremely dangerous to test) to warn you away. There have been reports of them forming hybrids with other types of amanitas, a strong reason for leaving this entire group alone!

Do not touch these. Handle them with disposable materials if you must move them. Do not carry any of these in an open container in your vehicle. If they have been close to, or touch, any other species which you are collecting, destroy the entire lot. Thoroughly wash any object that has been in contact with them.

PLEUROTUS MUSHROOMS

Pleurotus sapidus (Sapid Mushroom)
Pleurotus ulmaris (Elm Mushroom)
Pleurotus ostreatus (Oyster Mushroom)
Photo page #30

Also known as: Savory mushroom, tree mushroom, fall tree mushroom, spring tree mushroom

Season: Sapid and oyster, spring through summer; elm, fall

Habitat: Hardwood trees, dead or cut wood with bark still on

There are three commonly found pleurotus mushrooms. The oyster mushroom, *Pleurotus ostreatus*, the savory mushroom, *Pleurotus sapidus*, and the elm mushroom, *Pleurotus ulmaris*, are all edible and fine. The name of the last one gives away their preferred habitat: All three generally grow on elms or other broad leaf trees. There is little to really distinguish one of these from the others, except for minor differences in spore color or growing season.

Pleurotus mushrooms grow ***only*** on trees. The stem is attached to the cap off-center (it is never central) and sometimes the mushroom seems to lack a stem entirely. The gills are cream to white; some of the pleurotus species have gills which extend down the stem, while others are rounded or notched at the point where they join the stem. None of the pleurotus mushrooms are hairy or scaly on the cap. They differ only slightly in outward appearance, varying in color from light tannish-white to grayish or nearly pure white. It is doubtful that the beginner would confuse these with any harmful species; indeed, this is one of the first groups of mushrooms we dared to pick. They freeze well, and cook nicely to a golden brown. They shrink less in cooking than many varieties, and have an excellent flavor.

The oyster mushroom and the sapid are practically indistinguishable. The oyster mushroom varies from white to ashy gray, and may become yellowish as it becomes older. The sapid may run to slightly darker shades, being quite white when it is young, or at least a cream color. The caps of either kind vary in size, partly depending upon age and partly upon the conditions under which they are growing. They range from "baby" inch to inch-and-a-half caps on up. Generally, the mature caps are about six to eight inches across. The gills of either mushroom are white. They are broad, and rather well spaced. In the sapid mushroom they often run down the stem, while in the oyster the portion that extends down the stem may hardly be visible. In both species the stems may grow from a common base, and the caps overlay each other in shelves. The stems are usually whitish or cream-colored, and may be a little hairy. It does not really matter which one is picked, for either is a lovely mushroom. The oyster mushroom got its name from the fact it may be cooked as raw oysters are, and made into an oyster stew or any other oyster dish. This mimic usually escapes recognition! The oyster and sapid pleuroti are apt to be found from spring through summer, while in the fall it is the elm pleurotus which you've likely spied.

The elm pleurotus is found on wood only, as is the oyster or sapid. Generally these mushrooms are found on elm wood, and there is a large quantity of dead elm wood around since Dutch Elm disease has wrought havoc to these majestic trees. They will also be found on maples and occasionally on oaks, but we haven't observed them on anything else (though they are reported to grow on poplars, too). They will sprout from standing dead trees, wounds and dead branches, or even the wood in your wood pile. This mushroom is practically indistinguishable from the oyster and sapids. It prefers cool weather, and so is less apt to contain insect larvae. The cap is white, or white with a yellowish tinge, and the caps do not overlay each other so much as in the other two species. The gills are the same in appearance as those of the others, turning yellowish when old, and, rather than extending down the stem, are generally notched near it. The stem is attached to the side or off-center. It is seldom you'll see a central stem on any of these three: This happens only if the mushrooms are growing from a structure such as the top of a stump. Even then, some in the group will display the normal traits, and only a few will have centralized stems. If all in the group have stems springing from or near the mid-point of the cap, leave them alone!

It might be interesting to try cultivating some of these pleuroti. In Hungary, the sapid has been cultivated on cut elm branches. This is similar to the method used by the Japanese in their cultivation of *shiitake* mushrooms: They simply stack up the logs and sprinkle them at regular intervals with water containing the mushroom spores.

The name "sapid" means savory, and it could apply to any of these three cousins. They can be boiled, fried or broiled. They may, especially if older, maintain a somewhat chewy nature if just boiled. Frying or broiling seems to be the choicest means of preparing them.

These mushrooms freeze well. As with any mushroom, it is wise to cut through the caps to determine whether any insects have beaten you to your meal, especially in spring or early summer. If there are any tunnels or holes through the flesh, discard the caps. The little insects known as "springtails" often hide among the gills, but these will wash away. The best place to throw invaded caps might be your wood pile!

After checking for invasion, we simply wash the caps well, pat them dry, and then wrap them tightly in plastic or aluminum foil and pop them into the freezer. Since mushrooms spoil rapidly, it's not advisable to wait too long before freezing or preparing them; the best time is right after you have brought them home. For this reason, we don't keep them in the freezer for more than four or five months. When we need some sliced mushroom caps, we remove them from the freezer and cut them into the thin slices which cook so well. Since they are still frosty, they are rewrapped and promptly tucked back into the freezer. We'll only do this twice before discarding any remnants, for it is dangerous to refreeze, and each time the wrapping is opened some of the tissue does thaw a little. If you're serving the mushrooms with meat or in a soup or stew, fry them gently and long until they are a light caramel brown. They add their own distinctive and lovely flavor. They make a great mushroom soup, too!

Older caps may be tough, especially toward the inner stem portion. We "feel" for this as we slice them to check for bugs. If the knife begins to meet resistance, the remaining tough portion is simply added to our front lawn — it needs any help it can get!

Some traits you might find under particular conditions, and which might worry you in your positive identification of these mushrooms, may include the presence of tattered or split edges on the caps. This is apt to happen under rapid growth conditions, or under severe drying. If you notice such variations, consider the weather during the previous few days. The gills may seem ripped or tattered, not smooth. This is often true of the sapids, and may occur in either of the others, especially if the mushroom is older or dry. For verification, check the younger caps. If no youngsters are present, be sure these are rips and tears and not regularly saw-toothed edges. ***Beware of tree mushrooms with gills that are truly saw-toothed.*** These are not pleuroti!

These are easy mushrooms to spot from your car as you drive down country roads. We've found the best hunting to be on roads which run generally east-west, but the pleuroti also like the side of a north-south road, facing southeast. Very often they are within reach, and we've collected literally a large cooler full from one or two trees within just feet of each other. Sometimes they grow high on the trees. At this point, the best bet is to wish them luck in spreading their spores into more convenient locations! Often, if you'll check the same spots a day or two after rains, you'll find more than one crop of pleurotus mushrooms growing on the same tree. This makes hunting so much more convenient! You're also sure to get those tender, insect-free babies that way.

COMMON INKY CAP

Coprinus atramentarius
Photo page #30

Also known as: Ink cap, ink mushroom, blackened toadstool
Season: Best in spring and early summer, early fall
Habitat: Rich soil, lawns, gardens, near bases of trees

THESE MAY HAVE HARMFUL EFFECTS IN COMBINATION WITH ALCOHOL

The common inky cap is seen not nearly so often as its little brother, *Coprinus micaceus* (see Little Inky Cap, which follows). It is worth looking for, though, since its caps are larger.

The specimens pictured here are not entirely typical. These had grown in the first true warmth of the season after very heavy spring rains — a situation entirely appreciated by inky caps. We must have turned a few heads as we sprawled on the lawn of a funeral home to photograph their shining glory! These lush specimens had grown from fertile soil above some decaying tree roots.

Normally, in less wet weather, the caps would have been less spectacular in color, perhaps a powdery, dull gray-brown with only yellow tinges rather than shimmering gold. It's likely, too, that the flakes would have been smaller and fewer. The caps may be nearly smooth if they've grown slowly, but generally their margins bear the same furrows and unevenness seen here.

Unless completely pulled up in their youth by someone careless of their worth, inky caps will appear year after year in the same spot. The fashion in which inky caps release their spores gives this group of mushrooms their generic name of *Coprinus*: The name literally means "filthy," and refers not to where the mushroom grows, but to the black, wet mess they produce. Enzymes manufactured within the two- to four- inch wide caps turn the gills to a liquid which transports the spores to the ground as it dribbles down the stalk. Of course, by the time they've turned this neat trick, the mushrooms are not exactly attractive for eating! You cannot stop this process, even by refrigeration. At least, seeing the adult caps in this condition, with mature gills gooey and partly missing, is reassurance that you have found true inky caps.

The gills begin as creamy white structures, thin and closely placed like pages in a book. Later they develop brownish tones with graying edges, finally turning black as the ebony spores develop. Inky caps are very pickable in the early stages. Waste no time in rinsing them lightly to check for visitors and to remove soil or grass. We've seldom found any insects on them, except for an occasional wandering ant.

Cook them to prevent further spore formation and the eventual ink formation. They will freeze cooked or raw. If you would rather freeze them raw, dry them as quickly as possible, wrap them tightly, and store them in the freezer for up to two months. If longer storage is anticipated, blanch them for a few minutes before freezing to destroy (by heat) the autodigesting enzyme. Those mushrooms which have been simply rinsed and frozen may retain enough active enzyme to continue the spore-releasing process when defrosted, so cook them without waiting for them to soften.

These mushrooms require little cooking. They nearly disappear if fried hard, for there is precious little cap tissue, and even the tender white, ringless stems are hollow. Most often, I cut them into bite size pieces and simmer them gently in margarine or butter, whereupon they may lend their delicate but nice flavor to a mushroom soup, or a clam or shrimp chowder. They're a terrific addition to gravy, too. Steam them slowly for just a few minutes, drain, and add to your gravy. (Let them mingle awhile in the warm gravy before serving.) They're good, too, in spaghetti sauce and even on pizza. They'll nearly disappear in the oven's heat, but their flavor doesn't shrink. If you have gathered a large number of inky caps, try baking them gently in a milk sauce.

Atramentarius is, however, an odd fellow among the inky caps. A material in these particular caps ***may produce nausea*** and disturbances of the nervous and circulatory systems in some people if they drink alcohol at the same meal in which this inky cap is eaten. (The other inky cap varieties, including *micaceus*, do not contain this substance.) Generically known as **disulfiram**, the substance was discovered separately and introduced in 1948 as Antabuse®, which has been used in treating alcoholics. Apparently, patients learn to avoid alcohol to avoid the symptoms brought on by the combination of the two substances!

In the body, alcohol is converted to acetaldehyde, and this is later changed to acetic acid. The conversion takes place in the liver. Acetic acid is easily handled by the body, but disulfiram prevents this final product from being formed by blocking the action of the liver enzymes. The presence of great amounts of acetaldehyde in the bloodstream can cause real discomfort. Symptoms include shortness of breath, sweating, nausea, vomiting, chest pain, drop in blood pressure, and possible loss of consciousness. The use of Antabuse® is discouraged if the person has heart disease or is taking any other medication, and any attempt to use the disulfiram contained in the inky cap for purposes of treatment must be considered unwise or dangerous — there is no way to determine the strength of the chemical in any given batch of mushrooms.

This little inky cap is a delicious and nutritious addition to your wild grocery list. There is just this one caution to be observed: Don't take alcohol in the same meal that features this mushroom. In fact, it might be better to avoid eating *C. atramentarius* if you have a medical problem, anticipate surgery, or are pregnant or nursing.

LITTLE INKY CAP

Coprinus micaceus
Photo page #32

Also known as: Sugar inky cap, granular inky cap, spring inky cap
Season: Early spring and fall
Habitat: Rich soil around living or dead hardwood trees, or over underground remnants and roots of hardwood trees

These are one of the harbingers of spring. You need to pick quite a number of these tiny (one to one and a half inch long) caps to make any use of them worthwhile, but the effort usually seems well rewarded when the other mushrooms are yet to bloom. Fortunately, these little inky caps spring up in such great numbers that there's no problem in picking enough.

Their close kinship with *Coprinus atramentarius* (see Common Inky Cap) is seen in their gradually dissolving mature caps, and this affords an almost instant first identification trait. The caps of these two- to five-inch-high mushrooms may vary according to growing conditions. If they've been spurred to sprout by spring or fall rains, and then the weather turns hot and dry, there may be cracks on the cap surface. Usually a central top flat section will separate from the rest. These golden brown caps will remain intact if there's normal moisture. All caps will usually bear ridges running in the same direction as the gills, and the edges of the caps may not be smooth, especially in the aged specimens.

The stem is white and hollow. There's neither a bulbous base nor a ring. The mushrooms seem to grow packed together like sardines in a can, cap pressing between cap. Often they'll be pushing up through the blackened, dry mess of the last generation's efforts.

Their gills begin as creamy white, closely packed, narrow structures. They turn gray, then deep brown-black as the spores mature, then autodigest into a soupy mass.

Look closely at the young mushrooms. If you see what looks like sugar granules, or mica specks, you're now nearly positive of identification. The fact that they will grow only in close association with a hardwood tree's remains usually nails the matter down.

Pick the young buttons when they're firm and unexpanded. If there's room, they'll spread out like opened umbrellas with age. There's hardly any flesh to these caps, but the stems are tender, too. Cook these as you would *atramentarius*, the common inky cap. The little inky cap has never been reported to produce any problems at all, though individual sensitivities may exist as with any food.

One word of caution needs to be mentioned. These are most often found around stumps: neighborhood puppy stops. Be sure to wash them well!

RUSTY BOLETE 

Leccinum insigne (Boletus rufescens)
Photo page #30

Also known as: Orange bolete, cinnamon-top bolete
Season: Early summer; fall
Habitat: Mixed woods, shaded roadsides and edges of woodlands

All the members of this genus, *Leccinum*, are reportedly edible. Of them, we've most commonly found the rusty bolete. This species crops up early in the summer during the days which follow rain, and may reappear in early fall. ***All members of this group of boletes have tiny spine-like structures, called scabers, on their stems***, and it is this characteristic that allows us to distinguish them from the other blue-staining boletes. The scabers are black, reddish-brown or deep brown in color; the background material of the stem is white, unless the tissue has been wounded. The stems are often quite plump, but are never enlarged at the base. There is never a ring around the stem.

Imagine a dull orange or cinnamon-colored bowl, its center full of cream cheese topped by fine-pored polyurethane foam. Turn this rusty-toned bowl upside down, and you have a model of the cap of this bolete. Unlike the familiar grocery store mushrooms, boletes have little tubes; the ends of the tubes form a porous surface over the area where you'd expect to see gills.

In the rusty-cap bolete, the pores are quite fine. They are whitish in the button mushroom. Frayed or solid edges of the cap extend beyond the pore surface. As the bolete matures, the pores change color through various yellow and yellowish-olive tones, becoming brown in the senile mushroom. A spore print will show a golden brown or yellowish brown color.

The last key identification feature is seen when you slice down through cap and stem, cutting the mushroom in half. If this is *Leccinum insigne*, or its close and edible cousin, *Leccinum aurantiacum*, the flesh will go through a color change. When first exposed to air the flesh is firm and white, but will show reddish-gray to reddish-blue tones and then blue-black shades. Old-time mushroom hunters warned to never eat a bolete which showed blue stains upon cutting, but these of the scaber stemmed *Leccinum* genus have proved to be quite good and edible.

By cutting each mushroom lengthwise, you are not only positive of its identity but are also able to check for the presence of any insects. If the tunnels of insect larvae are seen, let these specimens continue shedding spores to produce the next crop. Usually only the very young caps will be uninfested. Bring these home. Though they darken considerably upon cooking, they're tasty and good.

In the young mushroom the tubes are not very deep, and we cook them right along with the flesh of the stem and cap. It's not necessary, but we prefer to remove the tubes of the occasional uninfested mature caps we find. These may be fried, broiled or treated as you would any other mushroom.

MEADOW MUSHROOM

Agaricus species: *Agaricus campestris* and others
Photo page #31

Also known as: Pink bottom, lawn mushroom, pasture mushroom, field mushroom

Season: Best in late summer, early fall

Habitat: Lawns, meadows, pastures; never on wood or in forested areas

SEE ALSO WHITE LEPIOTA

If you think these might be related to the mushrooms you purchase at the grocery store, you're right! There are several forms, each showing minor variations on the overall theme, but, all in all, they are very similar. Some meadow mushrooms are pure white from top to bottom, except for the gills. In others, tan, gray or brown tones are intermingled in the silky whiteness of the cap. Often the cap's tone is dependent not only on the variety, but also on soil and weather conditions, as well as age. Some show yellow bruises where they have been handled, and some caps have brownish scales. ***Never, though, will you find an agaricus with warts or flakes on its cap.***

The stems generally are quite sturdy. There is never a bulbous base nor a volva (see *The Amanitas*). Sometimes the stem is thick to the very bottom; sometimes it narrows at the base. Unless it has broken loose, there's usually a ring about halfway up the stem, left by the tissue which once held the cap's edge to the stem. The elderly mushroom may lack this. Most often this ring has a somewhat tattered or fringed margin.

With the meadow mushroom, the gills are the most important identification feature. In the young unopened button, the gills will be a very pale pink or even grayish-pink, but never white. As the little mushroom expands, they become a more definite pink, and later ripen into red-brown tones. When the gills at last mature, their color will be a rich chocolate brown. Turn the fully grown cap (measuring two to seven inches across) upside-down: you'll see that these gills almost, but not quite, reach the stem.

As you should do with any mushroom, slice each from stem to stern, splitting cap and stem lengthwise. The flesh of some of the meadow mushrooms may show a pinkish tinge just below the cap's outer layer. Occasionally, you'll find that the flesh of the stem has turned pink where exposed to air. Even if the cap is quite full and firm and the stem solid, check for the tunnels of wee creatures who also find that "pink bottoms" make an excellent meal.

These caps will leave lovely, delicate blackish-brown spore prints if you'd care to check them further.

Sometimes you'll find a few agaricus late in spring or early in summer. At this time of the year, with insects wooing everywhere, it's difficult to find even an uninfested button. But even these we put to good use: Leaving a fair number of caps to reseed the area, we take the rest home, bugs and all, and toss them on our lawn.

We've successfully begun our own little agaricus farm this way!

Many people consider the buttons the best; still, don't waste the mature caps. If you suspect that you've been unable to remove all the little invaders, the gills may easily be scraped away. If you're using the older caps and stems in a light-colored gravy or chowder, you may wish to remove these dark gills anyway, to prevent discoloration. There is no reason to peel the caps unless they've been too stained to wash clean; a brief washing is all that is needed. Soaking only makes them absorb water which later cooks out, adding cooking time and taking nutrients with it. You'll prevent a lot of needless work if you'll remove dirty portions in the field after you're completely sure of identification.

Don't pick these lovely, free gifts only to spoil them on the way home. They may be carried reasonable distances in an open basket or other ventilated container. If the day is warm, or the trip apt to be long, bundle the mushrooms loosely in a paper bag and tuck them into a chilled cooler. They spoil easily, like meat.

The fresh buttons or young caps and stems are even good raw in a salad. There are many recipes featuring this close cousin of the commercial mushroom which is coddled to grow on sterile manure in specially equipped barns or mines. Wild meadow mushrooms, though, snatched from the wild or a neighborhood park, have had the full benefit of nature's nutrients; after sampling their freshness and flavor, you'll find the grocery store's product pale in comparison.

Can, pickle, or freeze agaricus to preserve excess bounty. The whole mushrooms may be cleaned, patted dry, wrapped, and frozen for short-term storage. Blanching extends their freezer life. We also find it good to slice the mushrooms before freezing. They're then ready to go, straight from cold storage, with no defrosting necessary. And we generally have a few packages of frozen, pre-sauteed slices, ready to flavor a stew, glamorize hamburger, or crown a steak. Stuffed caps may be prepared, partially cooked and then stored frozen tightly wrapped in foil. Zip them into the oven to warm for an instant, mouthwatering dinner.

Get to know them. Study the traits of the harmful amanitas: You'll find many differences. Agaricus is a good beginner's mushroom, for only reasonable care is needed to add mountains of flavor to your wild dinners. People seem to learn to spot these mushrooms quickly.

Are they good for you? Yes! The U.S. Department of Agriculture (Handbook No. 8) lists the commercially cultivated *Agaricus campestris* as containing 123 calories of food energy, 11.9 g of protein, 1.3 g of fat, 19.4 g of carbohydrates, 26 mg of calcium, 510 mg of phosphorus, 3.5 mg of iron, 66 mg of sodium, 1,822 mg of potassium, a trace of vitamin A, 0.40 mg of thiamine, 2.02 mg of riboflavin, 18.6 mg of niacin, and 14 mg of vitamin C in a one pound batch. A second listing is given for "other edible species" (type or types not mentioned). These are higher in carbohydrates and higher in calorie count, a bit lower in protein and higher in fat, but nearly equal to or higher than the cultivated mushroom all across the remainder of the board, especially in niacin, where they're nearly double. I'm sure trace minerals and other nutrients may vary according to the harvesting site. Reportedly, mushrooms are quite high in non-protein nitrogen, which may mean they have additional value to us as protein-forming food sources.

One word of caution to the meadow mushroom hunter: Beware of areas near gardens or ornamental bushes. These places are often sprayed with insecticides. Lawns boasting of weedlessness may have been layered with chemicals designed to destroy broad-leaved herbs. None of these materials belong in your diet. Look instead to the unkempt pasture. It's better, in my estimation, to dodge cow flaps than poisons!

HORSE MUSHROOM

Agaricus arvensis (Psalliota arvensis)
Photo page #31

Also known as: Large pasture mushroom
Season: Late summer through fall
Habitat: Same as meadow mushroom

These firm, full-flavored beauties usually make their appearance in late summer or during autumn's golden glory. They like sunny, temperate days and cool, dewy nights. If early summer imitates these conditions, a few may be fooled into sprouting.

They may form huge caps. We've found mature horse mushrooms measuring up to eight or nine inches in diameter, but these are exceptions. They normally boast four- to seven-inch widths. Each is almost a meal in itself. Even the buttons that become the giant caps are a sight to behold! The juvenile caps may measure two to three inches through. It doesn't take many of these to produce a hearty mushroom stew, and what stuffed mushrooms the mature caps make!

Button mushrooms of this variety may be a bit confusing to a novice, especially if they are of normal to small size. Their very immature gills are an off-white tone. They're not the chalk-white or creamy tone of the amanitas, but they would startle a wise hunter. Other traits help to differentiate these, however:

The gills gradually mature through grayish-pink and brownish-pink shades to their ultimate rich blackish-brown color. They are not attached to the stem. Though, like the amanita, the horse mushroom generally bears a ring around the stem, its ring is double-layered. As on the cap, some shades of yellow may be spotted on the ring. Sometimes the lower edge of this annulus is cracked. The ring tissue, while it still connects the stem and the cap's edge, is a very specific indicator of identity in the immature mushroom. In the horse mushroom it will appear to project, starlike, in a series of broad crown points; these will reach from around the stem midway to the cap's edge. These points are actually the tougher lower layer of this membrane. As the tissue pulls free of the expanding cap, some of the thinner ring skin may adhere to the margin of the cap and hang in remnants. The edge of the cap usually overhangs the gills.

The stem is chunky, and often large at the base, though it possesses neither a bulbous bottom nor a hint of a volva. Upon splitting the mature mushroom, you'll find the stem is hollow. Long exposure to the air, firm handling, or larvae invasion may cause the development of yellow pigments.

At the top, the cap's surface is typically a silky white. The central portion often is tinged yellow or tan. Yellow bruises may appear in this flesh, too.

To many people, the freshly cut flesh will have a licorice scent. This delicately flavored variety of *Agaricus* often grows slowly over a period of days, giving you ample time to spot it and pick. It keeps well and freezes or cans beautifully.

PUFFBALLS 

Calvatia cyathiformis (Cup-shaped Puffball)
Calvatia craniiformis (Skull-shaped Puffball)
Calvatia gigantea (Giant Puffball)
Photo page #31

Also known as: Poor man's French toast, muffin mushroom, bread mushroom

Season: Late summer through early fall

Habitat: Grassy fields, parks, lawns

These constitute an outstanding reason to stop mowing your lawn around the middle of August. Hands down, puffballs are probably the easiest and safest of the beginner's mushrooms, and you can usually manage to "farm" some on your own lawn. They are found in great numbers over a fairly short season. They're usable in many ways, but we've found no satisfactory way of freezing them. We simply have a puffball feast, from breakfasts through suppers, throughout the time we're blessed with their appearance. Even mushroom-hating children convert to puffball lovers.

Yes, these are the brown balls you kicked in the park or on a neighbor's lawn, or threw at your childhood enemies, laughing as the clouds of brown spores erupted from the shattered surface. You were actually doing this breed of mushrooms a favor, and perhaps it is the children with whom we should credit the widespread occurrence of puffballs in late summer. If you find a mature puffball, don't kick it; instead, bring it tenderly home and smash it onto an open area of your yard! You may be rewarded with your own crop of puffballs during their next growing season.

The skull-shaped puffball *(Calvatia craniformis)* looks like a bulky muffin which has overflowed to form a rounded, baked-bun top. The cup-shaped puffball *(Calvatia cyathiformis)* looks for all the world like a round loaf of bread, or a round tan stone, sitting proudly above a lawn's cropped height. Many times we've run eagerly to a spot only to find we've not found a puffball, but a very unchewable field stone. The giant puffball *(Calvatia gigantea),* king of the group, is not found so often as the others. When you do find one, be prepared for majestic slices of goodness which will feed an army. We've found these most often in pastures, rather than on lawns; one of these looks, at first sight, like a volleyball someone forgot to bring home. The giants are creamy white in color, whereas the smaller *Calvatias* are more often a baked-crust brown. We harvest these great "ostrich eggs" early in the fall, and have found some enormous ones that measured a good fifteen inches through and weighed nearly ten pounds. The average giant puffball, though, measures seven to ten inches across.

A puffball is a puffball, whether it is white or brown. The only thing with which you might confuse a small puffball might be a button of a large amanita before it has ruptured the all-encasing volva. The one test you need to perform is to slice down through the puffball. The inside of any good puffball will look like cream cheese or finely textured bread all the way through. If you have accidentally picked the button of a mushroom, you'd see the stem and gills, and the texture of the flesh would look more like white plastic. If the puffball is too mature for eating, the creamy inner flesh will have turned a dingier shade of dirty yellow, gray, purple, or brown. Although they are, at this stage, no longer good to eat, do take one or two home; if you'd like a patch of puffballs closer to your kitchen, you can allow them to inject your lawn or field with their spores.

The outer skin of a puffball often holds grit particles, and is best removed. We've found that the easiest way to prepare puffballs and to remove their outer skin is to slice them like loaves of bread. (The resemblance is remarkable!) The outer crust may then be skimmed off by passing a knife between it and the "cream cheese" interior. At this point you have a slice one quarter to one half inch in thickness that is ready to be used.

The marshmallow-like flesh of the puffball is nearly tasteless. Its adaptability lies in the fact it will take on the flavor of nearly anything. Cube this into a salad dressing, and let them mingle for a half hour while you prepare the rest of the meal. Puffballs don't need to be cooked! A sour cream dressing will seem to have lumps of cheese, a blue cheese dressing will seem to be positively wealthy, and a French dressing will have heartily flavored chunks of tongue-teasing softness which will amaze your family and guests!

For breakfast, prepare the slices as you would French toast and deck them with a little powdered sugar or syrup. Delicious! The aroma will capture the heart of even the most determined mushroom-hater. Fry them golden brown with other mushrooms to make a stew or chowder, and they're hard to beat. For something besides mashed potatoes with chicken, dip them in a little egg batter which has been laced with chicken stuffing herbs, gently fry, and watch everyone's eyes light up. Or, concoct your own seasonings to accompany puffballs—their usefulness seems endless.

Are they nutritious? I'm sure they are, though the U.S. Department of Agriculture doesn't list them in their handbook. Mushrooms in general are pretty worthwhile food, containing some protein as well as other nitrogen-containing materials. They're usually fairly well provided with minerals, and contain some vitamins. They are definitely not junk food! I feel they add some of the nutrients which may easily be missing when the hot days of summer make both the cook and the appetite lazy. So, as the dog days of August dwindle into cool nights, start stalking nearby lawns and parks for rocks or balls that seem to have cropped up overnight. If you can gain permission, check out the golf course before the golfers hit them out of the way. And next year, don't forget to look right outside your own door!

LITTLE STUDDED PUFFBALL

Lycoperdon candidum
Photo page #31

Also known as: Little spiny puffball, tiny meadow puffball, prickly puffball

Season: Mid- to late summer

Habitat: Nearly anywhere (except wood and woodlands); sandy soils near the ocean, lawns, pastures, waste places

There are several small puffball-like fungi, and most are reported to be edible, at least in their early stages. We know these particular little "golf balls" are nice!

Seldom encountered in the spring, they crop up in large numbers late in July amid the grass a local restaurant thoughtfully keeps clipped in a lot adjacent to its parking area. The well-manicured hospital lawn and golf course in a neighboring town, as well as our own lawn (which we've "seeded" with spores), provide for us amply each summer. A few crops appear as August slides by; these puffballs keep us happy while we impatiently await the appearance of larger forms.

This little puffball is spherical or shaped like a slightly sagged mound of fresh bread dough. The bottom may be crimped slightly where it shallowly enters the ground. There is no real stem. Little pyramid-like spines dot its surface. The fungi vary in size from one to about three inches in diameter, but smaller sizes are more common.

As with any rounded fungus, cut down through the center of each and every one. It should be white clear through. If any dingy yellow, gray or brown material has formed, the puffball has already begun to form spores. I don't know whether it is actually poisonous at this point, but this off-colored material is mushy and ill-tasting. These specimens may be scattered on your own lawn. If the conditions are to their liking, these inedible little balls may begin your very own puffball farm for you.

Most important, if this slice reveals any evidence at all of gill or stem structures, ***DO NOT EAT THIS FUNGUS!*** It may well be an abortive form of some unknown mushroom, or the button stage of a very deadly amanita mushroom. A good puffball will have a pure white interior resembling cream cheese.

This little spiny puffball will have a fairly thick rind surrounding its spotless white interior. It takes a bit of patience to pare enough of these to feed a family. We mainly use them cubed in salads, or fried until lightly golden brown to form the basis of a good mushroom soup. If only a few are found, they're plunked in with stir-fried vegetables or added in tiny hunks to soups, chowders or stews. They may also be pickled, but we find them a bit mushy. They do add a certain smoothness to mushroom catsup, and stretch the supply of other fungi so used.

CHICKEN MUSHROOM

Polyporus sulphureus
Photo page #32

Also known as: Sulphur polypore, chicken polypore
Season: Late summer to autumn, sometimes in spring
Habitat: Dead spots on nearly any kind of tree

The chicken mushroom certainly stands out! The overlapping shelves of this tree-dwelling fungus are generally peachy-red in color to salmon or orange on top, and a bright, sulphur yellow on the underside pore surface. The colors may fade with age; the mushroom is likely to be too tough for eating by then. There is no stem to this polypore. The inner flesh of the caps varies from white to yellow or pale tan. The cap's irregular, wavy surface is dry, and we have found it to be hairless, though some authorities claim it may be woolly-surfaced. The outer edge is somewhat velvety.

Though firm, these caps are not as deep as those of the scaly-top polypore. The flesh is most often less than an inch thick, though the caps themselves may grow to six or more inches in breadth. The outer edge of the cap is a paler tone than the cap's top. The portion of the cap nearest the tree may bear a talcum-powder dusting of white spores from the caps above.

This is one of the first mushrooms we ever ventured to add to our home menu. "Chicken mushroom" very aptly describes the texture, cooked color, and use of its meat. It may be broiled, fried, or deep fried, and used in nearly any recipe calling for chicken, including chicken salad. The meat of this mushroom shreds just like the real item. It has less flavor than the feathered variety, but does well with any of the seasonings that usually accompany chicken. The simple addition of a little more spice will fool nearly anyone into believing it is really chicken in the fritter, soup or salad. If you've been lucky enough to capture one of these chickens while camping, it may be washed and peeled, cut into pieces, skewered, and broiled over a campfire as a different sort of chicken kabob.

This mushroom freezes easily. It is best to gently peel the upper and lower surfaces and wash or blanch the meat before freezing. Cutting it into cooking-size portions before freezing helps, too. In mid-winter the frozen portions can be cooked without defrosting by simply adding a few minutes to the cooking time.

As with the scaly-top polypore, the portions of these caps which are closest to the tree may be tough. The younger the cap, and the moister the growing season, the greater the amount of the cap which will be tender enough to be considered for the table. Experience with your knife will dictate where to stop cutting. It's an easy and delicious mushroom for the tenderfoot hunter to experiment with!

SCALY-TOP POLYPORE

Polyporus squamosus
Photo page #32

Also known as: Scaly tops, spring tree mushroom
Season: Early spring, occasionally late summer-fall
Habitat: On hardwood trees

These mushrooms, probably the first you'll notice in the spring, will jar you from winter doldrums. They are in bloom early, around the time when the fern fiddleheads first appear and when the oaks begin to show young leaves. They grow on the dead or dying trunk of a hardwood tree, especially an elm or maple.

Developing from cylindrical, large buttons with flat tops, they push out erect, firm and proud from the tops of amputated tree trunks, or like solid shelves from the sides of trees. The first few warm weather rains will often produce a magnificent crop, with second growth springing from the same areas you've harvested earlier in the season. There may be a later bloom when the mature summer or fall weather approximates the conditions found in the spring. Seldom solitary, the caps on any one tree may vary from a few inches to a foot or more across. A hunter may fill a grocery bag in a short time with these!

This fungus is creamy in color, overall, with brown to dark brown hairy/feathery scales on the yellowish-tan cap. These scales grow in concentric curves from the offside stem outward. When the cap is dry, the scales will lift from the surface, giving the cap a shaggy appearance. The edge of the cap often curls downward along its edge onto the pore surface. Overall, the cap is found in the form of an indented, roughly bean-shaped shield.

The pores and cut pore surface are white to cream in color or even yellowish in older mushrooms. In youth the pores are fine, but they become angular and larger with age. Often there will be brown spots on the pores where insects have tried to invade, and sometimes pieces of bark or leaf tissue from the tree will be caught up in these pore surfaces. This spore-producing surface may extend down the stem for a distance, becoming net-like on the stem.

The stem is colored like the cap in the early stages, becoming quite dark brown in old age on some of these mushrooms. Typical scaly-tops have their stems attached at the side, or may appear to not have a stem at all. If your scaly-top happens to be growing on a cut-off stump, the stem may at first appear to be in the middle of the cap, but upon closer observation, you'll see the cap does not form a complete circle. The flesh of this mushroom is white, although there may be translucent tannish or grayish areas if it has grown in very wet weather.

Except for the odd circumstance where a stump has been severed at ground level, these mushrooms are never found growing on the ground. ***They always use wood for food.*** Since the appear so early in the season, they are a good beginner's mushroom. As there are few others in bloom at this time, they are not easily confused with other types of mushrooms. They are also easily spotted by the lazy hunter while he/she drives slowly by!

When we first discovered these mushrooms, we checked with several handbooks before tasting them. The authorities listed these as "possibly edible when young," or "non-poisonous." We carefully nibbled only tiny raw samples. They proved to taste like cucumber-flavored rubber erasers. We concluded it was no wonder the books had not spoken of these mushrooms in more glowing terms! They wound up in our garbage pail.

A few years later we decided to brave them again. Their raw flavor and consistency hadn't changed, but when cooked they were decidedly a "horse of a different color." Cooked well, scaly-tops are absolutely delicious. If not broiled or fried for a good length of time they can be rubbery, but harmless. In taste they remind me of the browned edge of a steak. They shrink little in cooking, and are a tasty addition to steak, stews or soups, rice dishes, or wherever you'd like them. Their flavor is one-of-a-kind, gently assertive, and enjoyed by all who have tried them in our home. Thinly sliced, they will cook more quickly. Add them at the last minute to preserve their crispness.

The scaly upper surface and lower pore-bearing surface may easily be removed by gently scraping or peeling with a knife, though this is not necessary. If the surface is sticky, it may have attracted dust, spores, insect droppings, etc., and should be well washed. We've never found these caps to be invaded by insect larvae, but it does not hurt to check for their presence. This is accomplished by slicing through the cap in several areas to look for tunnels in the flesh.

The portion of the cap nearest the stem may be tough. As you slice through the tender portion it will feel like a block of cheese, but if it begins to feel like a raw turnip, you have reached the too-tough zone. You could add these rubbery parts to your compost pile, or throw them at your wood pile to possibly start your own scaly-top garden.

These mushrooms also freeze well. We have held them for a year's time with only a thorough pre-washing before tightly wrapping and freezing the freshly picked specimens. They may be easily sliced while still frozen, so you may take what you need from a good-sized cap and return it to the freezer before it has begun to thaw. They also dry well, and may then be crumbled and added to stews or soups as a combination thickening and flavoring agent. (Please read on to Scaly Lentinus.)

SCALY LENTINUS

Lentinus lepideus
Photo page #32

Also known as: Scaly pine mushroom, train wrecker
Season: Spring through fall

Habitat: Timbers, stumps, railroad ties, and other lumber made from coniferous trees

Some authorities state that this mushroom is edible. Others say nothing. We haven't tried it, but it is included here to make the beginning hunter aware that it is not the same as the very edible scaly-top polypore. The top surfaces of these two kinds of mushrooms look very much alike, and the type of stump the mushroom has chosen (the polypore likes hardwoods, while this scaly fungus prefers conifers) might not be identifiable. However, these two varieties are easily differentiated, although at first glance they appear to be similar.

The scaly lentinus has gills beneath its cap. The gill edges are usually uneven, and most often saw-toothed. There are scales on the lower portion of the stem. The gills generally run down the stem, and the stem is attached centrally on the cap. The scaly-top polypore, on the other hand, has no gills; its undersurface contains tiny pores. The scaly-top polypore's stem is attached off-center, and most frequently at the side of the cap.

WHITE LEPIOTA

Lepiota naucinoides

Also known as: Smooth lepiota, little nut lepiota
Season: Late summer through fall
Habitat: Lawns, roadsides, pastures

DO NOT PICK THESE MUSHROOMS

Although the true *Lepiota naucinoides* is actually an edible mushroom, I sincerely advise against your consideration of it as a food. It too closely resembles the lethal white amanitas. However, since it fruits at about the same time as the lovely agaricus mushrooms and tends to grow in the same areas, it seems inevitable that someone's child or pet will sample these mushrooms. Perhaps this description may be a source of comfort to someone, somewhere, sometime.

The white lepiota is similar to the white amanitas in that it is chalky white, has a firm stem, a white annulus, white gills and leaves a white spore print. You'll have to look closely for the differences, but they are there. Usually this mushroom is smaller than the amanitas, generally standing about four inches tall. One of the white amanitas will have a skirt-like ring, normally found well above the midsection of the stipe. This lepiota has a firm bracelet-like ring, also above the midsection of the stem, but normally it is freely moveable like a ring on your finger. The bottom of the white amanita's stem widens broadly and is usually found to be encased in a volva. The base of the lepiota's stem may be equal in diameter to the stem or it may be smoothly enlarged; it will never show any volval remains.

As the white lepiota matures, the gills often turn pinkish-tan, a tone which might cause a beginning hunter to believe an agaricus mushroom has been found, but they'll never reach the rich umber hues of the agaricus.

There is an additional reason to leave the white lepiota to the mushroom experts: although we have never found them, there are reportedly other lepiotas which look very much like the one described here. Should you find a white lepiota with a basal bulb, and should the enlarged bottom portion curve to the side, you may have found the thinner-stemmed *Lepiota schulzeri*. According to several authorities, this close cousin can make you distinctly nauseous.

During the fall extravaganza of mushroom season, even a seasoned forager can become careless or overly enthusiastic. Impress upon your memory to ***leave white mushrooms with white or light-toned gills alone.*** Check the color of the gills of *every* mushroom you believe to be the delicious agaricus. If you locate a white mushroom which shows no ring, don't even touch the mushroom.

White Lepiota

Bibliography

There are many fine books available dealing with edible wild plants, their identification, preparation and preservation. This list includes some of the ones we have found very helpful.

Abbott, Isabella A., and Dawson, E. Yale — *How to Know the Seaweeds*, 2nd ed., Wm. C. Brown Co., Dubuque, Iowa, 1978

Agricultural Research Service, USDA — *Common Weeds of the United States*, Dover Publications, Inc., New York, 1971

Angier, Bradford — *Field Guide to Edible Wild Plants*, Stackpole Books, Harrisburg, Pa., 1974; *Feasting Free on Wild Edibles*, Pyramid Communications, Inc., New York, N.Y., 1975

Berglund, Berndt, and Bolsby, Clare E. — *Edible Wild Plants*, Charles Scribner's Sons, New York, 1977

Bleything, Dennis — *Edible Plants in the Wilderness*, Life Support Technology, Inc., Beaverton, Oregon, 1972

Crowhurst, Adrienne — *The Weed Cookbook*, Lancer Books, New York, 1972

Dawson, Ron — *Wilderness Is . . . Edible Plants*, Vols. 1, 2, and 3, Ron Dawson, Enterprise, Oregon, 1978

Dwelley, Marilyn J. — *Summer and Fall Wildflowers of New England*, Down East Enterprise, Inc., Camden, Maine, 1977

Fernald, M.L. and A.C. Kinsey — *Edible Wild Plants of Eastern North America*, Harper and Row, New York, 1958.

Gibbons, Euell — *Stalking the Healthful Herbs*, Field Guide Edition, David McKay Co., Inc., New York, 1975; *Stalking the Wild Asparagus*, Field Guide Edition, David McKay Co., Inc., New York, 1975

Gosner, Kenneth L. — *A Field Guide to the Atlantic Seashore*, Houghton Mifflin Co., Boston, Mass., 1979

Grimm, William Carey — *The Book of Trees*, The Stackpole Co., Harrisburg, Pa., 1966; *Recognizing Native Shrubs*, The Stackpole Co., Harrisburg, Pa., 1966

Hall, Alan — *The Wild Food Trail Guide*, Holt, Rinehart, Winston, New York, 1976

Harris, Ben Charles — *Eat the Weeds*, Pivot Edition, Keats Publishing, Inc., New Caanan, Conn., 1973

Klimas, John E., and Cunningham, James A. — *Wildflowers of Eastern America*, Alfred A. Knopf, New York, 1974

Knobel, Edward — *Field Guide to the Grasses, Sedges and Rushes of the United States*, Dover Publications, Inc., New York, 1977

Krieger, Louis C. C. — *The Mushroom Handbook*, Dover Publications, Inc., New York, 1967

Lange, Morten, and Hora, F. Bayard — *A Guide to Mushrooms and Toadstools*, E.P. Dutton and Co., Inc., New York, 1970

Madlener, Judith Cooper — *The Sea Vegetable Book*, Clarkson N. Potter, Inc., New York, 1978

Martin, Alexander C. — *Weeds*, A Golden Guide, Golden Press, New York, 1972

Mellinger, Marie — *Out of Old Fields . . . A Wild Edibles Cookbook*, The Hambridge Center, Rabun Gap, Georgia, 1975

Miller, Orson K., Jr. — *Mushrooms of North America*, E.P. Dutton, Div. of Sequoia-Elsevier Publishing Co., Inc., New York, 1978

Mohney, Russ — *Why Wild Edibles?* Pacific Search, 715 Harrison St., Seattle, Washington, 1975

Muenscher, Walter Conrad — *Poisonous Plants of the United States*, Collier Books, Div. of Macmillan Publishing Co., Inc., New York, 1975

Palmer, E. Lawrence, and Fowler, H. Seymour — *Fieldbook of Natural History*, 2nd edition, McGraw-Hill Book Co., New York, 1975

Peattie, Donald Culross — *A Natural History of Trees*, Houghton Mifflin Co., Boston, Mass., 1950

Peterson, Lee — *A Field Guide to Edible Wild Plants of Eastern and Central North America*, Houghton Mifflin Co., Boston, Mass., 1978

Petrides, George A. — *A Field Guide to Trees and Shrubs*, Houghton Mifflin Co., Boston, Mass., 1958

Rhoads, Sharon Ann, and Zunic, Patricia — *Cooking With Sea Vegetables*, Autumn Press, Inc., Brookline, Mass., 1978

Rinaldi, Augusto, and Tyndalo, Vassili — *The Complete Book of Mushrooms*, Crown Publishers, Inc., New York, 1974

Smith, Alexander H. — *The Mushroom Hunter's Field Guide*, revised and enlarged edition, The University of Michigan Press, Ann Arbor, 1977

Tatum, Billy Joe — *Wild Foods Cookbook and Field Guide*, Workman Publishing Co., New York, 1976

U.S. Department of Agriculture — *Trees—The Yearbook of Agriculture*, U.S. Government Printing Office, Washington, D.C., 1949

Watt, Bernice K., and Merrill, Annabel, et al — *Composition of Foods*, USDA Agriculture Handbook Number 8, December 1963 rev., Washington, D.C.

Weiner, Michael A. — *Earth Medicine—Earth Foods*, MacMillan Co., New York, 1972

Wiley, Farida A. — *Ferns of Northeastern U.S.*, Dover Publications, Inc., New York, 1973

Young, Hugh (English translator) — *Simon and Schuster's Guide to Trees*, Italian edition by Lanzara, Paola, and Pizzetti, Mariella, Simon and Schuster, New York, 1977

Glossary

additive — a foreign substance, organic or inorganic, added to a food to promote freshness, flavor, ripe coloration, or to inhibit the growth of bacteria and fungi.

agaric — an older name applied to many mushrooms, especially those closely related to the *Agaricus* mushrooms.

alga, algae — simple plants which lack true stems, roots and flowers. Algae generally live in water or very wet areas, contain chlorophyll, and carry on photosynthesis; they may contain other pigments which mask the green of their chlorophyll.

alkaloids — organic materials that are alkaline, or non-acid, in nature, including such chemicals as morphine, caffeine, and atropine. Alkaloids are found mainly in the higher plants.

allergy — a sensitivity to an alien material. Allergic reactions may be internal or external, and are most often responses to proteins of plants or animals.

alternate leaves — leaves that are placed step-wise along the stem rather than placed directly opposite each other.

amine — one of a group of organic compounds. Amines are often produced commercially from ammonia.

amino acids — often called the building blocks of protein, these compounds are necessary for a plant or animal to manufacture protein.

annulus — the ring-like structure around the stipe of some mushrooms.

anther — the uppermost portion of the flower's male reproductive parts, supported by the filament; it produces pollen. (Together the anther and filament make up the stamen.)

axil — the junction of the leafstalk (petiole) and the branch or stem to which it is attached.

bane — an old word meaning threat or nuisance; this frequently serves as a prefix or suffix on a plant name to indicate the presence of poisonous or harmful materials.

blade — the wide, leaf-like portion of a seaweed, or the wide portion of a leaf.

blanch — to cause to turn white or lose color; specifically refers to a few minutes' boiling when vegetables are being prepared for freezer storage.

bract — a leaf-like portion or structure just beneath the true flower; this is sometimes colorful, and may be mistaken for a petal.

button — the young, unopened stage of a mushroom.

calyx — the group of sepals which enclose the flower bud, usually remaining behind the petals when the flower opens. In some flowers there are no petals, and the sepals may be colored in their stead.

cap — the uppermost, umbrella-like part of a mushroom.

carbohydrate — a group of organic materials, made up mainly of carbon, hydrogen and oxygen, including sugars and starches.

central nervous system — the brain, spinal cord, and associated nerves.

circulatory system — the heart, arteries, veins and capillaries.

corm — an underground base of a stem that is swollen, containing stored food.

compound leaf — a leaf consisting of more than one leaflet; the leaflets are all developed within a single bud, whereas a simple leaf has a single blade that develops within its own bud.

concave — dished-in at the center; thinner in the central area than at the edges.

conifer — those trees whose fruits are cones; generally, evergreens with needle-like leaves such as the pine and spruce.

convex — thicker at the center than along the edges, having an outward bulge.

corolla — a flower's halo of petals.

crozier — a synonym for the fiddlehead or curved, unopened leaf and stalk of a young fern, derived from the hooked staff carried by shepherds.

dicotyledons — a class of plants that produce seeds with two "seed leaves" or food storage areas. (The young, sprouting plant will have two immediate leaves that may not resemble the mature leaves.)

diuretic — a material that increases the rate at which the kidneys remove water from the blood.

ecological niche — the role a given plant or animal plays in its surroundings.

ecology — the study of the interrelationships of living and non-living things within a given area.

emetic — a material which causes a person to vomit.

entire margin — a leaf edge that is smooth and unbroken rather than toothed, waved, or lobed.

evergreen — a plant which does not shed its leaves all at one time or in one season, but seems to keep its leaves year round; it is never devoid of leaves, though it may shed more leaves during one season than another.

fat — an organic material often used by a plant or animal as a reserve food. In animals, fat is called adipose tissue when stored in special cells. (Most fats are solid at room temperature, whereas related oils are generally liquid at room temperature.)

fatty acid — one of the organic building blocks of fats. Since fats and their breakdown products play many roles in the body, the fatty acids are necessary to life. Some fatty acids are produced from simpler materials within the body, while others must come from the diet.

fiddlehead — a common name for the young, curled fern frond and its stalk. (The shape of the young fern resembles the curled end of a fiddle.)

filament — a thin, hair-like structure; in flowers, it is the very thin stalk which supports the anther.

frond — the name given to the leaf-like portion of a fern or seaweed.

fungi, fungus — a group of plants which do not contain chlorophyll and cannot manufacture their own food; they usually exist as saprophytes (decaying materials) or parasites (living on living hosts). Mushrooms, tree fungi, mildews, yeasts and molds belong to this group.

gills — the thin, vertical sheet-like structures, found beneath the upper layers of a mushroom's cap, that produce spores (the reproductive cells) for the fungus.

g, gram — a metric unit of weight (one ounce equals about 28 grams).

hallucinogen — a chemical which acts upon the nervous system to cause a person to hallucinate. Under the influence of an hallucinogen, a person will experience an altered, dreamlike state of consciousness and may not have a normal perception of his/her surroundings, possibly performing abnormal actions.

herbaceous — refers to a plant without an above-ground, persistent woody stem.

herbicide — a chemical which kills plants.

holdfast — the root-like structure at the base of a seaweed, though it does not carry out the full functions of a root. A holdfast may be able to glue the plant to the substrate upon which it lives, but does not have root hairs, and does not transport water and minerals, as do the true roots.

hybrid — the offspring produced by the crossing of two different species of plants or animals.

inorganic — refers to chemicals not usually found in living systems; technically, not manufactured by living systems.

insecticide — a chemical used to eradicate insects.

intertidal zone — the area located between the normal high tide line and the normal low tide line; that area along the ocean's edge which is alternately covered and exposed by the changing of the tides.

kelp — a common name for many of the algae known as brown seaweeds or brown algae, especially those which have long, flat, ribbon-like blades.

lenticel — a space or opening in the bark or outer skin of a plant which allows gases to enter or escape.

margin — the outermost edge or periphery of a leaf.

mg, milligram — one one-thousandth of a gram (0.001 g).

midrib — the central vein or vein-like structure in a leaf or a simple plant.

monocotyledons — a class of plants that produce a seed with a single seed leaf and food storage area; the young plant will have a single initial leaf. (Grasses and corn are examples.)

non-protein nitrogen — nitrogen which may be used in the human body to form protein, but which is not a component of the protein in food that is eaten.

opposite leaves — leaves arranged so that one is directly across from the other on the support stem.

organic — original meaning, refers to carbon-based chemicals found only in living systems or produced by them. Organic chemicals have been synthesized in laboratories.

ovary — the female reproductive structure which manufactures the eggs or ova; in flowers, the portion of the pistil which containsthe ova and which will ripen the fertilized ova into seeds.

palmate — arranged from a central point, as the fingers are attached to the palm of the hand. Usually refers to leaflets of a compound leaf, or veins of a leaf.

parallel veins — veins in a leaf which do not branch one from another, but are arranged so that all follow the long dimension of the leaf. Monocotyledons have parallel veins.

parasympathetic nervous system — part of the autonomic nervous system; these nerves respond to changes within the body, mainly serving to slow down internal activities. (The other portion of the autonomic nervous system is called the sympathetic nervous system.)

peduncle — a stalk which supports a flower or fruit.

petals — the leaf-like structures which surround the reproductive parts of the flower. Often showy and highly colored, the petals serve to attract insects or other pollinators, and are sometimes specially formed to help ensure that the pollinators visit the reproductive structures.

petiole — the individual leafstalk.

photosynthesis — the process whereby plant cells manufacture food: the energy of light is stored by chlorophyll and utilized in combining carbon dioxide and water to form simple sugars and oxygen.

pinnate — an arrangement wherein the leaflets of a compound leaf are attached along a central stalk.

pistil — the female reproductive structure of a plant, comprised of the ovary, style and stigma.

pollen — the male reproductive cell of higher plants, containing sperm nuclei which will fertilize the ovum or egg within the ovary.

polypore — a fungus which has, instead of gills, a surface that resembles a fine sponge. (This many-pored surface produces spores.)

protein — an organic compound consisting mainly of carbon, oxygen, hydrogen, and nitrogen, in addition to smaller amounts of other materials. Protein is essential for growth, repair and reproduction in plants and animals. (There are many kinds of proteins.)

receptacle — the portion of a flower which may be beneath or around the ovary. The receptacle supports the ovary, and in some plants produces the fruit wall.

resin — a material produced by some plants; usually it is somewhat yellowish and sticky.

rhizome — an underground horizontal stem or runner, often fleshy with stored food, which may serve to send up new plants at a distance from the parent plant.

rosette — an arrangement of leaves or petals which spring from a central point of attachment, resembling the petals of a rose, rather than leaving the central stalk at intervals.

saponine — refers to chemicals found in certain plants which have the common trait of producing soap-like bubbles when shaken with water. These materials are believed to have the ability to break down or alter the fats in the membranes of some cells.

scurvy— a condition caused by the lack of vitamin C. Symptoms include blood vessels which hemorrhage easily, weakness, bleeding gums, and easy bruising.

sepals — the leaf-like structures which cover the bud and form the calyx of the flower; they may be highly colored, and may accompany or take the place of the petals in insect attraction.

sessile — stalkless; having no stem or stalk.

sori, sorus — the reproductive structures of a fern which produce the spores. They may be located on the regular fronds, or may be on special reproductive fronds.

spadix — seen in the skunk cabbage and jack-in-the-pulpit, among others, this is a thick stalk bearing the reproductive floral parts; instead of being surrounded by petals, the spadix is generally surrounded by a single leaf-like spathe.

spore — the reproductive cell of some of the simpler non-flowering plants; usually produced without a union of cells, it is an asexual reproductive cell, able to produce a new plant.

stamen — the male reproductive parts of the flower, consisting of the anther and filament.

stigma — the "landing field" for the pollen grains at the top of the pistil; often equipped with hairs, a sticky substance, or both. The stigma contains chemicals which will encourage pollen grains from like plants to grow, but which will discourage pollen from dissimilar plants.

stipe — the stem-like portion of simple plants which supports but does not conduct materials as does the stem of higher plants.

striation — a fine line.

style — the portion of the pistil which connects the stigma with the ovary in the pistil of a flower. The pollen grains must penetrate the style in order to reach the ova.

sympathetic nervous system — works with the parasympathetic portion to make up the autonomic nervous system. Mainly concerned with speeding up internal activities, this system of nerves is important in our "fight or flight" reactions.

taproot — a thick, central root such as that of the carrot. A taproot sends forth few branch roots; if present, they are usually very fine.

tidal pool — a pool of water, usually among rocks, left by the outgoing tide.

tidal zone — (same as intertidal zone)

toadstool — a common name given, usually, to any mushroom which is unfamiliar and which may be a poisonous mushroom.

tuber — an underground stem that is thick with stored food; this may be the starting point for new plants (example — white potato).

volva — the cup-like remnant of the universal veil of some mushrooms; it encases the base of the mushroom either loosely or snugly.

whorl — a group of leaves which arise from the same area of the stem, surrounding the stem in a circular fashion.

wort — an old name meaning plant or common plant.

Appendix

Flower Parts

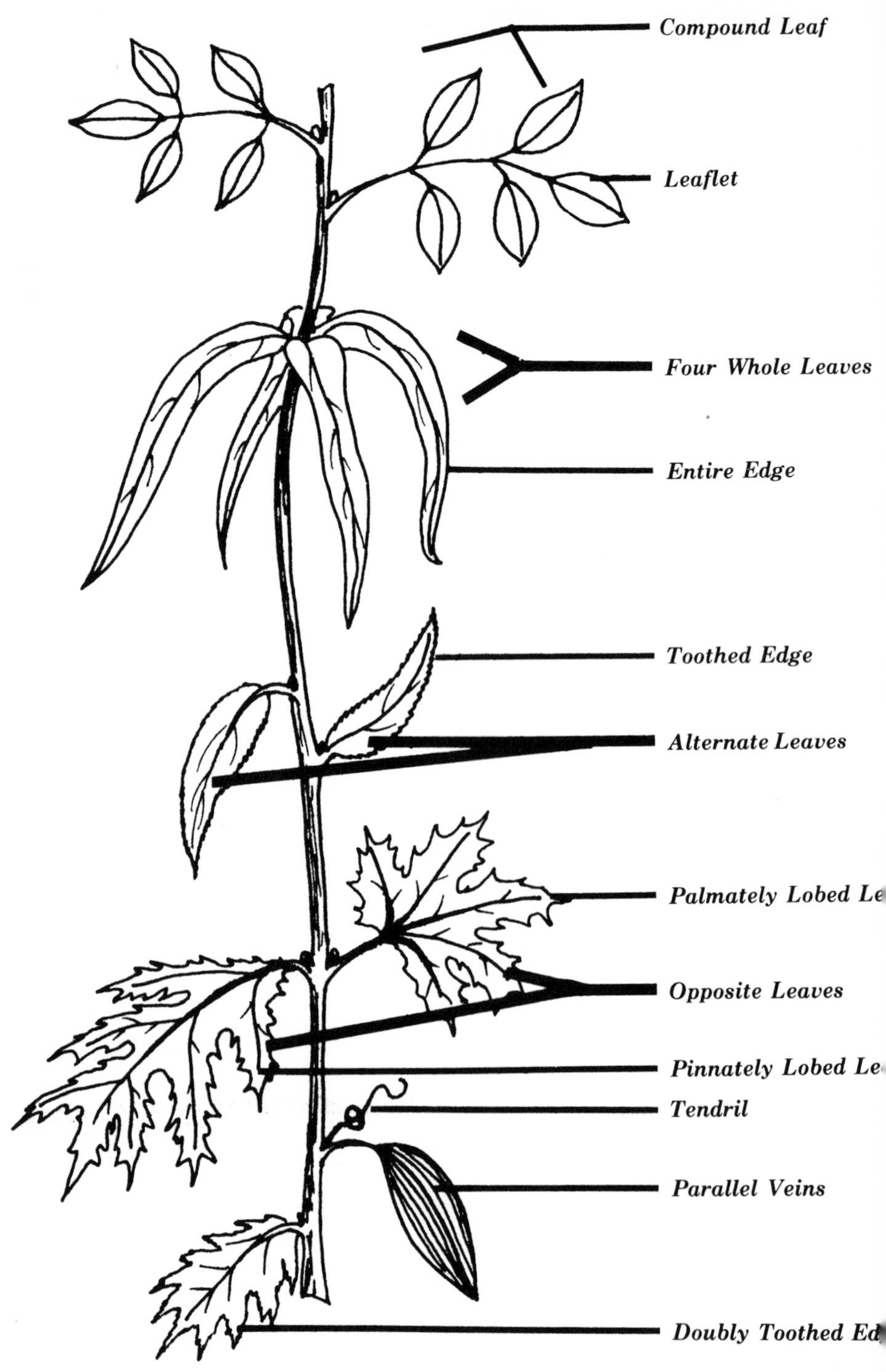

Leaf Placement and Types

Quick Key

to Plants by Flower Color and Fruits

Plant	Description page	Photo page	Illustration page
FLOWERS WHITE (OR PRIMARILY WHITE)			
Fragrant water lily	25	2	
White water lily	25	2	
Arrowhead	26	2	
Water plantain	28	2	
Cranberries	37, 52	4	14
Dwarf ginseng	41		41
Baneberry	42		43
Solomon's seal	44	5	45
False Solomon's seal	45	5	46
Spiderwort	49	6	
Checkerberry	50	5	
Partridgeberry	51	5	
Bunchberry	52	6	
Blue lettuce	53	7	
Wild sarsaparilla	56	7	
Bristly sarsaparilla	58	8	
American spikenard	58	8	
Common wood sorrel	60	15	
Strawberry	61	9	
Dogbane	62	8	
Milkweed (older blossoms)	63	9	
Chicory	65	10	
Wild mint	66	8	
Smartweeds	67	10	
Musk mallow	75	11	
Chickweeds	80	13	
Ox-eye daisy	81	13	
Bladder campion	87	15	
Evening lychnis	88		10
Night-flowering catchfly	88	15	
Bouncing bet	89	15	
Alsike clover	97, 98	17	
White clover	97, 99	17	
Rabbit foot clover	100	18	
White sweet clover	101	17	
Foxglove	106	18	

Plant	Description page	Photo page	Illustration page
Poor man's pepper	108	19	
Shepherd's purse	109		109
Cow cress	110		110
Field pennycress	111	19	
Galinsoga	111	19	
Plantains	112-115	19	
Horseradish	116	20	
White-flowered trees and shrubs; large, shrubby plants			
Japanese knotweed	121	26	
Pokeweed	123	26	
Mountain ash	125	21	
Juneberries	142	23	
Flowering quince	143		143
Chokecherry	145	24	
Wild black cherry	146		
Wild red cherry	147	24	
Elderberries	147-148	28	22
Hobblebush	149	23	
Wild raisin	150	25	151
Guelder rose	152	25	
Highbush cranberry	152		
Blackberries	153, 155	28	
Raspberries	153-154, 156-157	25	
Northern dewberry	153, 155	25	
Cloudberry	153, 155		10
Golden seal	156		10
Black raspberry	153, 157	25	
Blueberries, huckleberries, bilberries, deerberry	158-162	27	
Roses	164	27	
FLOWERS PINK/RED			
Cranberries	37, 52	4	14
Wild ginger	47	5	47
Spiderwort	49	6	
Partridgeberry	51	5	
Common wood sorrel	60	15	
Dogbane	62	8	
Milkweed	63	9	
Purple milkweed	65	9	
Chicory	65	10	
Smartweeds	67	10	
Musk mallow	75	11	
Strawberry blite	76	11	
Bouncing bet	89	15	

Plant	Description page	Photo page	Illustration page
Frogs' bellies	93	16	
White and alsike clovers	97-99	17	
Red clover	99	18	
Rabbit foot clover	100	18	
Fireweed	105	16	
Foxglove	106	18	
Flowering quince	143		143
Sumacs	144	24	
Golden seal	156		10
Blueberries, huckleberries, bilberries, deerberry	158-162	27	
Roses	164	27	
Redbud tree	165	27	
FLOWERS ORANGE/GOLD /YELLOW			
Iris	24	1	24
Bullhead lily	26	2	
Marsh marigold	28	2	
Wild lettuce	54	7	
Jewelweed	55	7	
Sunflower	70	11	
Jerusalem artichoke	72		73
Asparagus	79	12	
Goatsbeard	82	13	
Sow thistles	84	14	
Prickly lettuce	84	14	
Dandelion	85	14	
Pineapple weed	90	15	
Yellow wood sorrel	91	15	
Roseroot	93		93
Buttercups	94-97	16	9, 96
Hop clovers	100	17	
Black medik	101	11	
Yellow sweet clover	102	17	
Wild indigo	100		6
Mustards	117	20	118
Ground cherries	119	20	
Carrion flower	120	24	
Yellow-flowered shrubs, shrubby plants, trees			
Shrubby cinquefoil	141	23	
Barberries	142	23	
Sumacs (immature flowers)	144	24	

Plant	Description page	Photo page	Illustration page
Greenbrier	149	24	
Roses	164	27	
FLOWERS GREEN/BROWN			
Cattails	30	3	
Great bur reed	33	3	
Skunk cabbage	33	4	
Jack-in-the-pulpit	34	4	
False hellebore	35	4	
Solomon's seal	44	5	45
Wild ginger	47	5	47
Wild sarsaparilla	56	7	
Bristly sarsaparilla	58	8	
American spikenard	58	8	
Dock	68	10	68
Lamb's quarters	74	11	
Strawberry blite	76	11	14
Asparagus	79	12	
Pineapple weed	90	15	
Sheep sorrel	91	16	
Plantains	112-115	19	
Carrion flower	120	24	
Sumacs (immature flowers)	144	24	
Greenbrier	149	24	
Golden seal	156		10
FLOWERS BLUE/VIOLET /PURPLE			
Sea rocket	21	13	
Pickerelweed	23	1	
Iris	24	1	
Spiderwort	49	6	
Blue lettuce	53	7	
Bittersweet nightshade	56	7	
Purple milkweed	65	9	
Chicory	65	10	
Wild mint	66	8	
Chive	70	10	
Thistle	82	13	
Salsify	83	13	
Ground ivy	86	14	
Roseroot	93		93
Belladonna	119		
Frogs' bellies	93	16	
Red clover	99	18	
Alfalfa	103		103
Fireweed	105	16	

Plant	Description page	Photo page	Illustration page
Foxglove	106	18	
Creeping bellflower	107	18	
Burdock	115	19	
Purple-flowering raspberry	153, 157	28	
RED FLESHY FRUITS			
Checkerberry	50	5	
Partridgeberry	51	5	
Bunchberry	52	6	
Cranberries	37, 52	4	14
Bittersweet nightshade	56	7	
American spikenard (immature)	58	8	
Strawberry	61	9	
Asparagus	79	12	
Ground cherry	119	20	
Carrion flower (immature)	120	24	
Shrubby plants, shrubs and trees with red fruits			
Mountain ash	125	21	
Juneberries (immature)	142	23	
Barberries	142	23	
Sumacs	144	24	
Chokecherry (immature)	145	24	
Wild red cherry	147	24	
Red elderberry	148	28	
Guelder rose	152	25	
Highbush cranberry	152		
Raspberries	153-154, 156-157	25	
Golden seal	156		10
Purple-flowering raspberry	157	28	
Yews	164	26	
Roses	164	27	
FLESHY FRUITS, DEEP PURPLE/BLUE, BLACK			
Wild sarsaparilla	56	8	
Bristly sarsaparilla	58	8	
American spikenard	58	8	
Belladonna	119		
Carrion flower	120	24	
Pokeweed	123	26	
Juneberries	142	23	
Chokecherry	145	24	
Wild black cherry	146		
Common elderberry	147		22
Greenbrier	149	24	

Plant	Description page	Photo page	Illustration page
Hobblebush	149	23	
Wild raisin	150	25	151
Blackberries	153-155	28	
Northern dewberry	153, 155	25	
Black raspberry	153, 157	25	
Blueberries, huckleberries, Bilberries	158-162	27	
Deerberry	162		
Juniper	162	26	
FLESHY FRUITS, ORANGE /GOLD/YELLOW			
Ground cherries	119	20	
Barberries (immature)	142	23	
Flowering quince	143		143
Cloudberry	153, 155		10
NUT OR NUT-LIKE FRUITS			
Oaks	126-127	21	126
Hickories	127-131	21	22,166
Black walnut	131	21	
Butternut	133	22	
Chestnut	134	22	
Horse chestnut	135		166
American hazelnut	139	22	
Beaked hazelnut	140	22	

INDEX